RUSSIA, AMERICA, THE BOMB
AND THE FALL OF
WESTERN EUROPE

By the same author

The Indonesian Tragedy
The Third World Calamity

Brian May

RUSSIA, AMERICA, THE BOMB AND THE FALL OF WESTERN EUROPE

Routledge & Kegan Paul
London, Boston, Melbourne and Henley

For Brendan

First published in 1984
by Routledge & Kegan Paul plc
39 Store Street, London WC1E 7DD, England
9 Park Street, Boston, Mass. 02108, USA
464 St Kilda Road, Melbourne,
Victoria 3004, Australia and
Broadway House, Newtown Road,
Henley-on-Thames, Oxon RG9 1EN, England
Photoset in Times Roman by
Kelly Typesetting Ltd, Bradford-on-Avon, Wiltshire
and printed in Great Britain by
Billings Ltd, Worcester

Library of Congress Cataloging in Publication Data

May, Brian.
Russia, America, the bomb, and the fall of Western
Europe.

Includes bibliographical references and index.
1. Atomic weapons and disarmament. 2. United States—
Military relations—Soviet Union. 3. Soviet Union—
Military relations—United States. 4. Europe—Defenses.
I. Title
JX1974.7.M34   1984   327.1'74   83–19063

British Library CIP data available

ISBN 0–7100–9757–3

Contents

It is useless to maintain that [the advance of mankind] takes place by itself, bit by bit, in virtue of the spiritual condition of society at a certain period of its history. It is a leap forward, which is only taken if society has decided to try an experiment.

HENRI BERGSON, *Les Deux Sources de la morale et de la religion*

Preface

This is not primarily an exhortative work, although it unreservedly favours unilateral nuclear disarmament. If Western Europe has not already begun the spiritual, psychological and intellectual metamorphosis that is essential to save both itself and Eastern Europe from an atomic catastrophe, no book can help. There are some signs that a new, salutary trend is under way. If it is, then fact and argument could cast light on the path to be followed.

The disturbing element in international wrangles over nuclear weapons is not merely the horror of the prospect, but the irrationality and primitive emotion that make war seem inevitable. To an observer on a planet more civilized than ours the perpetrators of a nuclear conflict would appear no less foolish than the warring factions of Ireland are to those who view Irish strife with the advantage of distance; the rights, wrongs and fears of both sides would vanish in the holocaust.

Arnold Toynbee saw the West heading for destruction by its demoniacal dynamism; he inclined to the view that there would be one world, led by a single power, perhaps voluntarily accepted by the others, or none. He found the West to be unsuitable for the leading role because, while it could 'galvanize and disrupt', it could not 'stabilize or unite';[1] China, subject to certain developments, was, in the light of its long record of unification, a better candidate.

We may or may not see the future through Toynbee's eyes. But it is suggested that at this awesome stage we should try to step aside from history, as he did, and view it with all the detachment we can muster. We shall then be in a better position to assess the risks of retaining nuclear weapons or abandoning them unilaterally. This is surely a method that would be adopted by an intelligent civilization concerned with its survival.

Brian May
Brussels, Zierikzee, London

Introduction

The challenge

Europe is confronted with a historic challenge that transcends, but includes, the issue of nuclear disarmament. From the Atlantic to the Ural mountains – which mark the limit of Russia's European territory and separate Europe itself from Asia – it is afflicted by a complex crisis. Both East and West are threatened with atomic annihilation and the effects of environmental pollution. The West is also faced with chronic unemployment, dwindling mineral resources and the urgent need to restructure industry in order to enjoy, rather than suffer, the proliferation of robots and computers. Associated with inability to come to grips with all these problems is a growing malaise, symptomatized by uncertainty of values, indifference, slovenliness, irresponsibility and crime. Russia's problems will be examined later. But both societies are handicapped by anachronistic thinking, which, while it answered past challenges, could be disastrous to the future. This, or the moral failure that gives rise to it, is the fundamental problem, from which all the others stem. Its resolution will require fresh insights no less radical than those that lifted north-western Europe from feudal stagnation to social dynamism. The change will probably have to blow from the West; for, ever since Peter the Great set about Westernizing Russia, all of its social innovations, notably its adaptation of Marxism, have had a Western component.

The challenge is daunting, but it could be met. Large demonstrations against nuclear missiles could presage a broadly-based movement of historical importance. Already politicians have been frightened into greater caution. At first Helmut Schmidt, then Chancellor of Western Germany, complained that the demonstrations amounted to war against the German government (they were); later he said they had their positive side. It is unlikely that Washington would have resumed its arms talks with Moscow when it did had it not been necessary to conciliate European opinion.

But disarmers alone cannot bring about disarmament. Because of primitive fears and the inadequacy of extreme leftists, West Europeans are unlikely to vote governments into office at this stage on the sole ground that they would abolish nuclear weapons. Both the Russians and the Americans are doing their best to manipulate public opinion. What was seen as a sinister Russian move could in certain circumstances cause the UND movement to collapse. The present society is too steeped in conventional attitudes to abandon the nuclear weapon. If the bomb is to go the old order will have to go first. This will not happen unless the disarmers are joined by large numbers of people who are disillusioned by unemployment and other social ills. There are signs that these conditions are gradually forming. The question is whether or not they will ripen before nuclear missiles are fired.

Influential Japanese have taken an alert interest in Toynbee's views on the rise and fall of civilizations. Noting Japan's rapid ascent, they were quick to look for signs of decline, in the hope that they might arrest them. West Europeans would do well to emulate their sagacity. If Western civilization is declining, it is unlikely that its present leaders will decide wisely on so vital an issue as nuclear weapons; for in the past fatally wrong decisions on matters crucial to survival – failure to see that a qualitatively new challenge requires a qualitatively different response – have been the hallmark of civilizations that were disintegrating. On the other hand, decline could lead to a regenerative upheaval, with entirely new leaders – new in policy and new in character, bearing little resemblance to right, left or centre as now conceived. It is possible, as we shall see in the last chapter, that these have already begun to appear.

This book, while placing nuclear disarmament in the larger setting of a moral crisis, nevertheless examines the issue in itself, using orthodox political and military criteria. It begins with an outline of signs that could indicate the approach of war. It then pauses to look at the two main adversaries, the United States and the Soviet Union. After that it considers the decline of Western Europe, then its economy, which itself contains the seeds of war. The subsequent chapters deal in one way or another with the relative risks of retaining or abandoning nuclear weapons; a systematic assessment in chapter 9 leads logically to the conclusion that Western Europe should get rid of them. The last chapter looks at the future. The book argues that Western Europe is threatened more by disintegration than aggression and that its alliance with the United States imperils rather than assures its survival. Identifiable constraints make it impossible for Russia to administer or exert undue pressure on it. What is required to secure Western Europe's future is not atomic missiles, but nothing less than a regeneration of the socially creative spirit that, virtually in a single bound, set it apart from the rest of the world only a few centuries ago.

Part 1

Fundamentals

Chapter 1

Signs of war

Specialists' studies have revealed a number of signs that can indicate the imminence of war.[1] These include high unemployment (in this century), for which war and war preparations provide a solution; inflation and high interest rates; sharp rises in the price of gold – a haven for funds in dangerous times; a spurt in arms expenditure; outbreaks of domestic violence; and exceptionally vehement exchanges between nations. All these signs are present today. They do not mean that war is inevitable; but it seems that only the prospect of nuclear destruction has prevented it from breaking out already. The present peace is uncertain. Increasing recklessness of speech and action, particularly in the United States, suggests that belligerence could dominate fear, perhaps quite suddenly.

In modern history major wars have become shorter and less frequent, while civilian casualties have risen as a proportion of the population.[2] The pattern is not immutable, but it is none the less alarming. It could point to an atomic war – at once shorter and more deadly than its predecessors. If the graph that has been established were to remain reasonably continuous, the casualties would have to be fewer than the worst we imagine. This could be the consequence of a limited nuclear war – limited, but terrible, and not the last nor the worst.

This century has already provided a curtain-raiser. The two major wars killed more than 60 million people. In the first war 8,418,000 servicemen were killed or died of wounds and 1,374,000 civilians were killed or died of injuries. In the second servicemen casualties were 16,933,000 and civilian were estimated at 34,305,000; the rise is partly accounted for by the entry of China into the war, with 2,220,000 servicemen and 20,000,000 civilians estimated to have been killed.

In April 1979 the United States Arms Control and Disarmament Agency published what it light-heartedly called the results of 'large-scale computer war game simulations of general nuclear war between the United States and the Soviet Union'.[3] Both sides used the forces that they were to have been allowed under the SALT II (Strategic Arms Limitation Talks) agreement. The Russians were assumed to have launched a first strike against ICBM silos, bomber and submarine bases, other US military installations and industry. The US then hit back at similar Soviet targets. Among the consequences in each country were: 25 to 100 million deaths within thirty days; 65 to 90 per cent of industry destroyed; 200 of the largest cities flattened and 80 per cent of all cities of 25,000 inhabitants or more attacked by at least one weapon. The sixty warheads that struck within Moscow city were in total 1,400 times as powerful as those used in Hiroshima and Nagasaki. As for bomb shelters, even with a limited attack of one 20 megaton bomb, a symposium at the Harvard Medical School found that in Harvard:[4] 'Bomb shelters would become ovens. There would be about 10,000 severe burn cases in Boston – unmanageable even if medical personnel and facilities were left intact, since the whole country has no more than 1,000 intensive burn-care beds.' After a study lasting nearly two years the British Medical Association warned in March 1983 that a single strike at Britain would be extremely improbable. But even a 1 megaton bomb dropped on one city would completely overwhelm the nation's medical facilities. In the wider, more likely attack decaying corpses would litter streets, and there would not be enough doctors, drugs or equipment to ease the sufferings of millions of burnt, irradiated and starving people who would die slow, agonizing deaths.

Faced with such a risk, a Europe bent on surviving would hasten to clarify its attitude to the installation of nuclear weapons in its territory. Apart from indifference, there seem to be six possible policies:

1 *Planning to win an atomic war.* This has had notable exponents, such as Herman Kahn.[5] He thought that America would come off best, and soon recover, after a nuclear exchange with the Russians, who would be virtually wiped out. Kahn's thesis reflected a streak in official thinking. Robert McNamara, former Secretary of Defence, has disclosed that on 21 November 1962 he sent a memorandum to President John Kennedy saying:[6] 'It has become clear to me that the Air Force proposals are based on the objective of achieving a first-strike capability.' McNamara said it still scared him 'to even read the damn thing'. Despite the existence of nuclear-armed

submarines on both sides, this school of thought has re-emerged in Washington.

2   *Limitation.* This is a mere reduction in surplus killing power and is no help. As long as any nuclear weapons existed the danger would remain.

3   *A gradual reduction in all nuclear weapons to zero.* This must be ruled out. In the first place it entails the elusive idea of initial parity, on which the diversity of weapons and their location makes assessment arbitrary and agreement impossible. Further, present Western leaders will never forsake nuclear weapons as long as the Russians retain what NATO sees as conventional superiority in Europe. The Russians would be sure to counter any increase in Western conventional strength. Hence the point at which both sides would agree to abolish nuclear weapons will never be reached.

4   *Confidence that nuclear weapons will remain a certain deterrent to war.* In the popular mind this is usually based on the assumption that nuclear attacks would begin and end with the annihilation of cities on both sides and that nobody would be mad enough to launch them. It ignores the likelihood that an atomic war would begin in the field, either in Europe or the Middle East, with the intention that it should be limited. The possibility of errors of judgment in highly-charged situations, in which decisions are often impetuous, reduces the deterrent argument to an act of faith, upon which it is irrational to depend.

5   *Hope that the deterrent will be effective, qualified by resignation that if it is not it would be better to be dead or maimed than suffer or risk Russian domination.* This reflects an attitude not to be found in a civilization with the qualities needed for survival. It is like huddling behind a wall, knowing that it might well blow up in your face, instead of assessing what the real risks are and preparing to tackle them.

6   *Unilateral nuclear disarmament.* A conclusion on this option will be reached in chapter 9.

Before developing the main arguments of this book, it is perhaps worth while to consider, though briefly, some aspects of war as a phenomenon. Research workers have looked at the subject from various angles. For instance, war is considered to be sometimes caused by disease, to cause disease, and even to be a contagious disease itself. Pathological disorders may predispose leaders to belligerence, particularly in times of crisis. The cruelty of Idi Amin, the former Ugandan leader, has been positively attributed to syphilis. Studies have suggested, but have not proved, that neuro-syphilis accounts for the behaviour of Julius Caesar, Charlemagne, Mussolini and Hitler.[7] Some psychologists find that professional military men are given to strong belief in national myths, dogmatism and desire for power and achievement – characteristics that are seen to be accompanied by feelings of insecurity and low self-esteem.[8] The subject is controversial; but when assessing the risk of nuclear weapons, an intelligent society concerned about its survival would take the psychological and pathological factors into consideration.

As nations approach the brink of war, or when they have embarked upon it, fatigue and illness may warp leaders' judgments. This is such a serious hazard that it would require a very sound reason for a community to entrust so horrific a weapon as an atomic missile to anyone subjected to the heavy strains of leadership in a crisis – which means, in effect, anyone at all. In his book, *Fit to Lead?*, Dr Hugh L'Etang, editor of the *Practitioner*, finds that people have a 'touching faith in the mental and physical superiority of their chosen or self-elected leaders', although illness need not invariably lessen their effectiveness.[9] It is clear in L'Etang's book – although this is not a point that he makes – that Churchill provides no exception to the rule that nobody should be entrusted with an atomic bomb. During the war his military assistant, General Ismay, wrote to General Auchinleck, then Commander-in-Chief Middle East:[10] 'He is either on the crest of a wave or in a trough. . . . He is a child of nature with moods as variable as an April day.' A naval officer who visited Churchill in an underground cabinet room in April 1941 wrote: 'He was very depressed and desperately tired – in a sort of coma almost. His speech was rather slobbery and very slow. . . . It was a terribly depressing interview.' On 13 July 1943 Anthony Eden's Private Secretary said of Churchill:[11] 'The battle has gone to the old man's head. The quantities of liquor he con-sumed – champagne, brandies, whiskies – were incredible.' The battle was not the one against the Germans; it was merely a differ-ence with the United States over recognition of the new French Committee. On 14 April 1944, a few weeks before the Allied invasion of Europe, Cecil King, the newspaper proprietor, was informed that Churchill was 'drinking again'. Churchill, L'Etang thinks, was dependent on alcohol, although not necessarily addicted to it.

L'Etang recalls that when in July 1956 Gamal Abdel Nasser reacted to what he saw as a threat from the United States by nationalizing the Suez Canal, Anthony Eden, British Prime Minister, in his turn interpreted the move as a threat to Britain's survival.[12] As the United Kingdom mobilized for 'what was virtually an undeclared, unofficial and clandestine war a number of key ministers dropped out'. R. A. Butler, Lord Privy Seal and Leader of the House of Commons, went down with a virus infection; Lord Salisbury, Lord President of the Council, suffered a heart attack; and Sir Walter Monckton, Minister of Defence, was stricken by physical exhaustion. Selwyn Lloyd, Foreign Secretary, confessed on 22 October: 'I am so confused and exhausted that I honestly have no advice to offer any more.' Finally Anthony Eden broke down early in November and was forced to take refuge in Jamaica.

Roosevelt has been criticized for having yielded too much to Stalin at the Yalta conference in February 1945. The important fact is that he was seriously ill. Sir Alexander Cadogan, Permanent Under-Secretary at the Foreign Office, saw in Roosevelt 'the early signs of dementia'.[13] When he presided over a meeting he made no attempt to guide it, but remained speechless; if he made any comment at all it was irrelevant. L'Etang says that not fatigue 'but a dangerously high blood pressure was responsible for his mental failure'. Two months later Roosevelt died from a 'massive cerebral haemorrhage'. In an age of nuclear arsenals a man in his condition could make an error of judgment that would bring much of the world down with him. President Richard Nixon appears to have constituted a potential danger. An article in the *Atlantic Monthly* claimed that he was regularly drunk at crucial periods, and on one occasion told Henry Kissinger to 'nuke (nuclearize) them' – presumably the Russians.[14]

Fit or not, leaders are unable to make completely rational decisions whether or not to launch a war. Historical fact is far removed from Carl von Clausewitz's statement that 'war is an instrument of policy. . . . The conduct of war . . . is . . . policy itself which takes up the sword in place of the pen.' As Beer points out:[15]

> The rational calculation of national interest is extremely difficult. . . . The traditional view gives foreign policymakers qualities that they may not possess, capabilities of rational processing that may be absent, particularly in the difficult conditions of wartime choice.

The difficulty of deciding rationally whether or not to fight is apparent in the different opinions expressed by historians on the causes of particular wars and in their unexpected consequences. During the Second World War nobody, to the author's knowledge, expected that the vanquished Japanese and Germans would soon emerge as the most economically successful peoples in the Western bloc. According to one study three-fifths of war decisions throughout the world since 1910 have been based on 'errors of perception, judgment and expectation of outcome'.[16]

Statesmen are sometimes unable to explain the outbreak of the war for which they are directly responsible. Soon after the eruption of the First World War Prince von Bülow, former German Chancellor, asked his successor, 'How did it happen?' The reply was: 'Ah, if only we knew.' Sir Edward Grey, Liberal Foreign Secretary, who led Britain into the war, wrote afterwards: 'The enormous growth of armaments in Europe, the sense of insecurity and fear caused by this – it was these that made war inevitable.' In his 1981 BBC Reith lectures Lawrence Martin disagreed with Grey and said he was more inclined to look for the causes of the war in the decay of East European empires. The only constant amid differing opinions is that nobody now believes that Britain entered the war because of the emotional issue that was whipped up to persuade the people to fight – the German invasion of 'little Belgium'. Perhaps the first to expose this myth was Bertrand Russell, who denounced it in a letter to the *Nation* as early as 15 August 1914, eleven days after Britain had declared war. He wrote of 'secret arrangements, concealed from Parliament and even (at first) from almost all the Cabinet' and of 'an obligation suddenly revealed when the war fever had reached the point which rendered public opinion tolerant of the discovery that the lives of many, and the livelihood of all, had been pledged by one man's irresponsible decisions.'[17] Russell quoted Grey's report, dated 1 August, of a conversation with the German Ambassador:

> He asked me whether, if Germany gave a promise not to violate Belgian neutrality, we would engage to remain neutral [in an imminent war with Russia arising from the Austro–Serbian dispute]. I replied that I could not say that. I did not think that we could give a promise of neutrality on that condition alone. The Ambassador pressed me as to whether I could not formulate conditions on which we would remain neutral. He even suggested that the integrity of France and her colonies might be guaranteed. I said I felt obliged to refuse definitely any promise to remain neutral on similar terms, and I could only say that we must keep our hands free.

Russell commented: 'It thus appears that the neutrality of Belgium, the integrity of France and her colonies, and the naval defence of the northern and western coasts of France, were all mere pretexts.' The outcome was the quickening of 'all this madness, all this rage' which to Russell was already evident. As B. H. Liddell Hart was to point out, President Woodrow Wilson later tried to bring about peace, but failed because the war had developed into 'a struggle of peoples dominated by a primitive instinct of self-preservation', and could not be settled politically.[18] Perhaps the most succinct comment on the war, with all its suffering and devastation, comes from Henry Kissinger:[19] 'World War 1 – senseless in its origin, pointless in its outcome – produced a catastrophe out of all proportion to the issues at stake.' Kissinger has yet to see that this statement would apply to any war between Eastern and Western Europe; we shall return to this subject in subsequent chapters.

At any time when explosive forces of various kinds have accumulated a haphazard event can ignite them, as the assassination of Archduke Franz Ferdinand by Serbian rebels showed at Sarajevo in 1914. A warning of what could happen today was given when President Reagan was shot (1 December 1981). Reflecting the power struggle that is a chronic cause of instability in American foreign policy, the Secretary of State, Alexander Haig, defied protocol by proclaiming on television that he was taking charge of the White House. Haig was quickly obliged to withdraw to his proper function. No harm was done, but in a time of critical relations with the USSR an impetuous action by someone inspired with a mission to save the world from communism could cause immediate disaster.

Such a man could be a general. In February 1982 declassified documents revealed that in 1955 the US Strategic Air Command discussed a plan to reduce the USSR to a 'smoking, radiating ruin' in a two-hour first strike.[20] The exact battle plan was known only to General Curtis Lemay, who had sole authority to carry out the attack. A force of 735 bombers was to drop 600 to 750 nuclear bombs. While airfields and atomic installations were to be the main targets, the command estimated that 118 large cities would be destroyed and 60 million people killed. We do not know what contingency plans, of more recent origin, lie concealed in files that remain secret in the USA and USSR. But it cannot be ruled out that if dangerous relations between the superpowers coincided with a vacuum or instability in the leadership of either of them, some person or clique would decide to push the nuclear button.

The chances are high of a decision based on false or wrongly assessed information. President John Kennedy's sponsoring of the abortive invasion by Cuban émigrés in the Bay of Pigs in 1962 was based on both. Among the blunders was failure to calculate that Castro's armed forces would outnumber the invaders by 140 to one.[21] Strong objections were raised in three memoranda, but one of these was withheld from the President, who in turn, did not circulate the other two among the decision-making group. At the end of February 1982 William Casey, Director of the Central Intelligence Agency, said that the guerrilla war in El Salvador was being organized by 6,000 Cubans, Russians, East Germans, Bulgarians, North Koreans, Vietnamese and members of the Palestine Liberation Organization in Nicaragua – a charge described by the BBC's Latin America correspondent as 'the most remarkable' yet to have come from Washington. Whether or not Casey's information about the number and variety of foreigners was correct, he grossly distorted the situation in El Salvador, where poverty and exploitation, not foreign intervention, were the cause of rebellion.

'Executive deception' was at the 'very basis of America's vastly expanded involvement in Vietnam' in August 1964.[22] The Johnson administration claimed that North Vietnamese torpedo boats had attacked two innocent American destroyers that were on a routine patrol in the Gulf of Tonkin. It was this that 'excited Congress to give the Johnson Administration a virtually free hand in conducting the Vietnam War' and 'excused the bombing of the North'. But Senate Foreign Relations Committee hearings in 1968 disclosed that the destroyers were on an intelligence mission, not a routine patrol, and that, in any case, there was no certainty that they had been fired at. A few hours before the administration ordered retaliatory strikes against North Vietnam, the commander of the American task force in the gulf, who was aboard one of the destroyers, sent a telegram to the Pentagon casting doubt on the attacks. He said that no torpedoes had been sighted from his ship and that freak weather and 'over-eager sonarmen may have accounted for many reports' of attacks and contacts. Three and a half years later Senator Fulbright said he regretted 'more than anything I have ever done in my life' steering the Gulf of Tonkin resolution through the Senate; it had never occurred to him that there was the slightest doubt that the attacks had taken place. Senator Albert Gore said: 'I feel the Congress and the country were misled. . . . I know I have been misled.' Fulbright had profound reasons for his regret. In 1965 the number of American lads sent to fight a futile war – described by de Gaulle as a scandal – rose from little more than 20,000 to nearly 200,000. Yet in his 1964 election campaign Lyndon Johnson had promised not to increase the American commitment. Even as late as 21 October 1964 he said: 'We are not about to send American boys nine or ten thousand miles away from home to do what Asian boys ought to be doing for themselves.' Johnson's deception led to the death of 47,000 Americans and 235,000, mostly South Vietnamese, in the allied forces; the North Vietnamese and Vietcong are estimated to have lost 444,000 dead; and the number of civilians killed in the north and south has been put at 587,000, bringing the total to 1,313,000.[23] South Vietnamese civilians admitted to hospital, some of them children maimed by napalm, numbered 475,488. Added to the casualties are the ruin of forests and farm land, the massacres in Cambodia, which were a consequence of the war, and demoralization in the United States. The war served no good purpose of any kind. It would be a naïve people, indeed, who entrusted nuclear weapons to the judgment and integrity of men such as those who launched it.

Propaganda lies are a normal product of wartime administration. A Jesuit historian, Father Robert Graham, found that lies proposed by British intelligence and the Foreign Office and perpetrated by the secret Political Warfare Executive during the Second World War were sufficiently insidious to impede subsequent historical research.[24] In the Falklands campaign official prevarication and concealment for political rather than security purposes evoked protests from both the BBC and ITV.

War, or belligerent talk that can lead to war without anyone going as far as to desire it consciously, offers a special temptation to leaders. What the political philosopher, Jean Bodin, said in the sixteenth century remains true:[25]

> The best way of preserving a state and guaranteeing it against sedition, rebellion, and civil war is to keep the subjects in amity with one another, and, to this end, to find an enemy against whom they can make common cause. Examples of this can be found in all commonwealths.

When they come to recognize their impotence in handling domestic problems, leaders may project their frustration into international disputes, consciously or without knowing it. With atomic weapons at their disposal, they then constitute an intolerable danger. Unemployment, which more than anything threatens the existing order in the West, is thus the most disquieting of the signs that can presage war – without necessarily being the direct cause of it. Hitler and the British and American governments all solved their unemployment problems by increasing the manufacture of arms. In January 1982 President Ronald Reagan proposed a $257,000 million military budget, by far the biggest since the war. Doubtless it would have crossed his mind that this burst of expenditure could help to reduce unemployment, although it probably did not occur to him that his general economic policy would offset the benefit.

With or without morbid elements, the psychological factor in war is strong. As Beer says:[26]

> War can appear . . . as a liberating experience. Society imposes severe limits on the natural tendencies of individuals. The frustrations of everyday life – stored as alienation, hostility, anger, hate, rage – can be relieved through external aggression and violence.
>
> Normal taboos, prohibitions, and limits to violent behaviour are lifted in wartime. . . . Death comes out into the open, allowing individuals to see it directly and deal with it face-to-face. Constraints against suicide and murder disappear. The sin and guilt of destruction can be transformed into the glory and bravery of heroism.

With such dark psychic forces at work it appears to be impossible for people and their leaders to see clearly the processes that are impelling them towards war and to assess the risks they are taking. This human helplessness is perhaps the most dangerous element in the nuclear threat. While the subject has been intensely studied in recent years, politicians and the public at large are almost totally unaware of its vital importance. Among the findings of psychologists, Britten says, is that 'subjects in test situations commonly believe their knowledge and capacity to estimate uncertainties to be more accurate than it is.'[27] Beyond the limits of their data, experts are as 'prone to overconfidence as anyone else'. Groups usually take greater risks than the individuals within them; once the group has decided, the doubters tend to join the risk-takers. When war looms, people are often hesitant at first about fighting. But, as Britten points out, if a British admiral threatens the Soviet Union with 'They'll get a bloody nose if they start anything', he helps the public to 'avoid the torment of weighing for themslves the risks of armament as well as disarmament'. Accustomed to peace, people cannot seriously imagine a war that would destroy them. Politicians' decisions are not based on fresh assessments of what is the greatest risk to the community, but are incremental on previous policy. Asked in March 1981 why Britain should have independent nuclear weapons, the Secretary of State for Defence replied: 'Because we do not start from here. By history we happen to be a nuclear power.'.

It is such irrelevant considerations that make possible the lunatic situation in which society allows drug addicts and psychotics to man and guard its nuclear weapons. Urine analysis disclosed that 2.3 per cent of an élite US brigade were heroin addicts; this would be the equivalent of 2,749 soldiers among its nuclear units, assuming the same proportion.[28] Instances have been documented in which men suffering from severe psychiatric disorders and others taking LSD or marijuana have guarded nuclear weapons or manned batteries capable of firing nuclear warheads.[29] Telecommunications and missile launch crew have transmitted hoax messages to relieve their boredom; one went so far as to record a launch signal and play it when the relief crew came on duty.[30] Systems for firing Pershing I missiles were stolen from West German air force depots. It is not at all fanciful to imagine a crew of drugged Americans letting loose atomic weapons. Given the opportunity, a maniac of the kind that tries to murder the President could just as easily attempt to annihilate the Soviet Union.

But official miscalculations could be enough to begin a nuclear war. Carter gambled on rescuing the American hostages from Tehran, without taking into account the well-established technical shortcomings of the US armed forces. Three of the eight helicopters broke down. The rotor blades of another cut the fuselage of a Hercules troop carrier, killing eight men, whose bodies were abandoned. Rescue helicopters in the aircraft carrier *Nimitz* were drenched with salt water and chemicals when fire extinguishers were set off by mistake. A confidential army report leaked in September 1980 said that six of ten combat divisions, including the 101st Airborne Division, were unfit to fight. Fewer than 65 per cent of their men were qualified to perform their duties and each division possessed less than 65 per cent of essential equipment.[31] Other official information showed that ships could not go to sea because they lacked petty officers and sailors with essential skills while a high percentage of air force planes were 'in no shape to fly'. Twenty-one per cent of US Army tank gunners in Western Germany did not know how to aim their guns, and other soldiers could not tell the difference between an enemy and a friendly aircraft in silhouette, and had difficulty in reading instruction manuals. Twenty-five per cent of men in all services were in the lowest intelligence category – the fourth – although regulations limited the proportion to 10 per cent; the consequence was a shortage of men who could handle high technology weaponry.[32] On 16 June 1980 the BBC World Service broadcast a discussion on the state of the US armed forces, following the failure of the operation in Iran and two false alarms in the nuclear alert system. Paul Beard, a member of the US Congress, said 90 per cent of soldiers maintaining nuclear weapons had failed in their qualification tests; only 1 per cent of tank turret and artillery repair men had passed in basic skills. The volunteer system had broken down because, as another speaker said, skilled men preferred civilian jobs. Asked whether Europe could afford to wait until America produced an army, navy and air force that could be counted upon, Brigadier Kenneth Hunt, Director of the British Atlantic Committee, said: 'Europe has no option. These are the Americans we have got. We have to make do and hope that they will put it right.' The army has disclosed that 20 per cent of men use drugs once a month and 6.8 per cent take hard drugs often. US army anti-drug squads and West German police rounded up 8,875 drug addicts – the equivalent of half a division – in one year.[33]

While war has long been reviled as cruel and sordid, society has none the less been at pains to dignify it and make it respectable, thus effecting a compromise between the savage instinct without which no battle can be fought and the demands of civilization. Remote from bloodthirsty cries in the field and the weeping of wives and mothers at home, learned men have drawn up concepts such as that of the 'just war', one of the pillars of the relevant international law. We have *jus ad bellum*, justice in waging war, and *jus in bello*, justice in the way war is conducted. There are two main schools of thought on this dual concept: one, that it is a mere charade, the other that it limits war and its effects to some extent, however small, and is therefore useful. But the view taken here is that its main interest is as an example of man's split personality – of the contradiction between his desire for peace and his violent urges.

Since each side always considers its cause to be just, *jus ad bellum* can at most delay a war while leaders whip up the ruled into a state of self-righteousness. In 1974 the United Nations established the priority principle, according to which the aggressor is the one that initiates the action. But there is an inevitable loophole: 'other relevant circumstances' must be taken into judicial consideration. Myres McDougal, an authority on international law, says that a state 'is not obliged to be a "sitting duck" ';[34] a first strike can be justified as a defence against clear and immediate danger. Israel has used this argument to justify attack against the Arabs. The destructive power of atomic weapons reduces the priority principle, and with it that of *jus ad bellum*, to the absurd. After the holocaust, when the radiation had finally drifted from the lunar landscape, and what was left of the leadership had emerged from its underground shelters, a solemn inquiry into whether the first strike had been legally justified would seem like a grotesque comedy to observers on the more civilized planet envisaged in the Preface.

Jus in bello may be similarly demolished. Its two main elements are proportionality (weapons should not be disproportionate to their immediate purpose) and discrimination (between combatants and non-combatants). Even if chemical and biological warfare is excluded, we are still left with nuclear missiles, which make proportion and discrimination impossible. Both elements in the idea of just war are thus inapplicable to modern conditions. Their irrelevance is part of a complex of thinking which assumes that man is still living in the nineteenth century and earlier. An entirely new approach, a veritable revolution of the psyche, is essential if the gains of civilization are to be preserved and developed.

If the prediction offered by Beer in his comprehensive analysis of war and war studies is correct, this change is unlikely to occur.[35] While Beer recognizes that existing patterns do not necessarily constitute a trend, and is cautious about extrapolations in general, he believes that past tendencies will persist – not only in outbreaks of war, but in the creation of international institutions to contain it. He thinks it likely that the human race is faced with increasingly long periods of peace interrupted by wars of greater violence. Because casualties will be much higher, the average length of life will be reduced. The periods between peace and war will be clouded more and more by the clandestine operations of secret services. At the same time guerrillas and terrorists, eventually armed with nuclear weapons, will increasingly menace governments, cities and corporations. If Third World rulers acquired nuclear arms they could threaten or attack the more advanced countries to obtain food for starving, rebellious populations.

Beer does not think that present technical knowledge makes it possible to destroy the human race. This leaves open the continuation of another part of the pattern, termed aggregation. Fewer and more disastrous wars will be accompanied by the continued formation of international institutions designed to maintain peace and effect co-operation in various fields; or, we could say, the process that began with the Concert system established after the Napoleonic War in 1815 and led to the formation of the League of Nations in 1918 and the United Nations Organization in 1946 will go on. But aggregation contributes to polarization, Beer says, and hence strengthens tendencies to war; this is clear in the United Nations, which has become a political rostrum divided into hostile blocs.

Given the persistence of established patterns, Beer finds that the task confronting humanity is to reduce further the frequency of violence, to limit its incidence and to adopt measures to create peace, partly by the sublimation of aggressive drives in individuals. But he fears that proposals he makes on these lines have only a slim chance of success. War, he finds, is deeply and even mystically rooted in the human predicament, while in the minds of many foreign policy makers, war is not the worst evil that can occur – a sentiment expressed by Alexander Haig when he visited West Berlin, which war could totally destroy. If Beer is right we can expect human history, or what is left of it, to be punctuated by a series of hollow declarations like that in the preamble to the UN charter: 'We the peoples of the United Nations determined to save succeeding generations from the scourge of war, which twice in our life-time has brought untold sorrow to mankind. . . .' But the graphs implicit in Beer's predictions are not binding, unless it is assumed that human beings have no will.

Chapter 2

The Americans

If Western Europe were annihilated, the United States would be qualified to preserve, at least in specialists' books, the essentials of West European culture. American scholars have contributed to Europe's understanding of its past and to the evaluation of its arts. While the publisher and editor of the new *Grove's Musical Dictionary* are British, most of the contributors are American; the English translation of C. P. E. Bach's important book on the art of playing keyboard instruments was made by an American, with useful annotations. The European spirit of inquiry is sustained in scientific research and the Americans are said to be first in mathematical discovery, with the Russians second. American analysts of current events are probably second to none within the generally accepted reference frame. And so on.

But when we look at America's record as a world power, the picture is starkly different. Its attempts to fill the vacuum created by the exhaustion of Europe after the Second World War, the liquidation of the British Empire and the winding up of French, Dutch and Belgian colonies has been a momentous failure. Yet this was to be expected; for America had neither the experience nor the ethnic homogeneity required for this exacting and delicate task and its only qualifications were wealth, partly acquired through two wars that it entered on the right side at the right time, and technology, which the wars helped to stimulate. Now even its wealth is in jeopardy and its technology is tending to lose its advantage to Japan and Western Europe.

It was at no time reasonable to suppose that Americans were eligible for a leading world political role. Henry Kissinger says that the United States 'entered the twentieth century largely unprepared for the part that it would be called upon to play'.[1] In Kissinger's account of events this defect remained at least until 1968, when the Nixon administration took over; at that time America's history had 'ill prepared' it for its commitment to 'shape a world'. This brings us close to the present. Closer still was 23 April 1973 when Kissinger suddenly announced, without publicly consulting members of the Atlantic alliance, that this was 'the year of Europe'. The Atlantic debate that ensued has been described by two American analysts as 'maladroit in form'.[2] It was not long before the French Foreign Minister, Michel Jobert, complained that Western Europe was being treated as a 'non-person, humiliated all along the line', while Willy Brandt, West German Chancellor, protested that 'partnership cannot mean subordination.' But if Kissinger did not always please Europe, he displayed none of the inconsistency and incoherence with which Washington has dismayed its allies and perplexed its adversaries since his departure from office. As the end of the twentieth century approaches, America is no more fit to lead a Western alliance than it was at the beginning of it. That it should have been allowed to do so indicates the depth of West European decline.

In terms of blood the United States has bought its ascendancy relatively cheaply. The First World War erupted at the beginning of August 1914. The United States entered it on 6 April 1917. By the time of the armistice on 11 November 1918 the Americans had lost 126,000 servicemen dead compared with 1,774,000 Germans, 1,700,000 Russians, 1,200,000 Austrians and Hungarians, 1,363,000 French, 908,000 from the British Empire, 460,000 Italians and 325,000 Turks; American losses were only 1,000 more than tiny Serbia's 125,000.[3] In the Second World War dead American servicemen totalled 292,000, Russian 7,500,000 (plus 7,500,000 civilians), German 3,250,000, Chinese 2,220,000, Japanese 1,507,000, British 557,000 and French 202,000. America's relatively light casualties and its immunity from civilian losses in both wars may account partly for its recklessness in foreign policy, although this would be a far less important factor than inexperience and the naïvety and sheer brashness that are found to a significant extent in the very style of its diplomacy.

The USA's fundamental weakness in its dealings with the rest of the world is the assumption by too many people in high places that all societies have similar motives and aspirations and that, given the opportunity, they would become like America, or nearly so. This is a handicap in its relations with Russia, Western Europe and the Third World. In *American Civilization*, Daniel J. Boorstin, Director of America's National Museum of History and Technology, says that in the twentieth century the USA had become 'a pole-star by which peoples around the world guided themselves and took their bearings'. Amplifying this attitude, which clearly informs American foreign policy, Boorstin goes on:[4]

> There was good reason to see the United States as an extrapolation, a preview, or even perhaps a caricature, of what the future held for mankind. For this continent had offered Western man an opportunity to broaden his very notion of civilization, to give new emphasis to man's restless quest for novelty.

But while a restless quest for novelty may characterize a nation consisting essentially of individual migrants and the descendants of individual migrants, as compared with those who migrated earlier in ethnic groups in other parts of the world, it is not found in all societies, most of which became almost stationary in structure and slow to change their artefacts until the West disturbed them. In Western Europe, the greatest technological innovations were a by-product of something quite different – a spirit of fundamental inquiry; while, for example, Faraday's research made the electric motor possible, his primary aim was to 'divine God's pattern'. None of the great inquirers who did most to distinguish Western civilization from all others was concerned with such a trivial aim as novelty.

When new nations sprang up after the Second World War Americans who would otherwise have been obscurely engaged in professions and businesses were sent in droves to staff the large embassies that Washington set up throughout the world. With little tradition of colonial experience to guide them, some diplomats and their families were so overwhelmed by unexpected Third World attitudes that in 1978 the State Department engaged a psychiatrist, Dr Elmore Rigamer, to treat them for what was described as acute cultural shock. Incomprehension of foreign behaviour is sometimes matched by serious ignorance of fact. An American ambassador to Singapore was surprised when told that India and Pakistan had fought a war not long previously. A year before his appointment as President Reagan's National Security Adviser, William Clark admitted that he did not know the name of the French President. America has produced some widely respected diplomats. But generally its inexperience has placed it at a disadvantage in its attempt to 'shape a world', not unlike that suffered by barbarian invaders when they tried to govern civilized states. Of these Toynbee says:[5]

A barbarian successor-state blindly goes into business on the strength of the dishonoured credits of a universal state that has already gone into bankruptcy; and these boors in office hasten the advent of their doom by a self-betrayal through the outbreak, under stress of a moral ordeal, of something fatally false within.

Toynbee's words serve as an apt description of America's failure to take over and extend the world role once performed by the British Empire and of the unfortunate consequences for Americans. Its inability to cope with the task that it undertook after the Second World War, symbolized by its defeat in Vietnam, has shattered both the morale and the morality of the people, and 'something fatally false within' is evident. The United States has become a breeding ground of weird and murderous cults. Its crime rate has soared: in 1980 23,000 murders and 82,000 rapes were reported, compared with 9,000 and 17,000 in 1960; in Japan, on the other hand, in spite of rapid urbanization, crime remains low. With states unable to afford more police, people are demanding the death penalty. Paul Reynolds, the BBC New York correspondent, reported on 31 October 1981 a meeting at which a speaker urged the amputation of the little finger of the right hand for the first crime, the fourth finger for the next and so on; by the time he got to the thumb the audience were on their feet – cheering. The correspondent said that usually when a small group of people met in New York, at least one had been robbed or attacked, or knew someone who had. Reagan lamented in September 1982 that crime had touched one-third of American households. His answer was harsher penalties. Drugtaking has become such a 'socially approved adventure' that a gramme of cocaine can be bought for $100 on the floor of the New York Stock Exchange; a psychiatrist explained that it made people feel 'smarter, faster, more able to cope'.[6]

American society, with crime spreading among the masses and drug-taking to some extent fashionable among the élite, has become increasingly less fit to compete with Europe and Japan, now that they have recovered from the war. In 1978 Washington began to express concern that the United States was 'losing its technological lead'.[7] The aircraft industry, under competition from Europe, appeared to be 'starting a decline'. The Japanese were challenging US computer superiority while the Germans, French and Russians seemed to be 'equal to or ahead of the United States' in breeder reactors. The US steel industry could not compete with foreign producers; not only were high-quality special steels imported, but 44 per cent of all nuts, screws and bolts in the United States were made abroad. In 1963 other countries issued to Americans 4.5 times the number of internationally significant patents that the United States granted to foreigners; by 1975 the ratio had fallen to two. US research and development spending fell from 3 per cent of the gross national product in 1963 to 2.25 per cent in 1976, while that of Western Germany rose from 1.4 per cent to 2.2 per cent. American motor manufacturing executives in Detroit felt obliged to take notes while a Japanese lectured them on how to produce efficiently and conduct industrial relations. In a climate of declining standards scholarship is for sale, probably more than in Western Europe. Daniel S. Greenberg wrote in the *International Herald Tribune*:[8] 'If oilmen wish to support US studies of the Middle East, they need not guard against an unfriendly outcome.' A major university refused to publish the Pentagon Papers for fear of losing research funds provided by the Defence Department. Yet despite the general malaise, the brains of leading scientists continue to function; the United States won 47 per cent more of Nobel prize awards in the period 1961–77 than in 1946–60.

A sure sign of incipient disintegration is that the people have become increasingly alienated from the politicians. During the 1980 presidential election campaign voters had become so disillusioned that many felt they were not so much voting for a candidate as against his opponent. Dissatisfied though they were with Jimmy Carter, they had little confidence in Ronald Reagan, whose staggering campaign blunders included an assurance that trees caused more pollution than cars – a mistake in gas chemistry. Only 53.95 per cent of registered voters went to the polls – the lowest turnout since 1948 – and of these 50.7 per cent voted for Reagan. This meant that Reagan won the support of only 27.35 per cent of the electorate – a result that did not deter the London *Daily Telegraph* from saying that he had received a mandate from the people.

Corruption and general lack of principle have long characterized American public life. After his visit to the House of Representatives in 1842 Charles Dickens wrote of 'despicable trickery at elections; under-handed tamperings with public officers; . . . shameful truck-lings to mercenary knaves'. He said:[9]

It is the game of these men, and of their profligate organs, to make the strife of politics so fierce and brutal, and so destructive of all respect in worthy men, that sensitive and delicate-minded persons shall be kept aloof, and they, and such as they, be left to battle out their selfish views unchecked. And thus this lowest of all scrambling fights goes on; and they who in other countries would, from their intelligence and station, most aspire to make the laws, do here recoil the farthest from that degradation.

Dickens found that there were exceptions, but they 'scarcely coloured the stream of desperate adventurers'. It would be hard to estimate the improvement that has taken place since Dickens's time, but it is certain that the American political machinery is such that principle can play little part in retaining control of it. The shock inflicted by the Watergate affair on Americans consisted in their being forced to see what their politics were really like. It would have been unreasonable to assume that Nixon had a monopoly of villainous henchmen or that he was the only president who would cover up if he could get away with it. Since Watergate there have been other scandals. Carter had to rid himself of his budget director, Bert Lance, who was accused of dubious banking activities; Reagan's National Security Adviser, Richard Allen, was replaced after disclosures that he had received money and two watches from a Japanese journalist, for whom he had arranged an interview with Mrs Reagan. In August 1982 Reagan's Secretary for Labour was under Congress investigation for alleged links with the Mafia, but was cleared for want of convincing evidence. Earlier FBI men, posing as oil sheikhs, had no difficulty in persuading congressmen to accept bribes to further Arab interests; it was reported that they called off this operation for fear that it would become embarrassingly fruitful. An Indonesian agent, who lobbied Congress on the question of political prisoners and other matters, claimed that he was successful, although there is no evidence of the methods he used. South Koreans are among those who have found ready takers of emoluments. The 'shameful trucklings' noted by Dickens may be less frequent than in the nineteenth century, but they undoubtedly persist and are a factor in the instability of American foreign policy.

But it is communal lobbying that makes formulation of a coherent foreign policy virtually impossible. The most feared lobby in Washington is the Jewish. There are as many Jews in America as in Palestine and nearly as many in New York as in Jerusalem. They exercise considerable control over sections of the information media. Most of them are concentrated in six states – New York, New Jersey, Massachusetts, Illinois, California and Florida – which are among the ten with the most votes in the electoral college that chooses the president. Such is the voting procedure that a candidate who won in the six states would already command 160 of the 270 votes needed for victory.[10] It has been said that Reagan's Middle East proposals, announced in September 1982, showed that he did not fear the Jewish lobby. The plan was, in fact, a compromise between his need to avoid antagonizing the lobby, on the one hand, and on the other to win the support of the electorate at large, which, through the press, was accusing him of having no policy at all. While the Begin Government rejected the proposals, the Israeli opposition found them to be an acceptable basis for discussion. It may be assumed that many, probably most, American Jews, who were concerned that Begin's intransigence and aggression in Lebanon were dragging Israel into disrepute, would have found them reasonable. What Reagan did not dare to propose, and what no American president is likely to propose, is that the Palestinians should have a fully-fledged, independent state and that Israel should withdraw to its original borders. Fear that a Palestinian state would become a Soviet client is an important factor in present American policy; but even if there were no strategic consideration, the Jewish vote would ensure American support for Israel.

The Polish–Catholic lobby is 'probably second in strength only to the Jewish'.[11] During the Second World War Roosevelt told Stalin that he agreed with the proposal to move Poland's frontiers westward, to protect Russia from Germany; but he said that he could not state this openly because with 6 or 7 million people of Polish origin in the United States and an election coming up he could not risk opposing the Polish Government in exile in London. Balfour comments:[12] 'As a result that Government went on thinking for fifteen months that they had American backing when they did not.' America's relations with Britain have not been improved by pressure from citizens of Irish origin or descent. In 1920, when immigration quotas were fixed, Americans born in Ireland totalled 1,035,680, Germany 1,683,298, Italy 1,607,458, Russia 1,398,999, Poland 1,139,578, Britain 1,133,967, Canada 1,117,136, Sweden 624,759, Austria 574,959, Mexico 476,676, Hungary 397,081, Norway 363,599, Denmark 189,051, Greece 175,701, France 152,792, Finland 149,671, Holland 131,262, Switzerland 118,647, Asia 110,586 and Rumania 103,007. Engraved on the base of the Statue of Liberty are the lines:

> Give me your tired, your poor,
> Your huddled masses yearning to breathe free,

The wretched refuse of your teeming shore
Send these, the homeless, tempest-tost, to me.

This message may well be consistent with the spirit of a more humane society, yet to be realized. But the ferment of lingering hatred for former oppressors and sentimental attachment to diverse ancestral lands is not conducive to clear and consistent foreign relations, despite the dominant feeling for America as a nation. Two years after it has won a presidential election a party has to fight for seats in Congress. This means that many politicians are almost continually bending to communal pressure. With Poles hating the Russians, and Jews the Palestinians, it would be difficult to develop a sound and stable policy on the two most dangerous international issues of our time – relations with the USSR and a settlement in the Middle East. A Western Europe intelligently appraised of the requirements of survival would regard Washington's vulnerability to communal coercion as disqualifying it from leadership.

Even if the United States were ethnically homogeneous, the executive structure would make instability in foreign policy inevitable, for there is never certainty about who will be in charge. Whether the State Department or the White House formulates foreign policy depends rather on the relative strength and interests of personalities than on rule or precedent. Immediately after his election President Richard Nixon told Kissinger that he intended to conduct foreign policy from the White House; he emphasized that he regarded the State Department as untrustworthy and the CIA as incompetent.[13] This gave Kissinger, the President's Special Assistant for National Security Affairs (National Security Adviser), an opportunity to play an increasing role in formulating foreign policy. In the words of George Ball, a former Under-Secretary of State:[14] 'Kissinger used his national security council post as a springboard merely to undercut the Secretary of State [William Rogers] and then to take his place. And I think Mr Brzezinski [Carter's National Security Adviser] tried unsuccessfully to do the same thing.' Reagan's lack of competence and interest in foreign affairs exacerbated the conflict. There was no struggle between the State Department and the White House as such. Instead a personality clash developed between the Secretary of State, Alexander Haig, and Richard Allen, who had no qualifications for his post. The squabbling continued after William Clark had replaced Allen, and was compounded by the intervention of the Defence Secretary, Caspar Weinberger, who also had his own ideas on foreign policy.

What emerged was a mixture of purely personal rivalry and genuine difference of opinion. It was this blend of frictions, combined with Reagan's vagueness, which precipitated the long series of contradictory policy statements and squalid wrangles that led to Haig's resignation in June 1982. It is true that Haig's character magnified the built-in possibilities of division. He had already shown what one Washington commentator described as a 'bit of paranoia'[15] when, violating precedent, he proclaimed on television as soon as Reagan was shot that he was taking over the White House – a bid for power that was quickly foiled; from the moment he took office he had tried to extend his territory in the administration and rejected the appointment of certain officials for no other reason than that they were not his men. His departure from the State Department reduced tensions in the executive, but it did not remedy the structural weakness, which remains one of the impediments in America's relations with the rest of the world.

America's involvement in Europe was only made possible by Europe's chronic internecine insanity. Its beginnings have been interpreted by Kissinger:[16]

> Our entry into World War 1 was the inevitable result of our geopolitical interest in maintaining freedom of the seas and preventing Europe's domination by a hostile power. But true to our tradition, we chose to interpret our participation in legal and idealistic terms. We fought the war 'to end all wars' and 'to make the world safe for democracy'. The inevitable disillusion with an imperfect outcome let loose the tide of isolationism.

This picture of a people reacting after a bout of simulated idealism can do with some modification. When the war broke out the United States expected to remain neutral until the end of it. At the same time there was what A. B. Hart, Professor of Government at Harvard University, called 'sharp division on questions of foreign policy'.[17] Irrespective of their sympathies with one or other of the belligerents, most Americans still shared the aversion to involvement in European wars expressed by Presidents George Washington, Thomas Jefferson and James Monroe. In his farewell address on 19 September 1796 Washington said that the great rule of conduct for the United States in extending its commercial relations with Europe should be to avoid involvement in the 'combinations and collisions of her friendships, or enmities'. In 1823 the British Foreign Secretary, George Canning, proposed a joint Anglo–American declaration to the effect that Spain could not recover South American colonies that had gained their independence. His aim was to forestall a plan of the three pillars of the Holy Alliance – Austria, Russia and Prussia – actively supported by France, to overthrow the new governments as part of a move to enforce the divine right of kings. President Monroe sought the advice of Jefferson, who said: 'Our first and fundamental maxim should be, never to entangle ourselves in the broils of Europe.' Monroe rejected the British proposal for a joint statement and in his presidential message on 2 December 1823 he enunciated what became known as the Monroe doctrine. This drew a firm line between American and European interests. Monroe said it was not American policy to take part in intra-European wars. The United States would not interfere with existing European colonies, but any attempt by a European power to control the destinies of those that had become independent would be regarded as an unfriendly act towards the United States, and the creation of further colonies in America would not be met with indifference. Monroe had thus refused to align the USA formally with one European nation against others, while at the same time making it clear that he did not want any more European intervention in the Western hemisphere.

It was therefore consistent with long-established policy that on the day that Britain declared war on Germany President Woodrow Wilson proclaimed America's neutrality. Two weeks later he issued a further proclamation advising the people to remain neutral 'not only in act but in word and thought'. Many Americans were anti-British by inheritance. Between 1820 and 1900 more than 5 million Germans and nearly 4 million Irish had migrated to the United States; the flow continued and by 1910 341,489 more Germans and 339,065 more Irish had settled there. The Irish persisted in their hatred of the British and many Americans of German origin or descent retained their ethnic emotional ties. Anti-British feeling rose when the Royal Navy, enforcing its blockade of Germany, searched American ships for goods that Britain had declared contraband. In the first weeks of the war trade with Germany was almost totally cut off. Late in 1914 Washington lodged a protest when the contraband list was extended; but Britain cooled hostile feeling considerably by permitting the passage of cotton and certain other goods, despite their military value to Germany; and its mere searching of vessels was dwarfed in the public mind when German submarines sank them. Dislike of German autocracy and reports of ill-treatment in the occupied areas of Belgium and France, embellished by British propaganda, won a strong preponderance of American public sympathy for the Allies; but it was a radical shift in the economy that gave it political substance. Great Britain, France and Russia borrowed heavily from the United States to buy munitions, food, clothing and horses. American industry swiftly geared itself to this opportunity. Immense profits were made. America's favourable trade balance rose from $690 million in 1913 to $1,770 million in 1915 and $3,000 million in 1916. This huge debit incurred by the Entente was balanced by about $3,000 million sent to the United States in securities and gold and $2,000 million in foreign war bonds. In these circumstances genuine neutrality became impossible and Germany increasingly regarded the United States as a *de facto* enemy. But neither belief that the Allies were fighting for democracy nor the fact that the United States was profiting from their sacrifice was sufficient to draw Americans into the conflict. One of the slogans in Wilson's successful presidential election campaign in 1916 was: 'He kept us out of the war.'

Nor was the German torpedoing of American ships that were supplying the Allies enough to provoke American participation. After the sinking of the Cunard liner, *Lusitania*, on 7 May 1915, when 139 Americans were among the 1,198 dead, Germany had agreed not to torpedo merchant ships without warning and without ensuring the safety of non-combatants. When on 31 January 1917 Germany announced that it would resume unrestricted submarine attacks, the United States immediately broke off diplomatic relations with it. Yet even after American ships had been torpedoed in February and March, Congress opposed the arming of merchant vessels – a decision that the administration ignored. About this time the Germans offered an alliance to Mexico, which was to recover territory it had lost to the United States, and tried to woo Japan. The United States then declared war. While the spirit of Washington and Jefferson was a factor in keeping the United States out of the fighting for two years and eight months, Monroe's amplification of it played an important part in the decision to participate, which was not taken until the government saw a European threat to the Western hemisphere in general and US territory in particular. Ironically, it could hardly have fought at all, but for the stimulus that the Allies gave to its war industries. In 1914 the United States had no military aeroplane of approved type, no trench bomb or mine-thrower and only four modern heavy field guns, which lacked transport. Its only considerable supply of weapons was 800,000 rifles.

The doctrine evolved by Washington, Jefferson and Monroe expressed the feelings – wisdom, one might say – of a considerable body of Americans. It was probably this traditional thinking, rather than disillusionment at predictable European behaviour, that brought about America's return after the war to what is loosely called isolationism. Wilson's sponsorship of the League of Nations was under strong attack even before the Peace Conference began. There was widespread misgiving that the President's idealism would entangle America in foreign quarrels. Danger was seen in Article X of the Covenant, by which the League undertook 'to respect and preserve as against external aggression the territorial integrity and existing political independence of all members'. The fears entertained by Wilson's opponents soon proved to be justified. France refused to join the League unless its security was guaranteed; Wilson, with astonishing blindness to feeling at home, signed a treaty of alliance with France and Britain, under which the United States promised to give France armed assistance if Germany invaded it. This violation of traditional policy provoked bitter opposition, which cut across party lines. In November 1919 the Senate refused to ratify the Treaty of Versailles, with which the Covenant was inextricably interwoven. The United States thus abandoned the League of Nations, which fell under the sponsorship of Britain, and remained technically at war with Germany until a peace declaration was signed in 1921. Untidy though it was, this end to America's first venture in Europe was not negative. Americans had not simply failed to show the qualities required for world leadership; true to the sagacity of their forefathers, they had positively rejected their president's attempt to do so.

Traditional American foreign policy persisted until the Second World War when, as Kissinger says:[18]

> Only with the greatest difficulty could President Roosevelt take the first tentative steps against the mounting threat, aiding Great Britain by subterfuge and rebuilding our military might. The Second World War was well under way before we were shocked out of isolation by a surprise attack on American soil [the Japanese bombing of Pearl Harbor on 7 December 1941].

While the United States had been giving substantial support to the Allies in word and deed, there is no saying when it would in fact have entered the war had it not been for the Pearl Harbor attack. On 8 December Britain, the United States, Canada and the

Netherlands, which saw a threat to the East Indies, declared war on Japan; but the United States did not declare war on Germany and Italy until after those two powers had precipitately declared war on it on 11 December. Meanwhile Roosevelt had been shepherding the American people towards the verge of participation. Public sympathy had been overwhelmingly with the United Kingdom, particularly since 17 June 1940, when France asked Germany for an armistice and left the British to struggle on alone; but this did not mean that Americans wanted to fight. In September 1940 the United States agreed to recondition and exchange fifty old destroyers for the lease of bases in the British West Indies and Bermuda. By 9 February 1941 Churchill was able to tell America: 'Give us the tools and we will finish the job.' The reply came in March when Roosevelt won Congress's authority to lend or lease equipment or installations to any country whose defence he considered essential to US security; in the necessary bill America resolved to become the 'arsenal of Democracy', a function highly satisfactory to those whose task it was to manufacture the weapons. In the same month the government ordered the seizure of 300,000 tons of Axis shipping tied up in American ports. With shrewd deference to traditional doctrine, Roosevelt declared on 27 May that the war was 'approaching the brink of the Western hemisphere itself' – an allusion to the Battle of the Atlantic – and that it would be suicidal for America to wait until an enemy was in its front yard. In the following month he acted against espionage by ordering the closure of all German and Italian consulates and agencies. In July American troops replaced the British garrison in Iceland, which became part of the Western Hemisphere defence system; and in September US naval vessels escorted British convoys sailing to Halifax, while Roosevelt ordered the navy to 'shoot first' at raiding Axis warships. Despite the tension of an undeclared sea war, in which eleven American ships had been sunk by 27 October, aversion to involvement in a foreign conflict remained strong; and in November 1941 Congress repealed the Neutrality Act, which Roosevelt had signed two years previously, by a margin of only eighteen votes – 212 to 194; US merchant ships could then be armed and were allowed to sail anywhere.

The bombing of Pearl Harbor, though unexpected, did not occur in a diplomatic void. In July 1941 Japan, with the concurrence of Vichy France, had occupied bases in French Indo-China. The United States and Britain immediately cut Japan off from vital tin, rubber, oil and steel. In October a militaristic government under

General Tojo took over and demanded that the 'orient be purged of the United States'. In the next month a series of Japanese–American conferences in Washington broke down when Japan insisted on no obstruction of its activities in China, the lifting of the Anglo-American blockade and no spreading of the European war to East Asia. The Pearl Harbor attack followed.

After the war the United States was transformed from a nation that had eschewed involvement in the affairs of Europe into one that intervened belligerently in all the major affairs of the world. Yet this development was not without ideological and economic roots. Since early in the nineteenth century, when for a time it was the world's only republic, the United States had become imbued with a sense of mission. Jefferson, while opposed to becoming embroiled in Europe, said in his first inaugural address that the United States was 'the world's best hope'. In the words of Ernest R. May:[19] 'There was a widely held conviction that the United States had a mission to perform on behalf of other lands and peoples.' The economic counterpart of this belief was a policy of expansion. As May points out:[20]

> Of great importance in the early decades of the country's history was simple territorial expansion. Movements in favour of annexing New Orleans, the Louisiana territory, the Floridas, Texas and the Great Southwest were all, at one time or another, elevated to the level of noble national objectives. . . . Territorial expansion was said to increase the 'area of freedom'.

Describing what he regards as America's isolation between the two world wars, Kissinger says that economic action was seen as the only legitimate involvement abroad; its objectives were either humanitarian, as in Herbert Hoover's relief work, or free trade, as advocated by Cordell Hull (Secretary of State).[21] To a statesman like Kissinger, concerned above all with power balance, the pursuit of free trade may appear to be a relatively unimportant element of a policy that was politically isolationist; but in fact this seemingly innocuous activity provides a link between American assertion in the nineteenth century and that which followed during and after the Second World War. During the general imperialist scramble for slices of China in the 1890s the United States urged an Open Door policy, under which concession-holders would have no exclusive trade advantages; a similar policy was urged upon the Ottoman Empire. In this period a clear and enduring relationship was established between America's professed belief in national self-determination and its desire to maintain trade and investment openings. This policy, in both its aspects, was to render difficult, if not impossible, a *modus vivendi* with the Soviet Union, whose virtually closed economy extended to a group of satellites, which it controlled to ensure its security.

At no stage does it appear to have occurred to any United States leader that an Open Door does not suit all peoples. As Balfour has pointed out, the Open Door policy loomed up even in the lend–lease negotiations.[22] By this time America's need was less to increase than to maintain its prosperity. In 1938, after the depression, seven million Americans were still unemployed; only war production reduced this number to three million at the end of 1941. The question was how could industry be kept going when the war ended and America ceased to be 'the arsenal of Democracy'. The answer was seen to lie in increased exports, and Britain's financial predicament appeared to offer the United States an opportunity to gain them. In December 1940 British currency reserves were only within a few days of exhaustion; the government had either to make a compromise peace or find foreign funds to finance the war. Roosevelt knew from experience between 1915 and 1932 that large loans would never be fully repaid and embarked on his lend–lease policy. Cordell Hull, continuing his pre-war campaign, proposed that in return Britain should commit itself to a post-war world of free trade; in other words the price of help was to be fulfilment of the American dream of an Open World. This proposal was as absurd as it was brash and in this respect may be likened to more recent attempts by the United States to enforce its will on Europe. It took no account of the fact that other countries would lack the means of paying for increased exports rolling off American production lines. Keynes, who was the British Government's chief economic adviser at that time, said privately that it was 'lunatic'. There was no reason to believe that the entire world would become open; in any case, Britain could not expose her markets to all and sundry in the expectation that other countries would automatically buy enough from her to pay for her imports. Nor could the United States be relied upon to adhere in practice to the doctrine that it preached. Congress already had a long record of submitting to protectionist lobbies. In the 1930s high American tariffs had blocked imports and made it difficult for other countries to earn dollars; importers from the United States were thus forced to pay in gold on such a scale that America acquired three-quarters of the world's stocks. Cordell Hull's plan would have reduced still further, if that were possible, chances of economic development in what became the Third World, which cannot compete against more technologically advanced nations; if an Open World had existed in the 1930s, Australia, which established industry behind a strong tariff wall, would have remained a purely agricultural country. Looked at from any point of view, the idea was impracticable. It was eventually lost in the loopholes of the Lend–Lease Agreement.

The desire to organize an Open World on the one hand and traditional aversion to entanglement in Europe on the other produced anomalies in American policy that took some time to resolve. In the Atlantic Charter, drawn up with Churchill on 14 August 1941, Roosevelt vetoed the insertion of any reference to a post-war international organization; doubtless the possibility that the American people would reject a new league, as they had the original one, made some contribution to his decision. Subsequently he said to Churchill: 'Do please don't [sic] ask me to keep any American forces in France after the war. I just cannot do it. I would have to bring them all home.' There was also a contradiction between the concept of a flourishing Open World and Roosevelt's determination to crush Germany and keep it down. In this Roosevelt was supported by his Secretary for the Treasury, Henry Morgenthau, who wanted to destroy Germany's industrial plant and reduce its economy to a primarily agricultural footing; in one version of this plan population rendered surplus was to be transferred to North Africa.[23] But in 1946 it became obvious that the cost of feeding an impoverished Germany was too high. On 6 September James Byrnes, Harry S. Truman's Secretary of State, said in Stuttgart that Germany must be given a chance to export enough to make its economy self-sustaining. In the same speech he made it clear that American troops, instead of going home within two years of the end of the war, would stay on as long as the occupation lasted. America's economic, political and military involvement in Europe was now beyond doubt.

Western Europe was economically prostrate. With the Marshall plan, the United States set about putting it on its feet again. The Russians saw this as a first move in building up the West militarily in order to deprive them of the buffer formed when they set up the satellites. Consequently Marshall aid 'deepened the split between East and West, bringing in Eastern Europe a consolidation of Communism and Soviet power'.[24] Whether or not Moscow's suspicions were justified, 'a main objective had undeniably been to win the mouths and minds of the West European peoples so as to prevent them from turning Communist'.[25] Thus it was no longer a question of America's becoming embroiled in the quarrels of Europe, but of an attempt to influence the destiny of the entire Western part of it, as a step in the creation of an Open World – a world as open to the United States as the vast southwestern plains were seen to be in the nineteenth century.

Chapter 3

The Russians

Dominance

The first point to note in assessing the Russians is that they have already achieved a walkover in what appears to have been the last of the great conflicts between European nations. In 1939 Hitler's invasion of Poland to enforce his demand for the return of Danzig and the right to construct a military highway and railway between Germany proper and East Prussia, across the Polish Corridor, was enough to trigger off a world war; Nazism was not the issue. But now the Russians, when they find it essential to their security, may freely invade countries such as Hungary, Czechoslovakia and Afghanistan. They may, or may not, decide that they need to occupy Finland, described by Molotov as a peanut, or think it advisable to intervene in Poland. While they do not ignore world opinion, the initiative is always theirs. If another war breaks out in Europe, it will not be primarily European, but Russo–American. It would be the United States, not Western Europe, which would decide whether or not a Russian attack or a real, imagined or fabricated threat would be substantially met. Immediate American participation, rather than tardy and shrewdly calculated intervention, would be essential to the conflict.

In the past, including the recent past, European countries ravaged the continent to achieve influence, on the one hand, and to maintain a reasonable balance of power, on the other. They dominated, bullied and bled a vast part of the world. But since the Second World War history has taken an astonishing and irrevocable turn. Only Russia has survived as a European power, in the sense in which that word had usually been understood; the term 'super-power' serves little purpose other than to blur that otherwise obvious fact. Russia's superior strength in conventional forces, backed by adequate industrial capacity, has finally shattered the concept of European balance; and Western Europe, unable to defend itself, is reduced to relying upon a brash and unpredictable ally on the other side of the Atlantic. Paying lip-service to the concept of Europe, the former powers have tried to pull themselves up by their shoestrings in forming what is euphemistically called the European Communities. Instead of facing up to the great issues of the era, they have spent an inordinate amount of time wrangling over such matters as budget contributions and food prices, in constant fear of enraged farmers and fishermen.

The magnitude of Russia's rise to power can only be compared in the twentieth century to the dissolution of the British Empire, one of the most stupendous events in history, the significance of which for Western Europe does not appear to have been fully grasped. The achievement becomes all the more startling when it is recalled that Russia was trounced by the Japanese soon after the beginning of this century, and reduced to an apparently hopeless shambles, with fearful casualties, in the First World War. Yet if Western Europe is weak, so, in its own way, is Russia. This chapter will attempt to establish where the weakness lies. We shall begin with relevant aspects of the Russian character and civilization. It will be argued that Russia, in spite of its having been fired to some extent by the Western spirit, retains psycho-cultural traits that impede, but do not prevent, its further development.

Cultural limitation

In the first version of his *A Study of History* Toynbee called the Russian civilization Orthodox Christian; subsequently he added that it was also a Western satellite. But when we look for the sources of Russian despotism, there is more to be taken into account. Referring to the period of Mongol–Tatar domination from the thirteenth to the fifteenth centuries, Marx said: 'The bloody mire of Mongol slavery . . . forms the cradle of Muscovy, and modern Russia is but a metamorphosis of Muscovy.'[1] On the other hand, the historian, Richard Pipes, while recognizing the Mongol–Tatar influence, maintains that the patrimonial state, conceived as the personal property of the ruler, originated in the early Slavonic communities.[2] To this he traces what he calls the police state of today. Christopher Duffy, the military historian, singles out the princes of Muscovy as enthusiastic and shameless Mongol surrogates. But this distinction could also be claimed for other Russian princes, who put down their own people to assure tribute to the

Mongols. Rival sons of Grand Prince Alexander Nevsky, who saved Novgorod from a Swedish invasion on St Vladimir's Day in 1240, competed for Mongol–Tatar support; in the ensuing war Tatars ravaged Russian lands. Early in the fourteenth century the Prince of Novgorod married Khan Uzbeg's sister. In the seventeenth century families of Tatar origin accounted for almost one in five of the service nobility, with Russian-sounding names such as Apraksin, Leontev, Rostopchin and Turgenev.[3]

Whatever its origin, absolutism characterized Russian government until the establishment of an independent judiciary in the second half of the nineteenth century. It then gave place to autocracy, until Stalin reinstated it in another guise. In other words, Russia, with the reform of 1864, achieved a separation of justice from administration that was in force in Rome in the second century BC and in modern Europe in the late Middle Ages; and even this step would not have been taken but for overwhelming Western intellectual influence. As late as the eighteenth century von Manstein, a Russian subject of German descent, wrote in his three-volume classic of Russian military history:[4] 'it is possible that no Russian has ever conceived that his country could be governed otherwise than by an absolute sovereign'. The tsar was paramount, like the shah; the law was his word. Despite the revolution, the mass psychology has undergone little change; during the 1980 Olympic Games Muscovites found it incomprehensible that the British Olympic Committee was present against the wishes of its Government.

The Mongol–Tatars, the so-called Golden Horde, were not entirely repressive; their main demand was tribute. Nor was their domination without benefit; in 1257 they conducted Russia's first census. The khans did not interfere with the church, even after the Horde had adopted Islam as its official religion early in the fourteenth century. Churchmen, monasteries and convents were exempt from tribute. The definitive conversion of Russians to Byzantine Christianity had been ruthlessly enforced by Vladimir I, of Scandinavian origin, when he and his soldiers set the example and were baptized by Greek clergy in 987. Earlier, after some Russians had been converted by missionaries, Vladimir had initiated a pagan revival in Kiev, the first important Russian centre, and built a pantheon to the East Slavonic gods, as a unifying measure. But he probably recognized the superiority of neighbouring civilizations and saw in their religions the source of their success. After considering four possibilities he rejected Western Christianity,

Judaism and Islam and chose Eastern Orthodox Christianity, because, according to legend, he preferred its ritual. In the Kievan civilization the name Ruś came to mean not only the country and its people, but its religion. In accordance with the Byzantine tradition, the church supported, legitimized and was subordinate to the authority of the grand prince. When power shifted to Muscovy, the Metropolitan, who by this time was established in the principality of Vladimir, moved his see to Moscow in 1328. Moscow then became the Russians' own Constantinople.

While Orthodox Christianity helped to foster Russian self-awareness, the effect of the church's subordination to the state was to abort any tendencies towards intellectual vigour, such as those that came to characterize the West. Toynbee found that this structure was fatal to the East Roman Empire itself. In the eighth century Emperor Leo Syrus turned the church 'into a department of state and the Ecumenical Patriarch into a kind of imperial Under-Secretary of State for Ecclesiastical Affairs'.[5] By succeeding in what Charlemagne failed to achieve two generations later, Leo Syrus aggrandized the state at the expense of all other institutions. The general effect was to sterilize tendencies towards social experimentation and creativeness. In Orthodox society there was nothing corresponding to Hildebrand's great achievement in asserting and substantiating the church's claim to moral leadership of Western Christendom. Toynbee says:[6]

> We also miss the rise and spread of self-governing universities, corresponding to the new Western centres of intellectual activity at Bologna and Paris, and of self-governing city-states, corresponding to the new Western centres of life in Central and Northern Italy and in Flanders.

In theory the Eastern church was in harmony with the state, but in practice it was subservient. The emperor summoned church councils and appointed bishops; even the tenure of the patriarch was insecure.

The choice of such a model showed that the Russians had little chance of becoming a socially creative community. In addition, the Orthodox church was extremely conservative in its theology. By the time of the Russian conversion Byzantium had resolved its important doctrinal conflicts and had arrived at what it believed to be the ultimate form of its faith. With its primitive belief that this, and only this, was the genuine revelation, Russian Orthodoxy became more rigid than the mother church, and relied on a repressive secular authority to prevent the land from being polluted by false faiths. Thus the church reinforced despotism. Church tradition was binding; the Gospels were secondary and the Bible was not translated into Russian and published until the second half of the nineteenth century. Ritual was all-important; magical elements were more widely influential than doctrine. Whereas in the West rationality, like Galileo's, and relative rationality, like Luther's, fought against dogma, in Russia such intellectual struggle as took place until Western influence asserted itself was between one form of irrationality and another. The importance of magic in the Russian religion is highly significant; for it is surely more than a coincidence that inordinate superstition and despotism are usually found together and – what matters in the present context – characterize many countries that did not undergo Western-style development. Despotism and subservience seem to be psychically symbiotic.

Toynbee's view that the state–church relationship was the primary factor in the East Roman Empire's stagnation, and eventual collapse, will not satisfy those, including this author, who find structures to be less a social cause than a reflection of a particular psychology; Pipes's statement that the embracing of Orthodox Christianity, rather than that of the West, had the 'most profound consequences for the entire course of Russia's historic development' is similarly incomplete. If one is to look to environment, whim or chance as determining structure and to structure as determining the development of a society, one is left with the unlikely proposition that in only one tiny patch on the globe were the extra-human conditions right for the extraordinary social and intellectual leap made by Western Europe alone about the seventeenth century. Toynbee's handling of this issue is inconsistent. While at times he implicitly accepts structural determinism and in his treatment of race rejects innate characteristics as a factor in the rise of civilizations, he nevertheless uses such a phrase as 'the Iranian genius' and begins an essay, 'Russia's Byzantine Heritage', with Horace's dictum: 'You may throw Nature out with a pitchfork, but she will keep coming back.' Russia's nature, in fact, has never left it, and its history is packed with examples of continuity. Some of these will be mentioned later in this chapter, but we may already note the correspondence between past enforcement of religious dogma and present insistence on the purity of Lenin's version of Marx. With no revised version allowed, the Russians have contributed 'revisionist' and 'deviationist' to the world's political jargon.

The persistence of despotism in Russia and Asia and of the institution of divine king, until this century, in Africa requires more than an unqualified structural or environmental explanation. The power of West European monarchs was reciprocal even as early as the Middle Ages, when in England Henry I (1100–35) traded a charter of liberties for London's support in his election as king. It is inconceivable that any structure could have restrained the intellectual and commercial vigour that led to the founding of West European universities and free towns, just as it is certain that Greece's adherence to the European Communities will not make most Greek industrialists as efficient and reliable as most German. It was not the social structure of Western Europe that induced in the later Middle Ages 'a passion for the mechanisation of industry such as no other culture had known'.[7] Political institutions foster the forces that give rise to them, but are not in themselves creative; they are an expression, subject to ethnic variation, of a particular civilization at a given stage of its development, and are rarely transferable. Similarly, a religion is created or adapted to fulfil the psychic needs of a community. It stabilizes attitudes that are already maturing and is more expressive than formative. An exceptionally superstitious people will produce an exceptionally superstitious religion. Or, as Pope John Paul II observed with dismay in Brazil, it will add its own superstitions to a religion that it embraces.

None of this means that the characteristics of a people remain fixed for all time. But ethnic differences have important consequences, such as those observed by Jung in his studies of Eastern psychology and by Marx when he saw the influence of 'natural predisposition – the clan character' in the formation of early societies.[8] If we are to attempt an assessment of Russian social potential, consideration of the psychological factors is essential. Certain Russian characteristics have long been clearly distinguishable, although not rigorously defined. The question is to what extent they have been changed or modified by the revolution, whether such change as has taken place is widespread or limited and whether the consequences have been creative, traumatic or both.

Wright Miller, who knew Russia well, found it unhelpful to distinguish Russians from people in the West by thinking of them as Asiatic; to begin with, the Slavonic languages were a branch of the Indo-Germanic. Miller was aware of Chekhov's letter urging his brother, Nikolai, to 'sweat the Asiatic' out of himself; but he thought

that in the nineteenth century the Russian intelligentsia, 'exasper-
ated by the sluggishness and backwardness of their country, took to
using "Asiatic" as a term of abuse'.[9] Squalor and idleness had
always been Russian characteristics, Miller maintained, and were
not acquired from Tashkent or Bokhara. Nevertheless, the term
'Asiatic' is useful as shorthand to denote traits that are more general
among Russia's Eastern neighbours than in the West. Among these
is superstition so widespread and of such psychic depth that it
obscured the observation of cause and effect in nature and thus
rendered impossible the birth of Western-type science and the
social development that is related to it. Christianity in Russia was
permeated with animism, as it is today in parts of the Third World.
Miller says that Russian peasants observed animist practices well
into the twentieth century. The old pagan gods were no longer
worshipped (priests supported by despots had seen to that), but
countless sprites of trees and waters were still honoured and
'ancestors were thought of as inhabiting birch trees instead of (or
perhaps as well as!) ascending to heaven'.[10] Many pagan rituals
persisted at weddings and funerals. Chekhov's peasants found
comfort in the external forms of religion as a kind of magic; there
were few who understood Christianity, but many were enraptured
when the Scriptures were read to them.[11] While there was little
awareness of the Christian God, people, particularly women,
turned to the Little Mother in times of stress.

Mariolatry began as an Eastern phenomenon. That it fulfilled a
particular psychic need is seen in the exuberance with which a
fifth-century Ephesian mob celebrated the exclusion from all
priestly communion of Nestorius, who opposed the designation of
Mary as the Mother of God. The strong emphasis given to the cult of
Mariolatry in pre-revolutionary Russia and present-day Poland is
clearly a significant psycho-cultural phenomenon. Hedrik Smith,
former *New York Times* correspondent in Moscow, finds that in
spite of indoctrination with Marx-according-to-Lenin, the Russians
remain a 'mystical, religious and superstitious people at heart'.[12]
They are 'easy-going, indolent and disorganized, rather than scientific, rational and efficient'. A Russian writer told Smith that it was
the ailments and ordeals of life that made Russians fear the power of
the evil eye and turn to omens, signs and portents. But since the
Russians have long been backward in many respects, it seems more
likely that their mentality leads to their ordeals and not their ordeals
to their mentality.

It used to be disputed whether the misery of the peasants caused their drunkenness and sloth or whether it was the other way round. History seems to have supplied the answer. Initially driven by Stalin, peasants and industrial workers have become very much better off materially than they were before the revolution. But drink remains no less a national problem and is a serious cause of low productivity. Down the centuries the addiction to alcohol of Russians of all classes has always astonished foreigners. In 1639 Adam Orleans, who represented the Duke of Holstein's court in Moscow, found Russians to be 'more addicted to drunkenness than any other nation in the world'.[13] Tito was shocked by excessive drinking in Stalin's entourage during the Second World War and condemned it as 'sheer decadence'.[14] Smith cites high officials as saying that drunkenness accounts for 90 per cent of Moscow's murders, more than half of traffic accidents, 63 per cent of accidental drownings and one-third of ambulance calls; it is a major cause in 40 per cent of divorces. It looks as if day to day reality is too much for many Slavs to bear – Poles as well as Russians – and that they are constantly seeking an escape from it. At the same time the Russians possess a possibly unique spiritual quality, which enables them to respond magnificently to exceptional challenge.

While Russians looked to the Little Mother to intercede for them in their immediate troubles, it was a male figure that inspired their veneration. This was the Little Father (*batyushka*), in the person of the tsar and later, to a considerable extent, Lenin and Stalin. Apart from the intelligentsia – a tiny minority under Western influence – all classes looked up to the tsar; the absolute monarchy was in no serious danger until the end of the nineteenth century. Throughout the period of serfdom and beyond, the peasants continued to honour the Little Father until about the time of the 1905 revolution, despite his link with the hated landlords, which they saw only dimly, if at all. But when some were flogged and shot for initiating self-government after the tsar had promised them a measure of liberty, they no longer saw him as their protector. Some accused him of failing to keep his promise and turned bitterly against him. The revolution had been crushed, but the tsar's role was now more clearly seen and his authority was doomed.

In the veneration of the tsar we have again a psychological trait found more in the East, and in the Third World generally, than in the West. The most extreme form of this phenomenon is the institution of divine king, of which perhaps the most carefully studied example in recent times is in the kingdom of Benin, which remained unchanged for centuries before the British intervened in 1897. The king, though chosen politically, became divine upon his enthronement, with power of life and death, and on his rare public appearances his subjects cowered in his presence as before a god. The Russians did not formally deify the tsar, but in the sixteenth and seventeenth centuries the church, acting on its own initiative, firmly established his divine authority and the idea that he was 'like God' in the exercise of his office.[15] The intensity with which veneration of the tsar flourished alongside primitive religious beliefs suggests a psychic condition that was closer to the non-Western than to the Western. The West's ideas of monarchy were significantly unlike those found elsewhere. There is, for example, a vast difference between the doctrine of the divine right of kings and belief that the king is divine. Again, the Teutonic kingship did not imply absolute authority. Kingship as a theocratic power, over which controversy raged in the seventeenth century, was an oriental idea imported from Byzantium with Christianity. Alien to the psychology of the people, it was successfully resisted. Russia, with its almost divine king, appears, as in other important respects, to lie somewhere between East and West.

Veneration of despots, though it varies in degree, and the submissiveness that accompanies it, seem to fulfil a psychic need. Catherine II (1762–96), usually referred to as 'the Great', aroused no popular opposition when she declared: 'Everything *for* the people; nothing *by* the people.' The American historian, John Meyendorff, has noted 'the extraordinary degree of political submissiveness which the Russians have shown in their history'.[16] Djilas, the Yugoslav dissident, concluded from direct observation that the cult of Stalin as a deity was 'at least as much the work of Stalin's circle and the bureaucracy, who required such a leader, as his own doing'.[17] The needs of those closest to Stalin could hardly have been less than those of a mass that had lost its Little Father. Most people, like Djilas himself until he became disillusioned, believed that Stalin's ruthlessness was necessary. Despite the revelations of Krushchev, this feeling persists. Smith reports a conversation in which a son argued with his father that while the terror was excessive, 'maybe Stalin had to use force to pull the country together'.[18] A number of Stalin's supporters whom Smith interviewed included a thirty-year-old Tashkent librarian, who claimed that the ordinary people disliked the removal of his body from the mausoleum in 1961, and a metallurgical worker in his twenties, who said Russian workers needed a Stalin, not a Brezhnev, to 'stand behind his broad back'. A factory director in his fifties regretted that Stalin was no longer there to discipline the workers, who were 'all slackers'. A state farm accountant said: 'The intelligentsia may dream of democracy but the huge mass of people dream of Stalin. . . . They want a strong boss to "put the shoes" on the petty bosses.' Under Stalin, he said, officials did not rob and mock the people. Here we have Stalin seen in the role of protective Little Father. This popular view is not, however, irrational. Stalin did, in fact, wage an incessant war against bureaucracy. In an address to graduates of the Red Army Academy in May 1935 he condemned the 'outrageous attitude' of leaders to workers and cadres and said they had not learned to 'value people'. He declared:[19]

> Leaders should display the most solicitous attitude towards our workers, 'little' and 'big', no matter in what sphere they are engaged, cultivating them assiduously, assisting them when they need support, encouraging them when they display their first successes, advancing them, and so forth.

There was, of course, no trace of democracy, as the West understands it, in these precepts, any more than in the efforts of Peter I ('the Great') to Westernize Russia in the eighteenth century. As Duffy says:[20]

> Tyranny of a governmental kind was taken over almost without a break from the old order. 'Dissidents' and the like remain a tiny, unrepresentative minority, and the people have proved perfectly ready to accept the apparatus of controls, passports and directions with which they have lived for centuries.

Andrei Sakharov confirms this picture of conformity, but puts it down to brainwashing. For the time being, he says, the Soviet citizen is the government's 'chief support'.[21]

Concurrent with lingering respect for Stalin is the virtual deification of Lenin. While statuettes of Marx are extremely rare, Lenin is a 'ubiquitous ikon'.[22] Smith finds that the veneration of his bodily remains, which is reminiscent of the worship of the relics of Christian and Islamic saints, and the illusion of immortality created by preserving them are obvious parallels with religion. Lenin's word is preached as a gospel. On the eve of the anniversary parade celebrating the Bolshevik seizure of power a ceremony that amounts to a communist sacrament is carried out with religious ecstasy. A chorus 'roars like the seas of eternity, Lenin [spotlighted] gleams, one hand in his pocket, an open book resting on his other arm – human, reincarnate'.[23] The effect is one of purity and resurrection. Tass, reporting the reopening of the mausoleum, which had been closed for repairs, said in 1974: 'From this day onwards new thousands and millions of people will be bringing worship to Lenin from all over the world.' At kindergartens Smith found a smiling, benevolent Uncle Lenin looking down at the children in almost every room. Pupils were forbidden to draw him because, a teacher explained, they lacked the skill required for so sacred an image. Lenin is allotted the role attributed to Jesus in Christian countries as the child's best friend. Teachers are instructed in their manuals that children of two and three must be taught to respect his portrait. As in other religions and religious movements, the hope of a second coming is offered: children sing songs depicting a resurrected Lenin playing hide-and-seek, picking strawberries and bouncing children on his knee.

It is out of the question to regard all this religious activity as no more than a function of the propaganda machine. There are cynics, opportunists and half-believers in all religions, particularly at the top, but there can be no doubt that vast numbers of people, including teachers, derive comfort from this worship. In the past the Russians prayed to ikons of Christ, the Virgin and the saints. Many still do, but today the predominant object of devotion is Lenin, whose image is placed in 'red corners' reserved in factories, institutions and apartment buildings. Doubtless the party is deliberately exploiting the people's religious urge. But that this urge persists, and that it is of a kind that can be absorbed in this way, is what we are concerned with here. Some Russians resent being rounded up for Leninist rituals and some make cynical jokes about them. But they, like the dissidents, do not represent the Russian masses, who are typified by what Smith describes as the long lines of people waiting hours 'for a glimpse of their entombed saint . . . their passive peasant faces reflecting a patience born of centuries'. Adherents of the higher religions experience no difficulty in seeing divine qualities or divine authority in figures dimmed by history, about whom insufficient facts are known to dissipate cherished notions. But to deify, or virtually deify, a man not long dead, or even to make a holy legend of him, is different; it requires a psychology close to that which enabled the Indian ruler, Akbar, to command the worship of his subjects when he founded a religion of his own in the sixteenth century.

An important question now arises in our assessment of Soviet potential. If Russia had some psycho-cultural affinity with its stagnant Asian neighbours, notably India and Iran, what were its chances of initiating development along Western lines? Before attempting to answer, it is necessary to state what is meant by Western economic development; this is nothing other than the rise of modern capitalism, for an explanation of which we shall recall the well-known theory of the German sociologist, Max Weber (1864–1920). In its simplest form capitalism is of ancient origin. It existed in India, China, Babylon and the Mediterranean coast of antiquity. This rudimentary capitalism was a considerable, though limited, step up the ladder of rationality. As Weber pointed out, its most important element was that a calculation of capital in terms of money was made, however crude the method. Associated with this was 'an actual adaptation of economic action to a comparison of money income with money expenses'.[24] From there the next development was not a step but a gigantic leap, which was to transform some of the world and dislocate the rest. This was the emergence of modern capitalism in northwestern Europe. It was this system that produced the wealth to which the occident has become accustomed. Weber denounced its moral outcome and Marx predicted its downfall; but that is not what we are considering at the moment. The essentials of modern capitalism, as seen by Weber, are the 'rational capitalistic organization of (formally) free labour', 'rational industrial organization, attuned to a regular market, and neither to political nor irrationally speculative opportunities for profit', 'the separation of business from the household, which completely dominates modern economic life and, closely connected with it, rational book-keeping'.[25]

We are accustomed to this system now, but its development required a drastic change in thought and action – an unprecedented application of reason to various walks of life. This is far from saying that Western society was, or is, anywhere near completely rational. But the seventeenth century, with its philosophers and scientists breaking entirely new ground, has not been called the age of reason without justification. Bacon, Galileo and Descartes all died in the seventeenth century and Newton and Leibniz had done their best work before the end of it. As this rational process developed, the natural sciences, based on mathematics and exact and rational experiment, though existing essentially in their own right, provided the basis of new technology.

But rationality in itself was not enough to set modern capitalism in motion. Weber found that the initial application of Western rationality to the economy was born of Protestant asceticism. The Puritan felt that God had called him to his task. Divinely ordained activity glorified God. Waste of time was thus 'the first and in principle the deadliest of sins'. It was not merchant or landed capital, but the savings of the small, carefully calculating Protestant manufacturer that financed the beginnings of modern capitalism. 'When asceticism was carried out of the monastic cells into everyday life, and began to dominate worldly morality, it did its part in building the tremendous cosmos of modern economic order.'[26] In every important social aspect Weber found differences between East and West: 'The concept of citizen has not existed outside the Occident. . . . Similarly, the proletariat as a class could not exist, because there was no rational organization of free labour under regular discipline.' For Weber the decisive difference of the Western culture from the Eastern was its particular rationality. He was aware that in the East rational processes took place, as in the rationalization of mystical contemplation. What was peculiar to the West was rationality in science, economic organization, political thinking and law.

If we are to join Weber in dividing societies in this way, there is no doubt about the group with which pre-revolutionary Russia is more closely identified. There was no concept of citizen and, until the emancipation of the serfs in 1861, virtually no free labour; the main economic drive was politically motived; and merchants fitted the oriental pattern. Pipes says:[27]

> The business mentality of the Russian merchant retained a strong Levantine stamp. We find here little of the capitalist ethic with its stress on honesty, industry and thrift . . . every transaction is a separate event in which each party tries to take all. The dishonesty of the Russian merchant was notorious.

This manifestation of the bazaar spirit (with no thought of operations rationally attuned to a regular market) disgusted the Western-minded intelligentsia and is evident in Chekhov's stories. Muscovite merchants felt at ease in doing business with Asia, particularly in the three Moscow bazaars, of which one in the seventeenth century contained only Persian merchandise. But in the more rational markets of the West they relied mostly on foreign intermediaries; although often rich, they were usually ignorant of book-keeping – one of the essentials of modern capitalism. The first successful banks were not founded in Russia until the 1860s. For a long time the sumptuous dress of the merchants resembled that of wealthy Persians; although it was modified, it remained eastern in appearance until the beginning of the present century. Fear of dispossession was a constraint on the birth of capitalism in Russia, as in India; in both countries – Russia in the sixteenth century, at least – traders lived in dread of the despot's marauding officials.[28]

Western influence

If there were similarities between Russia and the East there was one very important difference: the Russians had long been under Western influence to a much greater extent than their oriental neighbours. Significantly, this powerful stimulus was not the consequence of imperialism, as, for instance, in India; it was of the Russians' own choosing, although not without considerable dissent. In a sense it could be said that the Russians felt the Western impact from the beginning. Ruś, the name by which the Russians were first known, may be Scandinavian; it was applied to the inhabitants of the Kievan state, the earliest that is positively identified as Russian. A. D. Stokes, the Oxford historian, says it is 'difficult to escape the conclusion that the earliest Ruś were Varangians', or Vikings, and that they adopted the name after their arrival from Scandinavia in the ninth century;[29] but Soviet historians insist that cognate river names show that East Slavonic Ruś existed before the Varangian penetration. However this may be, the political foundations of the Kievan state were laid in 882, when the Varangian Prince of Novgorod defeated his Varangian rivals and made Kiev his capital. Stokes says:

it could be generally agreed that social and economic developments among the Eastern Slavs had made the emergence of new forms of political organization [compared with tribal forms] a question of time; nevertheless, it is clear that in the event it was the Varangians who acted as the catalyst.

Whatever the relative levels of the Varangian and Kievan civilizations were at that time, the Russians were to lag behind all their important neighbours in the coming centuries, for which clear records are available. The Scandinavians, the Baltic Germans, Prussians, Poles and Tatars were more advanced. Russian civilization was incapable of producing an astronomer such as Ulugh Beg (1394–1449), a grandson of Tamerlane, who founded an observatory at Samarkand and published astronomical tables that were a standard work for two centuries. In Poland Copernicus (1473–1543) began his career by studying mathematics at Cracow University; but Moscow's first university was not established until 1775.

When Peter I (1682–1725) embarked on his ruthless attempt to Westernize Russia, he was confronted with an intellectual and administrative backwater, by European standards. Some Western elements had been imitated, but Western science, scholarship and service techniques were little known. Peter, therefore, had to begin almost at the beginning. Since the Russian language then lacked the vocabulary required for adequate translation of works from other parts of Europe, people who were to acquire and spread the Western spirit had to learn foreign languages, of which German was at first the most used. Nobles were torn from their estates and families, pressed into state service and forced to undergo technical education, which few mastered and most resented. They were ordered to dress like Germans, shave off their beards and to conduct themselves in a 'civilized' manner when in public. Peter planned an academy of sciences, which was not established until after his death, when all of its initial members were foreign.

As his famous trip to the West shows, Peter was determined to learn at first hand the secrets that would lift Russia to the level of Western nations. With an entourage of about 250 he travelled simply as Peter Mikhailov, gentleman, to avoid ceremony. He spent more than a year in Holland and Britain learning about such matters as shipbuilding, astronomy (at Greenwich) and gunfounding (at Woolwich). Peter was passionately resolved to transform Russia from an Asian into a European power. This does not mean that his aim was ultimate domination; what he wanted was that his country should be a fully-fledged member of the European family and have a voice in its affairs. Partly to this end he built his new capital of St Petersburg (the last syllable is Dutch), his so-called window on the West, on the Baltic coast. Peter is generally credited with having extricated Russia from the slough of the Middle Ages within a generation. The French diplomat, de Campredon, reported to Louis XV in 1723:[30]

> He has worked to drag his nobility up from the subhuman lassitude in which they were sunk, and qualify them to serve in

armies and navies, for which they harboured an invincible aversion until very recently. We have seen him perform the duties of drummer and carpenter, and rise gradually to the rank of general and admiral, observing at every step the obedience and subordination due to his superiors . . . he has managed to form some excellent military and naval officers, an army of more than 100,000 regular troops, and a fleet of sixty vessels. . . . Russia, whose very name was scarcely known, has now become the object of attention of the greater number of the powers of Europe, who solicit its friendship.

Yet the change was not as profound as the letter might suggest. While Peter built up Russia's armed strength and in the process raised its metal industries to a leading place in Europe, he was far less successful in his vigorous efforts to Westernize the nation and radically transform its economy. Some of the more educated and travelled Russians understood and responded to his policies, but generally feeling was what would be expected of a stagnant society that had experienced no renaissance or reformation. Westernization was widely resented and St Petersburg was disliked 'as a forced, artificial creation, a symbol of Peter's military ambitions, and the home of foreigners and a *parvenu* nobility'.[31] The Old Believers, who had been persecuted since the seventeenth century for adhering to Muscovite ritual instead of that adopted by the Greeks, declared that Peter was the instrument of Antichrist when he introduced Western dress and further secularized public life. New taxes and military conscription aroused bitterness. Every important economic measure that Peter took was impeded by the culture or contradicted by itself. The government founded, subsidized and even managed industries, mostly for war purposes; but taxes needed to finance these operations reduced chances that private enterprise would exploit the impetus given to the economy. These possibilities were, in any case, negligible. Townsmen continued to live in Asian-type subjection, with no recourse to law. Nearly all of the nation's capital was irrevocably tied up in land. Most landlords possessed only small estates, with serfs producing subsistence for themselves and a modest surplus for the master, who was frequently misled by faulty accounting into believing that he was solvent when he was heading for bankruptcy; farm production for the market was usually of minor importance. To ensure that all classes served the state as required, Peter consolidated serfdom; the result was that free labour remained so scarce that he was obliged to attach serfs to mines and factories, while the perpetuation of serfdom inhibited the emergence of independent artisans. It has been said that serfdom made it unnecessary for landlords to become efficient and think in economic terms. But the evidence of Russian literature is that a deeply ingrained mentality, not structure, is the important factor here.

Peter's attempts to impose bastardized Western models on a society whose culture was unreceptive to them were to a great extent as blind as similar endeavours in the Third World today. The result was not real development, but the damaging of any indigenous potential. This is exemplified in his imitative enforcement of industrial standards: crafts that could have formed part of a much-needed infrastructure were discouraged and sometimes destroyed. Whatever the stimulus that Peter gave to the economy, in furtherance of his political aims, Russia was to remain economically backward compared with the West. It could be said, however, though not with certainty, that without Peter's educational innovations the intelligentsia, who were the first to exhibit convincing signs of a genuine Western spirit, could not have emerged. The intelligentsia were directly influenced by Western thought and literature. They are not identifiable until early in the nineteenth century; the term itself, variously applied, appears to have been coined in the 1860s.[32]

The Western impact on Russia has been formidable in every important activity except religion and politics, which have remained essentially immune. While eighteenth-century Europe is noted for an abundance of cosmopolitan military adventurers, Russia had far more than its share and it would require considerable labour to compute the number of foreign officers on its payroll; these ranged from men of high distinction to the worst throw-outs of other countries. Until the beginning of the eighteenth century nearly all senior artillery officers were foreigners. The navy, one of Peter's greatest achievements, remained dependent on foreign officers throughout his reign; and early in the nineteenth century Lord Cathcart, British ambassador and military commissioner in Moscow, said the worm-eaten Russian fleet depended on British expertise to keep it afloat. In the last stages of the War of the Austrian Succession (1740–8), half of the officers were foreign in a force that Russia was obliged by treaty to send to Germany. But by the time of Russia's German Empress, Catherine II ('the Great'), most leading commands were held by Russians, although foreigners, particularly Germans, were still given highly responsible positions; among these was Major-General Friedrich Bauer, who reconstructed the general staff in 1770.

Yet even in the period of greatest dependence on foreigners, there was more than a mere nucleus of brilliant and inventive Russian officers. Peter himself skilfully devised principles of combat based on his experience as a commander. Duffy says that his codes abound in phrases like 'because I saw it in the last action'. A flying corps on lines introduced by Peter raided Berlin in 1760, during the Seven Years War; after further successes it was last used in the Second World War, when a new version of it frequently attacked the Germans from the rear. Revolutionary canon invented by Peter Shuvalov (1710–62) was the 'foundation of the terrifying potential of the modern Soviet ordnance'.[33] In the field the eighteenth-century generals Alexander Suvorov, considered to be the greatest of all Russian commanders, and Peter Rumantsev, were among those who contributed far more than they learned from others to military thinking.

As it was with the soldiers, so it was with the scientists, scholars and writers, once the initial impetus had been given. Early in the nineteenth century nearly all Russia's university lecturers were Germans, teaching in Latin. But by 1855 education, with Russian as the medium, had 'attained equality with the technical and scholarly training offered in Western Europe'.[34] While it was not until the nineteenth century that a truly literary language was developed, Russia produced in the second half of it a unique literature that quickly became international. The Russian critic, S. Venguerov, said:[35]

Russian literature, which attains the very limits of the actual, is yet illumined by the ideal and is full of a love of humanity, of which there is not even a trace in the greater European realists. . . . The barbarians of yesterday were speaking a new language, which was to echo profoundly in European literature.

Scientists also rapidly repaid Russia's cultural debt to the West. D. I. Mendeleyev (1834–1907), with his periodic table, was able to predict three elements before they were discovered. Ivan Pavlov (1849–1936), although more widely known for his experiments on the conditioned reflexes of dogs, was awarded the Nobel prize in 1904 for his work on digestive glands. Another Nobel prize laureate was I. I. Mechnikov (1845–1916), who worked with Louis Pasteur. Among physicists was Alexander Popov (1859–1906), who was the first to make a radio signal actuate a tapper. Alexander Zasiadko (1779–1837) tested the first rocket in 1817 and rockets were used during the Russo–Turkish war in 1828–9. In 1903 Constantin Tsiolkovsky (1857–1935) published a project for a highly ingenious space ship, fuelled by liquid hydrogen and oxygen. Mathematics flourished following royal encouragement of the Swiss mathematician, Leonard Euler (1707–83), to work in Russia. Nikolai Lobachevsky (1792–1856) was a pioneer of non-Euclidian geometry. In 1888 Sophia Kovalevsky (1850–91), one of the world's few distinguished women mathematicians, won the prize of the French Academy of Sciences with an anonymously submitted paper on the rotation of a solid body about a fixed point. But, impressive though Russia's nineteenth-century scientific achievement was for a people that had lagged behind others of Indo-European language for so long, it cannot be compared to that of Western Europe.

The West's influence in trade began early; and by the twentieth century Western capital had penetrated on such a scale that Russian dependence on it resembled that of some Third World countries today. For hundreds of years after the establishment of German trading posts in Novgorod in the twelfth century, trade was dominated by the Hanseatic League, Swedes, Livonians, Dutch and British. In 1630 the Netherlands saw in backward Russia an opportunity similar to that which it found in the Indies: through a special ambassador it offered to finance exploitation of timber and to establish vast farms to grow wheat for export. The Russians rejected the proposal. But in the last quarter of the seventeenth century all trade in Archangel was in the hands of a few Dutch and German merchants, who had offices in Moscow. In the middle of the eighteenth century cotton weaving was monopolized by two Englishmen in St Petersburg. Elizabeth Petrovna (1741–62) and Catherine II borrowed heavily from Dutch bankers, and Paul I (1796–1801) and Alexander I (1801–25) needed British subsidies to fight the French.

Long before Peter I's attempt at Westernization, Ivan IV ('the Terrible') recognized the need for foreign craftsmen. In 1556 he ordered that German prisoners captured in the Livonian wars, who were familiar with metallurgy, should be taken to him personally. Alexinsky makes the important point:[36]

> The Livonian wars assisted the Europeanization of Russia in a very curious fashion. The prisoners taken by the Russians – Lithuanians, Poles, Germans, Livonians, etc. – were transported

into the interior of the country, and there became sponsors of Western culture.

Ivan assigned a quarter in Moscow to Germans and gave them fiscal privileges, but in one of his fits of rage he had them pillaged and ruined. Boris Godunov, recognizing their value, restored their rights.

Peter I, while modelling his administration entirely on Swedish lines, recruited large numbers of officials and jurists from Germany, Bohemia and Holland. When Anna Ivanovna (1730–40) ascended the throne she took her entire Baltic German entourage from Courland, where her husband was the ruling duke. Germans spread over Russia and monopolized lucrative administrative posts. Faced with revolt, Anna's successor, Elizabeth Petrovna, a daughter of Peter I, pensioned off Germans and reduced their influence, but bequeathed the crown to a German when she named Charles Peter Ulrich, Duke of Holstein, a ludicrous man, as her successor; he ruled briefly as Peter III until his German wife overthrew him and became Catherine II. Alexander I, who early in life professed liberal ideas, was supported by aristocrats and foreign bureaucrats – 'German bureaucrats in particular' – when he imitated what had become the German police state.[37] While Russian generals were uncertain what to do when the Decembrist insurrection erupted in 1825, Baltic officers took the initiative and it was a German baron who advised that the artillery open fire on the conspirators. Prince Eugene of Württemberg, a general in the Russian army, commanded the troops that crushed the revolt. German names 'gleam from every page' of the list of his officers.[38] Early in this century it was still being said that senior bureaucrats and military officers of German origin were so numerous that Russia was, in effect, 'ruled by a small German colony'.[39]

Catherine showed some interest in the French ideas that were spreading in Europe, but this was little more than a flirtation. On the whole French influence on Russians was superficial. Philosophic arguments that had evolved in a Catholic and feudal country were barely applicable in Orthodox Russia, where feudalism, in its true, ideological sense, did not exist.[40] In other words, the coherent values that the French sought to change were not present in Russia, any more than in India or Iran. The consequence was that French principles became mere dogmas or 'noble ideals, expressed in fine phrases, which gave one an air of distinction . . . but which must by no means be regarded as rules of actual conduct'.[41] For a time

Catherine was devoted to Voltaire; but after the French Revolution she moved his bust from her study to the lumber room. In the same year in which she set up an abortive commission to draw up a legal code based on Montesquieu's principles of civic rights, Catherine issued a ukase forbidding peasants from complaining to courts against their masters. Three who went to St Petersburg to protest against exploitation and torture received one hundred blows of the knout, had their noses burned with hot irons and were exiled to Siberia for life. Catherine frequently toyed with reform, but at the end of her reign the absolutist structure remained intact. Her successor, Paul I, was so hostile to the idea of representation that, when on a tour, he disgraced an official who described some trees as 'the first representatives of the Ural forest'.[42] His successor, Alexander I, authorized a Council of State, the decisions of which were to become law after imperial approval. But Alexander, an avowed absolutist, very often adopted minority recommendations and even those of single members.

Autocracy and revolution

Nicholas I (1825–55) organized a police state on a scale that had not been seen in Russia before, although Peter I had gone a long way towards it. By this time Western influence was no longer a mere fashion, like speaking French and talking philosophy. Some of the army officers who had marched to Paris when Napoleon retreated had returned home appalled at Russia's political and cultural backwardness; not a few landowners were conscience-stricken at the plight of the peasants. These and other elements took part in the easily suppressed insurrection of December 1825, in the hope of establishing a liberal constitution and emancipating the serfs. Nicholas was not unaware of what he called the 'evil' of serfdom, but he felt that emancipation at that stage would antagonize the landlords and threaten stability. He set up a committee to consider reforms, keeping it secret for fear that false hopes would arouse the masses. But his main measure was the establishment of the Third Division of his personal chancery, backed by a new *gendarmerie*, based on the Prussian model. The result, as one Russian writer said, was 'Byzantine–Prussian tyranny';[43] another described it as the 'slavery of the East with the discipline of the Prussian barracks'.[44] The Third Division became a dreaded, sinister state within the state. As during the terror of Stalin's period, local officials abused their power and sometimes sent minor noblemen into exile with no other justification than personal dislike. With 50,000 men working for it, the Division penetrated political groups, planted informers in blocks of flats, as today, harassed universities and secretly kept watch on religious organizations and foreign residents. It foreshadowed the Iron Curtain by trying to screen Russians from Western influence. A ban on French books, imposed by Catherine II and lifted by Alexander I, was restored and a special department, which still exists, examined all other foreign works before they could be distributed. The censorship covered all intellectual activity. Mazour says:[45] 'The censor came to know best how to write poetry, how to teach anatomy and aesthetics, geometry, and theology; and any deviation . . . was interpreted as incivism.' Nicholas was Pushkin's personal censor. Yet either because of ignorance or negligence works that might well have been considered seditious sometimes got through the censorship. Despite reforms in later reigns, civil rights were precarious, and arbitrary rule was enforced 'right up to 1917'.[46] Thus, in setting up their elaborate secret police system, the communists required no administrative originality; the structure was already there. They did not even need to devise new ways of repression: Peter Chaadayev, who wrote among other things that Russia had missed the cultural bus when it embraced Byzantium instead of Rome, was arrested during Nicholas's reign and officially declared insane.

While the Third Division could handle the intelligentsia, it was less successful against the peasants, who were driven by sheer misery to desperate acts. In Catherine's time peasants had joined a Cossack revolt, not in the name of freedom, but to support a bizarre pretender to the throne, whose followers are said to have hanged more than 1,400 landowners; inquiry might show that there is an element of messianism here. In the three decades of Nicholas's rule there were 674 peasant uprisings of various degrees, in which the army fought thirty-four battles. The revolts were spontaneous and mostly leaderless; the wretched instigators were shot at random by punitive expeditions, thrashed or sent to Siberia. By the time of the widespread but sporadic revolts of 1905 population growth and other factors had reduced the average size of the personal plot by 36 per cent compared with 1861, when Alexander II (1855–81) emancipated the serfs. The peasants had repeatedly rejected attempts of urban revolutionaries to politicize them; and it was starvation, not indoctrination, that impelled them to take over the landlord's estate, pillage his grain and empty his pantry. Peasants had long believed that all land, not merely that of the commune (Mir), rightfully belonged to the tiller; the landlord, who was rarely a good manager and often absent, seemed superfluous.

The peasants' sufferings are not attributable mainly to exploitation, but to underlying Russian backwardness. Stalin was on the right track when he told a managerial conference in February 1931 that Russia had been beaten by Mongol khans, Turkish beys, Swedish feudal lords, Polish and Lithuanian gentry, Japanese barons and French and British capitalists, 'for backwardness: for military backwardness, for cultural backwardness, for industrial backwardness, for agricultural backwardness'.[47] The most significant factor in this catalogue is cultural, since the others are merely expressions of it. In the time of Chekhov (1860–1904) villages were scarcely monetized and barter, in so far as any commodities were exchanged, was common. Although many villages looked pleasant at first sight, their inhabitants lived in dirt and squalor. The izba, or log hut, consisted of one room about sixteen to eighteen feet square. Since there was no chimney, the interior was blackened with soot. Slits in the walls served as windows. The family slept on a shelf, six or eight feet wide, running along a wall. A kitchen corner might be screened off.[48] Chekhov, as a doctor, was familiar with these conditions. In his story, *Peasants*, such a hut was the home of an aged, toothless couple, their two daughters-in-law and eight grandchildren; the husbands were working elsewhere. The family wore the same clothes day and night, had no proper bedding, a poor water supply and no sanitation. In villages generally, police, abusing their powers of distraint when taxes were not paid, were apt to seize hens and sheep. Former serfs felt they had merely exchanged one master for another; they called the regional police chief 'barin', the word previously used for the landlord.

On the other hand, landlords were increasingly in debt; the vacuous but amiable Simeonov-Pishchik, in Chekhov's *The Cherry Orchard*, who was saved from bankruptcy when Englishmen quarried his land, seems to be reasonably typical. When Alexander II freed the 11 million serfs, nearly 7 million of them and two-thirds of the land were mortgaged. It was then the peasants' turn to be crippled by debt; they had to pay for redistributed land over forty years at 6½ per cent interest. It was not until the uprisings of 1905 that these payments were abolished, with the government footing the bill. But there were still the taxes.

The emancipation of the serfs was one of a series of so-called 'great reforms' enacted by Alexander II in the 1860s. They followed the débâcle of the Crimean War (1853–6), which convinced even conservatives that the body politic could not survive the manifold challenges of Western Europe. At the same time a limited and distorted penetration of Western economic practices, not unlike that in the Third World today, made it necessary to Europeanize the judicial institutions, which, as Alexinsky says, were 'wholly archaic and Asiatic',[49] and to relax constraints on entrepreneurs that were incompatible with the new, free labour market. Trial by jury in open court, with the right of professional defence, was introduced; corporal punishment was abolished in principle, although not for peasants brought before rural tribunals; laws restricting association were eased; and rural self-government, overwhelmingly dominated by landowners, was permitted. Governmental commissions, strongly influenced by Western ideas, had proposed more radical reforms. But 'the spirit of caste had warped the work of reformation under Alexander II; the directing circles had limited the Europeanization of Russia by clinging as far as possible to the old order of things.'

Nevertheless, it should not be thought that the Tsar and his advisers were no more than a band of blind reactionaries. Some gave serious consideration to Russia's constitutional needs and genuinely believed that representative government would not work. Alexander's Minister for the Interior, Michael Loris-Melikov, said in a report dated 28 January 1881:

> Russia cannot accommodate herself to a national representation invested with forms borrowed from the West. These forms are not only foreign to the Russian people, but might even shatter all the foundations of its political conceptions, and occasion a complete upheaval of ideas, of which it would be difficult to foresee the consequences.

Hedrik Smith's picture of Russia today tends to confirm this judgment.[50] Russia's faltering adaptations of Western models were not progress towards Western-style 'political maturity', as one Western writer has put it; they were stages in the disintegration of an authoritarian order, which, when it became incapable of governing, was replaced in 1917 by another that was equally Russian. Loris-Melikov had the task of combating nihilist and anarchist terrorists, who, devoid of social roots, were as irresponsible, neurotic and self-dramatizing as they imagined themselves to be humanitarian and heroic. On 13 March 1881 Alexander signed a ukase setting up commissions to prepare further administrative reforms proposed by Loris-Melikov. He was murdered in a nihilist bomb attack the same day.

Alexander's heir, Alexander III (1881–94), had never been sympathetic to reform. Convinced by his father's murder that he was right, he immediately set out to eradicate sedition. The university autonomy granted in the previous reign was revoked and all student societies were forbidden. The press was again rigidly censored. Persecution of dissenting religious sects was so savage that the Dukhobors fled to Canada. Only a handful of the intelligentsia fought back at the repression. Terrorists led by Lenin's brother, Alexander Ulyanov, failed in an attempt to kill the Tsar and were executed. While the state was secure in the cities, danger loomed in the country. The arrival of American wheat in Europe had seriously reduced the demand for Russian. Because of increased rural poverty, the government, while tightening landlord control over the peasants by means of newly constituted tribunals, was obliged to reduce land redemption payments and finally to abolish the peasant poll tax. By this time the emancipation had strengthened a class of detested, grasping peasants – the *kulaks* (the singular means fist). If they were not potentially more greedy than others, they were certainly more hard-working and relatively efficient. By increasing their holdings they accelerated the growth of what had become an impoverished rural proletariat, which they ruthlessly exploited.

Soon after ascending the throne, Nicholas II (1894–1918) ruled out representative government when he declared that he would 'maintain the principle of autocracy just as firmly and unswervingly' as his 'unforgettable father' had done. But it was the communists, not the tsars, who were to continue this almost unbroken tradition. Meanwhile certain concessions had to be made. Although the Russo–Japanese war was opposed by the pragmatic Serge Witte, the Tsar's most senior minister, other advisers saw it as a means of averting an already feared revolution. But Russia's defeat weakened the Government's grip and 1905 was filled with strikes, mutinies in the armed forces and demonstrations, which, because of the reforms to which they led, are said to have constituted a revolution, although no coherent attempt was made to seize power. In January 150,000 people, led by a priest, Father Gaspon, marched peacefully to the Winter Palace in St Petersburg, some of them carrying ikons and portraits of the Little Father. They sought to present a petition stating that they were so 'strangled by despotism and tyranny' that they would 'rather die than bear these intolerable sufferings'. Father Gaspon had given notice of the march and Nicholas kept away from the palace. Without warning, palace guards fired repeatedly on the crowd while mounted Cossacks cut down men, women and children with sabres. More than one thousand were killed and thousands wounded.

After widespread protests Nicholas made what he called the terrible decision of breaking the sacred trust passed on by his father and promised that all new laws would be subject to approval by a Duma. This legislative body had a stormy history, during which some of its deputies were exiled to Siberia. From the beginning peasant representation was counterbalanced by that of landlords. By 1907, when the Third Duma was prorogued, a 'crude piece of gerrymandering' had reduced the people's voting power to insignificance.[51] Nevertheless the Duma did useful work, particularly in the expansion of education. While these reforms were being initiated, repression continued in the universities. One historian has written that freedom of speech and publication were 'almost total'.[52] The press was certainly less rigidly controlled, but it is necessary to add what Maurice Baring wrote in 1910:[53] 'The slightest breath of criticism is held to be subversive.' And in 1914 a Russian woman wrote:[54] 'Not only what is on the list of prohibited things is regarded as a crime, but also what is not on the unwritten list of things that are allowed.' Baring said the local officials were 'completely successful in sacrificing the spirit to the letter of the law'. At the centre the Government was flooding the Duma with trivialities to block consideration of serious affairs.

But neither reform nor reaction had any effect on the chronic misery of the vast majority of those living in the Russian Empire. People who had said they found life unbearable in peace found it even worse in the First World War, when Russian forces were routed with a loss of 1,700,000 servicemen dead (compared with 908,000 from the British Empire). Short of rifles, food and even boots, troops were slaughtered in offensives that were often requested by other Allied powers to relieve pressure on their own fronts. Hungry men deserted and returned to their villages in search of food. Along with a succession of bungling war ministers, Nicholas, who commanded the armies in the field, was despised by all classes and lost the support of his generals. While Cossacks were willing to lash at demonstrators with sabres and whips, troops refused to fire on the people. In February 1917 the regime simply collapsed, like that of the Iranian Shah in February 1979, and a small group of liberal politicians established a Provisional

Government. Nicholas abdicated in the same month. He and his family were murdered by a Bolshevik firing squad in a cellar at Ekaterinburg in the middle of the following year.

While the new Government did nothing to end the war, the troops did little fighting. Unprecedented civil liberties were allowed and political prisoners were freed. But these measures did not reassure the workers, who distrusted the new ministers as offspring of the discredited Duma. In 1905 workers had set up their own soviets (councils) in St Petersburg, Moscow and many other towns. This largely spontaneous eruption recurred in 1917, with one member of a soviet for every thousand workers in a factory and usually one for a company in the army. In St Petersburg (by this time Petrograd, now Leningrad) the soviet was so strong that the Government was careful not to offend it. At first the Bolshevik Party played little part in this movement. But the return in April of Lenin and other Bolsheviks, facilitated by the Germans, from exile in Switzerland transformed the situation. While leaders of other parties were aimless and hesitant, Lenin organized vigorous infiltration of the soviets and used them as a stepping stone to power. The Bolsheviks (majority) and the Mensheviks (minority) had split when the Russian Social Democratic Party broke up early in the century. On the whole the Mensheviks were more Western and more democratic and even had some middle-class following. Lenin's concepts were consistent with the Russian tradition of leadership by an autocratic minority, his own being thought of as the vanguard of the working class; the Bolsheviks were particularly strong among unskilled workers, who had no idea of liberty.

On the night of 24–5 October (6–7 November New Style), Lenin instigated an armed uprising, led by Trotsky, which seized all key points in Petrograd. Next day the Bolshevik-controlled All-Russian Congress of Soviets announced a new Provisional Workers' and Peasants' Government, which was to rule pending a meeting of an elected Constituent Assembly. At the same time Lenin issued decrees taking over the land for distribution among peasants and declaring an armistice. This – and not much else – comprised the October Revolution. The Provisional Government, led by Alexander Kerensky, could find few troops to fight for it and collapsed ignominiously like the Tsar's; lacking a substantial socioeconomic foundation, it had merely filled a vacuum. But the Bolsheviks were not yet securely in power. After elections more than one-half of Constituent Assembly delegates, who met on 18 January 1918, were right-wing Social Revolutionaries. The

Bolsheviks and their left-wing Social Revolutionary allies, who commanded fewer than one-third of the seats between them, left the meeting. Next day the Soviet of People's Commissars, chaired by Lenin, dissolved the assembly and Red troops fired on protesting demonstrators. The Constituent Assembly bore the closest resemblance to a democratic institution that Russia had ever seen. It lasted just thirteen hours; and even this brief life was only achieved by means of an all-night session that lasted until 5 a.m., when the officer in charge of the guard told delegates it was time to go home.

The left-wing Social Revolutionaries, who had opposed Lenin's acceptance of large territorial losses in the Brest–Litovsk Treaty with the Germans, left the Bolsheviks to govern alone and resorted to terrorism. They killed the German ambassador and seriously wounded Lenin. Such activities provoked the terror carried out by the Cheka (Extraordinary Commission for Combating Counter Revolution), which had been set up in December 1917. With its summary justice and countless executions the Cheka overshadowed the record of even the French Revolutionary Committee of Public Safety. In November Lenin admitted it had been wrong at times, but said it had made the dictatorship of the proletariat – in other words, of the Bolshevik Party – 'a living reality'. The party was renamed Russian Communist Party in March 1918.

Achievement and failure

There has been some discussion about whether or not Russia could have equalled or surpassed its extraordinary twentieth-century achievement if it had become capitalist; but the preceding digest of relevant aspects of Russian history and cultural traits shows this to be a false issue. There was no cultural base for an indigenous capitalist take-off. While the need to develop an entrepreneurial class had long been felt by some of the tsars, and steps had been taken to that end, the necessary spirit and rationality were confined to a very small minority, and money flowing from land sales and peasant redemption payments did not find its way into industry. Both in communications and industry much of the capital had to come from the state. While savings had increased substantially by 1914, they were still 'insufficient to support large-scale economic development'.[55] Accordingly a 'vital role' was played by foreign credit, both as inter-governmental loans and direct investment in industry. In 1917 Russia's foreign debt almost equalled the national income; some estimates are higher.[56] The Communists were to repudiate the debt, but it is doubtful whether, like loans to the Third World and Poland today, it could ever have been fully repaid. Western Europe invested in Russian industry both through its own companies and in joint ventures. At the beginning of this century 62 per cent of south Russian coal was produced by European concerns; of twenty-three large steelworks in the Donetz basin only two were Russian-owned. Youzovka (the town of Hughes), an important south Russian industrial centre, was named after John Hughes, a British pioneer of the Donetz metal and coal industries. In 1909 more than 45 per cent of Baku petroleum exports were produced by five European companies. Except in the Moscow region the textile industry was largely under foreign control until the revolution.[57] With its dependence on Western capital and its cultural impediments to development, Russia faced the prospect of becoming a permanent Brazil, whose export earnings, most of which come from the sweat of peasants, are insufficient to service debts to Western banks.

If the Russian culture had failed to generate modern capitalism, it could hardly have been expected to produce the political structure associated with it. Most Russians wanted land, not democracy, and the Bolsheviks immediately gave it to them, although, as it turned out, not on the terms expected. The politicians who attempted to impose a Western-style democratic edifice on an unreceptive culture were not in themselves impressive. Somerset Maugham, who was sent by British intelligence to try and keep Russia in the war by making contact with parties that were hostile both to the government and the Bolsheviks, wrote:[58]

I came away disillusioned. The endless talk when action was needed, the vacillations, the apathy, when apathy could only result in destruction, the high-flown protestations, the insincerity and half-heartedness that I found everywhere sickened me with Russia and the Russians.

In 1917 Russia was simply not a going concern. Politicians who were devoted to imported abstractions could never have got it moving.

Since investment funds were virtually non-existent, agriculture offered the only means of accumulating the capital required for industry. Here the communists were faced with a major problem, which Nicholas II's Prime Minister, Peter Stolypin, had tackled brutally but without success. In 1910 the wheat yield per acre was as low as India's, lower than Algeria's, slightly less than one-third of that in both Holland and Sweden, which was the highest in Europe, and a little more than one-third of the yield in the United Kingdom. Despite malnutrition and starvation, exports of wheat, rye (the staple food), oats and barley were estimated at 51.1 per cent of the total surplus above farm consumption.[59] Stolypin's answer to Russia's agricultural inefficiency was, as he said, to encourage the 'diligent and capable against the lazy and stupid'; to 'wager not on the poor and drunken, but on the enterprising and strong'. For this purpose he set about breaking up the communes. Communal land consisted of strips to ensure a fair qualitative distribution. Consequently an individual's strips were narrow and often far apart. Communal work was essential. While the commune owned the land, the peasant's right to till his holding was inalienable. In 1906 Stolypin took the drastic step of allowing the peasant to withdraw from the commune and enclose his land, which then became his property; the better off were expected to buy out the indigent, who would add to the millions of rural landless – 8 million as early as 1861 – or drift to the towns. Uneconomic though the commune was, it gave the peasants a feeling of security and they continued to shelter in it; by 1917 barely 10 per cent of them had enclosed their land. In some areas violence was used to drive off the poorer peasants. Lenin wrote in 1905 of 'forcible ejection from the countryside, eviction, starvation, and the extermination of the flower of the peasant youth with the help of jails, exile, shooting and torture'.[60] Later communists were to use similar methods on a gigantic scale. Their victims were not the 'lazy', 'stupid' and 'drunken', but Stolypin's 'diligent and capable' – the kulaks, who were the most effective opponents of collectivization.

The agricultural problem was too much a part of the entire Russian cultural impasse to be solved by such a superficial device as strengthening the kulaks. The fundamental situation when the communists took over was well described by Stalin in 1935:[61]

Ruined by four years of imperialist war, and ruined again by three years of civil war, a country with a semi-literate population, with a low technical level, with isolated industrial oases lost in a welter of minute peasant farms – such was the country we inherited from the past. The problem was to transfer this country from the lines of mediaeval darkness to the lines of modern industry and mechanised agriculture. . . . The question that confronted us was that *either* we solve this problem in the shortest possible time . . . *or* we do not solve it, in which case our country – technically weak and culturally unenlightened – would lose its independence and become a stake in the game of the imperialist powers. . . . There was not that elementary technical base without which the industrial transformation of a country is inconceivable. . . . A first-class industry had to be created. . . . And for this it was necessary to make sacrifices and to impose the most rigorous economy in everything; . . . to economise on food, on schools and on textiles, in order to accumulate the funds required for the creation of industry.

It was not until some years after Lenin's death on 21 January 1924 that Stalin set about trying to solve this immense problem in earnest. In December 1929 he announced that the liquidation of the kulaks as a class – by driving them off the land – had begun, and in the following month launched a campaign to collectivize most peasant households by 1933. He admitted that peasants – kulaks or not – disliked socialism, but believed that the benefits of mechanization would win them over. Kulaks were forbidden to join collective farms, for fear that they would sabotage them. Instead they were executed when they resisted, exiled to Siberia or forced to dig canals or embankments. It is estimated that 3 million died in one way or another. One old man told Wright Miller that he was classed as a kulak and sent to Kamchatka because he owned a cow; 90 per cent of those with him died.

The collectivization itself appears to have gone more smoothly. By the end of February 1930 half the peasants throughout the country had joined the collectives, 'seeking safety in the new communities, and fearing the requisitioning of their produce if they stayed out of them'.[62] Not satisfied with these gains Party organizers began to force small peasants to hand over their livestock to the common pool, sometimes at gunpoint. This provoked the catastrophic wave of animal slaughter from which Russia was not to recover for many years. Stalin evidently became alarmed. In an article in *Pravda*, the Party newspaper, on 2 March 1930, entitled 'Dizzy with Success', he condemned the use of force as a violation of Lenin's principle that membership of collective farms must be voluntary, and asserted that the term 'kulak' had been too loosely interpreted. 'Collective farms cannot be set up by force,' he said. 'To attempt to do so would be stupid.'[63] Zealots had also been mistaken in thinking that everything was to be collectivized. The aim was an agricultural *artel*, in which the main means of production were socialized but 'small vegetable gardens and orchards, dwellings, a certain part of dairy cattle, small livestock and poultry' were not. Stalin ridiculed the infantilism of some of his activists: 'And what about those "revolutionaries" – save the mark – who *begin* the work of organizing an *artel* by removing the church bells. Removing the church bells – how r-r-revolutionary indeed.' But if Stalin had fully appreciated the backwardness of his people, he would have expected both the absurdities that were committed by his mindless followers and the barbarity of the reaction. Rebels murdered peasants who had joined the collectives, and whole communities fought bloody battles with security forces. The opportunity to settle personal grievances was not missed. This grim period of execution and murder and of looting carried out by the poor is vividly described in Michael Sholokov's novel *Virgin Soil Upturned*. It was followed in 1932–3 by a famine in which another 1 million people died. Because of the livestock slaughter the number of horses fell from 24 million in 1929 to 15 million in 1933, cattle from 67 million to 38 million, sheep and goats from 147 million to 50 million and pigs from 20 million to 12 million.

Yet collectivization eventually achieved Stalin's aim. Agriculture, instead of being a liability, became an asset that funded the industrialization without which Russia could never have driven back the Germans.[64] Stalin also thought he had taken a step towards that humanitarian goal for which he was always prepared to sacrifice countless lives. He told a conference of business executives on 23 June 1931: 'We have supplied the rural districts with tens of thousands of tractors and agricultural machines; we have smashed the kulaks, we have organized collective farms and have given the peasants the opportunity to live and work like human beings.'

Soviet agriculture has been misrepresented. Newspaper accounts of Russia's need to import wheat from the United States, although not inaccurate, give to those without other knowledge the false impression that the Russians are threatened with starvation. What has happened is that higher purchasing power has increased the demand for meat, as for other commodities. This creates shortages. As one economist put it:[65] 'There is so much pent-up demand (cash) in the U.S.S.R. that price measures [increases] would have to be of an extremely drastic kind if they were to have a real effect [in reducing it].' In the past the government killed off livestock when a bad season made feeding impossible; more recently it has bought grain, as fodder, from the United States, to enable it to increase its stock. While agriculture still suffers from undercapitalization and chronic Russian inefficiency, it is vastly more productive than the old system, as Harry G. Schaffer has demonstrated. In 1975 David M. Schoonover, of the Economic Research Service of the US Department of Agriculture, said that Schaffer's study was long overdue and should stimulate agricultural economists 'to rethink . . . accepted beliefs about Soviet agricultural performance'.[66] While the number of farm workers was reduced to just over 25 per cent of the labour force in 1976, compared with more than 75 per cent before the revolution, grain production rose from 86 million tons in 1913 to 223 million tons in 1973, although it fell to 140 million tons in 1975, when the harvest was particularly bad. The rise was proportionately much greater than the growth of the population, which was 170 million in 1916 and 265,500,000 in 1981. Recovering from the blow of 1930, cattle had risen to 109 million in 1975. While Schaffer is aware of the shortcomings of Russian agriculture, he finds that it has played a reasonable part in the 'remarkable' increase in the USSR's Gross National Product (GNP), which, he says, rose from 33 per cent of the United States GNP in 1950 to 54 per cent in 1970 and 61 per cent (estimated) in 1975.[67]

Huge sums have been spent not only on armaments, but on development and education, rather than on producing consumer goods. As J. J. Hooson says: [68] 'The cumulative fruits of this single-mindedness in terms of national power and the transformation of the Soviet Union in world status in the last three or four decades have been impressive.' Large-scale easterly displacement of industry began with Stalin's inauguration of the Urals Kuzbas Combine in 1930. This was followed by the establishment of a 'new type of zone, authentically Soviet in character', between the Volga and Lake Baykal, in Siberia. Among recent projects is the gas pipeline from Siberia to Western Germany, which is providing considerable employment in Western Europe, whose technology, along with that of the United States, is convenient but not indispensable to the Russians in this enterprise. Gas has been piped from Central Asia to blast furnaces in the Urals for some time. When the Germans invaded the USSR, more than four-fifths of its oil came from the exposed Caucasus region; now more than two-thirds of a greatly increased output comes from the new Volga–Ural fields.

Despite the diversion of vast sums to finance Russia's swift rise from agricultural and industrial backwardness, living standards have improved steadily; increases in real wages are included in every five-year plan. Stalin's purposeful neglect of housing, the transfer of most of the labour force from rural to industrial work and the destruction of the war created a serious accommodation shortage. From 1956 to 1975 44 million housing units were built, but the population rose by 45 million. By early in 1974 two-thirds of Soviet families had television sets, nearly 60 per cent had sewing and washing machines and about half had some kind of refrigerator. Savings deposits were more than 80,000 million roubles ($92,000 million). An American economist calculated that from 1950–70 Soviet food consumption per head doubled, disposable income quadrupled, consumption of soft goods tripled and purchases of hard goods rose twelvefold, while welfare benefits increased and the working week was shortened.[69] A Russian scientist, who was highly critical of the Soviet system, told Smith:[70]

You must understand that the majority of people here are satisfied with their lives. Many of them have city apartments. They may seem small to you, two or three rooms, small rooms. But these people remember that their parents lived in the countryside in those *izbas*. . . . And there have been other improvements.

It is a commentary on the superficiality with which the media handle world affairs that the CIA's finding that the Soviet economy was 'in good shape', to quote a British newspaper, should have been regarded as surprising news.[71] In a 401-page study submitted to Congress in December 1982 the CIA appeared to go out of its way to counter the dangerous ignorance of the President, whose belief that the Soviet edifice is so fragile that it could be toppled by a puff from Poland encourages him to adopt belligerent policies. The CIA said that it did not consider 'an economic collapse – a sudden and sustained decline in the gross national product – even a remote possibility'. It added:

Western observers have tended to describe Soviet economic performance as 'poor' or 'deteriorating' at a time when Soviet defence spending continues to rise, overall Soviet gross national product in real terms continues to increase, and Soviet GNP is second in size only to that of the United States.

Despite a large increase in agricultural imports, the Soviet Union was basically self-sufficient in food; grain production 'was more than sufficient to meet consumer demand for bread and other cereal products'; the Russian calorie intake was about 3,300 a day, compared with 3,520 in the USA. The Soviet Union's GNP had grown at an average annual rate of 4.7 per cent (the Soviet figure is 7.4) between 1951 and 1980. It had slowed down since 1978, reflecting four consecutive poor harvests. The CIA predicted a steady growth of 1 to 2 per cent per annum, but added that if Yuri Andropov succeeded in his drive to increase efficiency the forecast would be too low. (Novosti Press Agency subsequently reported that in 1981–2 the national income rose by 2.6 per cent.) Soviet capital investment – the key to the future – had risen from 14 per cent of the GNP in 1950 to 33 per cent in 1980 – a strikingly higher figure than in Organization for Economic Cooperation and Development (OECD) countries, where, with the exception of Japan, the general tendency is to consume increasingly at the expense of investment; in Britain it is 16 per cent and in the USA 11 per cent.

It now remains to consider what are the capacities of the society that has undergone such momentous upheaval and transformation. In looking at this question we should be cautious in examining the evidence of the intellectual dissident, who now as in the past represents only a small group or even just himself. He is certainly not the tip of an iceberg of emerging Western-style democracy; to assume so is probably to make the worst possible error in assessing Russia. Smith found that the dissident, like the official or the ordinary citizen, did not seek 'decency or fair play' but only total loyalty within a limited circle, who shared his thoughts and feelings. Smith does not mention Andrei Sakharov, the physicist, and Alexander Solzhenitsyn, the novelist, in this context, but each symbolizes an opposing current in the Russian culture. Toynbee saw Russia as a Byzantine civilization that disliked Western culture, but was obliged to assimilate its technology to protect itself from domination. Solzhenitsyn, as a Slavophile – more accurately, a Russophile, since he isolates Russians from other Slavs – rejects the entire complex of Western values. He believes in the spiritual superiority of Holy Russia, expressed through and maintained by the church. Pavel Litvinov, the dissident grandson of Stalin's Foreign Minister, Maxim Litvinov, said of Solzhenitsyn: 'He does not want democracy. He wants to go from the totalitarian state back to an authoritarian one.' Henry Kissinger is reported to have placed him 'somewhere to the right of the tsars'.

Sakharov represents the Western influence. He has given us useful information about the deliberate creation of an élite that is morally corrupt; privileges that have become virtually hereditary;

bureaucratic scheming, irresponsibility, cruelty and abysmal incompetence; the 'frightful' conditions in hospitals; and a general malaise. But there is a lack of balance in his picture. His statement that consumption of alcohol per head is three times what it was under the tsars needs the qualification that people now have very much more money to spend; his claim that before the revolution Russia was the breadbasket of Europe, but now has to import food, is seriously misleading; and his charge that education is on a low level is contrary to other information, such as that of Wright Miller, who noticed that every other book being read in a bus or tram was a textbook,[72] combined with that of Mazour, who finds that graduates from high schools, where there is a strong emphasis on mathematics, chemistry and physics, are better educated than those in the United States.[73] Above all, it is hard to see how a theoretical physicist as well trained and as creative as Sakharov could have been produced in the society that he so starkly depicts. Sakharov's Western mind cannot accept the Byzantine streak in Russian society, of which, on the other hand, Solzhenitsyn wants not less but more. In his chagrin he tends to attribute to communism what belongs rather to Russia.

Hedrick Smith is at pains to avoid this mistake. Towards the end of his 639-page work, which contains much significant detail, he says:[74] 'The longer I lived in Russia the more Russian it seemed to me and hence the less likely to undergo fundamental change.' Along with the persistence of particular kinds of public ritual he found continuity in 'the centralized concentration of power, the fetish of rank, the xenophobia of simple people, the futile carping of alienated intelligentsia, the passionate attachment of Russians to Mother Russia, the habitual submission of the masses to the Supreme Leader and the unquestioned acceptance of the yawning gulf between the Ruler and the Ruled'. There is resentment at privileges cornered by the *nomenklatura*, a self-perpetuating hierarchy that thrives on an oriental system of patronage; in proportion to rank members of this exclusive class appropriate professional opportunity, the best hospital accommodation, luxurious housing, imported clothing and appliances, preference in admittance to schools, and food provided in special shops at prices that diminish as the rank of the beneficiary rises and vanish altogether for the top people, who receive their supplies free. But the emergence of a new ruling class is in itself accepted and what is wanted is not Western democracy, but simply a fairer deal. This, in fact, is the spirit of the old Mir, where equality was only sought in local matters of direct concern to the peasant, who did not dream of a voice in determining larger issues. While the endurance of the Russian masses is great, it is not inexhaustible, as the revolution showed. But the revolution took centuries to arrive and before Russians revolted again they would need to suffer on a scale and for a period that seems highly improbable today. It would be erroneous to imagine that there is some kind of spirit of freedom abroad in Eastern Europe, which, having begun in Poland, could spread to Russia. The Russians would have to be sorely pressed indeed before antagonism towards the government matched that of the Poles towards theirs, which is seen as a tool of the long-detested Muscovites. While continued improvement in living standards has given rise to increased expectations, these are not as disproportionate to possibility as those in the West. It is true that after the Polish rebellion Leonid Brezhnev said that Russia's economic problems were a political danger. But his purpose was to rouse bureaucrats from their lethargy and what he called lack of responsibility; the worst that the Kremlin has to fear from the people at this stage is, as Michael Binyon, *The Times* Moscow correspondent, put it, a decline in respect for authority, which would take place if food became too scarce.

It would be absurd to think that the Soviet achievement was simply brought about by a docile mass sweating under a despotic lash. While docility and tyranny are always present in Russia, there is more to it than that. With little precedent to guide them, the Russians plunged into economic planning on a scale never seen before. The difficulties were immense, given the size of the country and the lack of skilled labour, which had to be educated and trained. Whatever may be thought of planned economies in principle, the Russians achieved a technical triumph, which required enthusiasm and detailed co-ordination that would have been beyond a merely servile people. The revolution was led by men who believed fervently that they had a historic mission to found a better society. Trotsky wrote a pamphlet romantically entitled 'A Paradise on This Earth'. Lenin thought that the Russians only happened to be the first in a chain of revolutions that would sweep Europe and create a new world; he sought no national domination, but believed that the 'German comrades' would soon take the lead in building socialism because they were technologically more advanced. Industrial construction in the cruel Siberian climate was not carried out merely by forced labour, but by men and women imbued with idealism and a spirit of self-sacrifice. In general the need to endure hardship to ensure future prosperity was understood to an extent perhaps never seen before or since in any part of the world. Among more earnest Russians nostalgia for the moral strength of those days looms larger than memories of the terror that accompanied it.

The decline of communist idealism in Russia is comparable to that of the Protestant ethic in northwestern Europe, including parts of the Catholic world, where it has had considerable influence. In this respect Russia, with its Byzantine but Western-influenced civilization, shares the disease that afflicts Europe as a whole. But of the two European branches the Russian is the more seriously degraded; for whereas the social conscience that found expression in both Western Christianity and Marxism retains some vitality in the societies in which it originated, it is less sustained among an essentially Byzantine-minded people, who merely imported it. A singularly unhealthy self-indulgence has reasserted itself in the top social layers. The *nomenklatura* appears to have become more powerful than any leader since Stalin, although Andropov may yet curb it; according to Sakharov, one reason for Kruschev's fall was that he tried to limit its privileges. The Party has been directly involved in this consolidation of the new ruling class. Students who had graduated with honours at various colleges were given a month's stay in Leningrad. At a lavish dinner they were asked, 'Would you like to live like this for the rest of your life?' and told, 'If so, go to the VPSh [Higher Party School].' As Sakharov says, such an example of unprincipled career-making would have been impossible in the 1920s.[75] It reflects a significant reversion to pre-revolutionary days, when 'many came to think that only those kinds of efforts were worth while which were recognized by the bureaucratic slaves of the autocracy, and that the supreme art in life was to advance in *chin* [grade] and earn a safe pension, no matter how immoral the means involved.'[76] In this environment the conscientious, enterprising administrator can be an outcast. Sakharov records the tragedy of Khudenko, head of a large state farm.[77] In an experiment authorized by Krushchev he reduced the work force, while raising output and wages. But his methods were counter to the 'conservatism, cowardice and selfish interests' of the *nomenklatura*, who got rid of him. When he filed a court petition asking that the workers be paid what they had earned, he was sentenced to eight years' imprisonment for having attempted to damage the state; he died in gaol.

This brings us back to the important subject of Russian characteristics resembling those found in countries that have not developed.

The crudely materialistic exhortation to the students in Leningrad, on the one hand, and Khudenko's fate on the other, recall a nineteenth-century observation that in Iran, the USSR's neighbour, a 'violent death' would be the likely end of a good man who tried to reform the government and 'wealth that of one who would accept the place and swim in the stream of corruption'.[78] There are other resemblances to Iran – a fear of foreign spiritual pollution, common to both the tsarist and communist regimes, and a bizarre wave of imagined conspiracies, along with real ones, which marked both the terror of the Stalin period and that which followed the Iranian revolution. What is significant for Russia's social potential is not the cruelty of the terror, but its almost total irrationality, which remains unsurpassed, even in Tehran, and the number of people involved in perpetrating it. It required a very numerous corps of security men, informers and vindictive neighbours – and a great surging of primitive emotion – to spy on, inform on, round up, imprison, torture and kill the many millions who perished in the terror of 1935 to 1938 and in its resumption after the war. Wright Miller says the fantastic aspect is that everyone arrested was implausibly accused of at least one, usually all, of four crimes – counter-revolution, working against Stalin and the Party, sabotage, and acting for a foreign power.[79] As in the summary trials of Iran, suspicion was treated, and genuinely believed in, as fact. A single meeting with a foreigner or a receipt of a letter from abroad, was enough for a death sentence. Wright Miller goes a long way towards explaining the irrationality of this period. He says the Russian Orthodox believe that people sometimes sin without knowing it. Minds attuned to this kind of thinking quickly assumed that a person who put himself in the path of temptation by greeting a foreigner or gossiping with a malcontent might well have sinned; even those arrested often came to believe that innocent contacts were as heinous as active conspiracy. 'Everyone is guilty of something,' a former prosecutor told Wright Miller, and it was better that the innocent should be punished, 'if that would help the community', than that the guilty should go free.

In religion the community has always taken precedence over the individual. The Orthodox belief is that the individual cannot control his violent impulses alone and needs the community to sustain him. Confession is public rather than private. If one accepts that a religion expresses and satisfies a particular psychic need, it follows that there is something in the Russian psyche that eschews individual responsibility. At all events the failure of officials to take responsibility was berated by Stalin and has been lamented by Brezhnev. It is one of the impediments to Russian economic progress and, like other Russian cultural barriers, is often found in the Third World, as is overriding attachment to family or other exclusive groups. Smith observed:[80]

> Their ['officials, dissidents and people in between'] friendship is tribal, inclusive and excluding, and they gauge each other by friends, cliques, group, reckoning these ties – in high politics as well as in personal relations – as far more meaningful than some abstract loyalty to the system or the Party.

Weber identified this kind of mentality among obstacles to the creation of modern capitalism in China.[81] Since it precludes impartial assessment and unqualified adherence to impersonal institutions, it would hamper large-scale socio-economic development of any kind, to the extent that it was not offset by contrary social currents.

Bursts of highly energetic activity, followed by periods of lassitude, which have been observed in some Third World societies and are certainly not characteristic of northwestern Europe, even today, have been regularized in the Soviet Union by the exigencies of planning. The factory worker thinks of the month as divided into three periods of ten days: the first is sleeper time, the second hot work time and the third fever time (*spyachka*, *goryachka* and *likhoradka*).[82] In addition, there is a pre-holiday feeling before each of the two pay days in a month; and for two or three days afterwards, a worker told Smith, 'people are practically sick from drinking and they have to drink off their hangovers'. Because of this cycle and the late arrival of essential materials, there is a tremendous rush known as storming to complete quotas in the last ten to fifteen days of the month; about 80 per cent of goods are produced in this time. Since the practice is widely known, consumers try to avoid articles (which are tagged with the production date) manufactured in the last part of the month, when quality is disregarded in the scramble to fulfil the quota. Military production is not immune from this 'wildly erratic work rhythm', but much greater care is taken with quality. Factories making anything from a teapot to an instrument employ special brigades to supply orders from the armed forces. These artisans are more highly paid than those working for the home market, as are export workers, although their premium is lower. The quality of Soviet arms appears to be well controlled, but not always well enough to ensure that tanks do not produce metal shavings in their crankcases after only twenty-five hours of running.[83]

Stalin (a Georgian) thus faced formidable obstacles when he set about creating modern industry in a country that he saw as culturally backward – 'culturally different' would be a better phrase. In 1931 he was accusing managers of 'an absolute lack of personal responsibility' for 'work that is entrusted to anyone', and for machinery and tools. Proper accounts were not kept; costs were rising through inefficiency and reliance on the state bank to advance money; in a number of factories labour was 'abominably organized'. These complaints read like a summary of chapter 4 ('Pointing backwards') in *The Third World Calamity*,[84] in which failure to keep accounts and neglect of maintenance, even disdain for it, are conspicuous among socio-economic indicators. If these defects persisted under Stalin's grim discipline at a critical time in Soviet history, they are hardly likely to have lessened during the more relaxed period that followed his death.

Even if no other information were available, a future historian could deduce Third-World characteristics from trade figures. About four-fifths of Soviet exports consist of raw materials, mineral combustibles and precious metals, while more than two-fifths of its imports are machines and transport equipment. In 1974 the West bought only $220 million worth of Soviet machinery and equipment compared with its sales to the USSR of more than $2,670 million worth – twelve times as much. This is a Third World pattern. Eighty per cent of socialized Soviet farm work was still being done by hand in 1970.[85] A person who for special reasons received permission to make several trips through Uzbekistan and parts of Azerbaijan told this author that it would be difficult to distinguish the region from Iran, even when driving along metalled roads. While cotton-picking is mechanized, the scene on leaving the outskirts of Tashkent is 'almost mediaeval'. There are no shops and no villages, only settlements. In the evenings people sit on four-poster beds outside their mud-brick houses, drinking tea. Some are in traditional costume, some in a kind of Western dress. The men converse apart from the women.

Despite the cultural drag on activities of Western origin, the USSR's scientific and technological achievements are greater than is generally recognized in the West. It has, for instance, held world air records in load-carrying combined with speed and with height, both by plane and helicopter, as well as the absolute height record;

it has also held the absolute speed record.[86] Its biggest concentration of effort in this direction was in 1961, since when certain records, including highest speed, have been captured by the United States. Since the Russians were the first to put a man in space there is no reason to believe that the Party's directive role is a serious hindrance. Achievements are probably proportionate to the amount of resources allocated and the innate capacity for innovation, which has never equalled that of the West. It would be pointless to ask whether the Russians would become better inquirers and inventors under a freer system. From what we have seen freedom is not in the culture and if it were tried it could well lead to anarchy. Again it is helpful to turn to Smith:[87]

> It is not only the chaos around them but the anarchy within themselves that Russians seem to fear. . . . The Russian obeys power, not the law. And if Power is looking the other way, or simply does not notice him, the Russian does what he thinks he can get away with.

The contradiction between Russian technological achievement and failure is resolved if activities of Western derivation are seen to comprise a multi-pronged enclave that penetrates with varying degrees of effectiveness both regions and factories, where much of the labour force merely goes through the motions of Western-style work. While Russians circle the earth in space, cashiers in Moscow shops are using age-old wooden abacuses to add up bills; projects will be ceremoniously opened on the scheduled date of completion, even when, because of muddle and bad workmanship, they are not in fact ready for months or even years afterwards. Raymond Hutchings, in his by no means unfavourable study of Soviet science and technology, finds that most new products, including aeroplanes, are basically of foreign design.[88] This recalls Toynbee's view that on the whole the Russians have merely felt obliged to respond to the Western stimulus; for design is an affair of the spirit, and the often drab imitation of Western forms in the USSR reflects the general failure of the Western culture to take firm root. Excluding the arts, the Russians have not been highly creative in those techniques that evolved as an expression of a very different culture. Russia's cultural impediment, from a Western point of view, was observed by Marx, although he did not use that term. He said that its capitalists in the textile industry were incompetent and dependent on protection and foreign management.[89] More significantly, in a discussion of Adam Smith's ideas on wealth creation, he drew a harsh distinction between indifference to certain kinds of labour in a developed capitalist country, such as the United States, where choice of work was intentional, and in Russia, where the indifference was spontaneous. He said: 'There is a devil of a difference between barbarians who are fit by nature to be used for anything, and civilized people who apply themselves to everything.'[90] Marx saw that Russians were 'embedded by tradition within a very specific kind of labour, from which only external influences can jar them loose'. As it happened, the jarring, though provoked by a threat from outside, was administered from inside – by Stalin. But, as we have seen, its effects have been more limited than those of the spontaneous industrial revolution in Western Europe.

Conclusion

From the survey made in this chapter it appears that while culturally Russia has become more Western since change got under way in the nineteenth century, and is less removed in this respect from north-western Europe than parts of southern Europe are, it retains characteristics that are found more in the Third World than in the West. Russia's achievements are limited because they are built on a foundation that remains to some extent alien. On the other hand, if capitalism, and the institutions that evolved with it, are outliving their usefulness (see chapters 5 and 10), a society experienced in planning, and amenable to authority, may have a more stable and prosperous future than one which is not.

To the cultural factor must be added the burden of empire. When the time came for Europe to liquidate its empires and re-adapt them to its needs by means of neo-colonialism, Russia remained saddled with all its territorial acquisitons. It could not have brought itself to follow the Western example, because its possessions, with their mineral and vegetable resources, were not overseas but contiguous and were also required as a buffer against China. The continued rigid centralization needed to control the subject peoples stifles economic development, which is further hindered by additional cultural obstacles in the non-European population, which are as formidable as those in the Third World. This centralization tends to defeat itself; for the consequent economic retardation exacerbates rebellious feeling among those peoples most prone to it, such as the

Balts, who, with their Germanic traditions, are said to produce the highest quality goods in the USSR, and the Armenians.

With such profound internal weaknesses, it is almost inconceivable that the Russians would seek to over-extend themselves further by adventures in Western Europe or that, if they were to embark on such folly, they could provide the personnel necessary to ensure their dominance, even by means of surrogates. We shall look at these factors again when assessing whether the risk of Russian domination merits the risk entailed in retaining nuclear weapons. At this stage it will be useful to consider the state of Western Europe.

Chapter 4

The West Europeans

The social weaknesses of the USA and USSR, as depicted in the previous two chapters, make it all the more remarkable that Western Europe, which only recently dominated the world, should now be reduced to relying on its offshoot across the Atlantic to defend it with weapons that could easily lead to its destruction. The present abject state of Western Europe is one of several symptoms of a great decline in the civilization; the loss of influence in the world does not arise merely from lack of military power, but from a general weakening of the creativity on which the strength and growth of a civilization depend. It does not follow from this that the American and Russian societies are healthier. What has happened is that Western Europe has long ceased to produce new ideas and values of the kind that formed a vital part of its marked, but historically brief, advantage over the rest of the world. Its decline will now be examined in the light of: (1) Toynbee's criteria of the disintegration of a civilization; (2) Plato's description of the last days of a democracy; and (3) Marx's view that increasing capital accumulation accompanied by rising unemployment would spell the end of capitalism – he could have been on the right track, even though his reasoning was wrong.

1 Toynbee: For the present purpose it is of no great account whether or not the whole of Toynbee's work is acceptable. It does not even matter if one disagrees (as this author does) with his principle that a national state is not an intelligible field of historical study because it is inextricably linked with the other components of a civilization. But it is desirable, none the less, to heed his view that nationalism is a grave spiritual malady.[1] We shall not be concerned with Toynbee's distinction between breakdown and the first of three stages of disintegration, as he saw it; rather we shall see his criteria as indicating a general decline, without particular stages, that could be catastrophic. In adopting this approach we are still drawing on Toynbee's remarkable insight into the frailty of civilizations. This great contribution to our understanding constitutes the fourth and fifth volumes of his masterpiece, *A Study of History*, of which the first six volumes appeared in 1939.[2] At that time Toynbee said it was not possible for the present generation to be sure whether or not his criteria fitted the modern West; this could not be known until the voyage had come to an end.[3] But by 1972 symptoms were such that in a revised and abridged edition he unequivocally identified certain characteristics of present-day society as signs of disintegration. This he saw, not as defeat, but as a challenge:[4]

> Those who neither acquiesce in the disintegration of their society nor seek to hold it back with artificial substitutes for creativity, but who have the vision and the spiritual courage to confront the challenge, have it within their reach to participate in a greater act of creation than is witnessed in even the most vigorous stages of social growth.

Looking at past civilizations, Toynbee saw that in a growing society the majority was drilled into following the lead of a creative minority.[5] Breakdown was characterized by three main elements: failure of the minority's creative power, the majority's consequent refusal to imitate, and disruption of social harmony leading to a total loss of the civilization's capacity for self-determination. With their vitality dissipated, leaders were deprived of their power to influence the uncreative masses. The majority ceased to admire and imitate them spontaneously; the creative minority degenerated into a mere dominant minority; and the majority were reduced to the status of underdog. Rebellion ensued. 'The piper who has lost his cunning can no longer conjure the feet of the multitude into a dance.'[6] If we accept Toynbee's concept of minority and majority, we may dispense with Marx's oversimplified ideas of bourgeois against feudal, and industrial proletarian against bourgeois, which are, at best, only particular examples of it. Taken over a long period of history, Toynbee's concept works much better; it is certainly more pertinent in this century, when any revolution that takes place is extremely unlikely to be brought about by proletarians, even if we include among them members of the middle and upper classes who style themselves the vanguard of the working class. There has, in fact, been no proletarian revolution as conceived by Marx in any part of the world.

In the light of Toynbee's criterion of political breakdown, the UND demonstrations that startled Europe and shocked the United States are significant. They were confined to no one traditional class and, far more importantly, they could not have taken place without a growing disenchantment with politicians, irrespective of party. In times when external attack is feared people in a society that is not in an advanced stage of decline form up behind their customary leaders. But now, in increasing numbers, particularly in Western Germany and Holland, they distrust them and are turning elsewhere – to clergymen, environmentalists and others not involved in traditional politics. It remains to be seen whether this movement is the spearhead of a regenerative force or whether it is no more than a symptom of disintegration. Inevitably it is supported and exploited by the stereotyped extreme left, but that is not the source of its moral strength. In Britain the Labour Party, unlike its approximate counterparts in Western Germany and France, was identified in the press with the anti-nuclear campaign. But CND activists expressed scepticism about the intentions of its divided leadership. The policy enunciated in the party's election manifesto, issued on 16 May 1983, was incompetently reported as unilateralist. It did not amount convincingly to more than a nuclear freeze – cancellation of the Trident programme, to which there is also considerable Conservative opposition, and refusal to deploy cruise missiles. The promise that Labour would, 'after consultation, carry through in the lifetime of the next Parliament' (during which Europe could be blown up) its 'non-nuclear defence policy' was not an unequivocal commitment to unilateral nuclear disarmament. It was qualified by the statement that Labour would 'propose that Britain's Polaris force be included in the nuclear disarmament negotiations in which Britain must take part'. Consultation and negotiation were no more necessary to liquidate Polaris than to abandon the Trident and cruise plans. The hollowness of the undertaking was put beyond doubt by the assertion of the parliamentary party's Deputy Leader, Denis Healey, that a Labour government would not abandon Polaris unless the Russians made matching concessions. Labour's carefully worded pronouncement represented a compromise within the party, which could be used in conceivable circumstances as a loophole. That the parliamentary party went as far as it did was an aberration, caused by the accident that its leader, Michael Foot, who had been elected to heal the breach between right and left on various issues, happened to be a unilateralist of long standing; the emphasis in the manifesto would have been different if the initiative had been in the hands of his rival, Denis Healey, a former Defence Minister, despite views within the party national executive. Showing their distrust of all factions in the dominant minority, some CND activists expressed scepticism about the Labour leadership's intentions as soon as the manifesto was issued. Labour's ambiguity resembled that of the Greek Socialist Prime Minister, Andreas Papandreou, whose deceptive campaign declarations before the elections of 18 October 1981 were naïvely reported as a commitment to leave the European Communities, which are an irresistible source of emoluments for the Greek élite, of whatever political colour, and NATO. Papandreou took his turn as President of the EC's Council of Ministers on 1 July 1983, for the usual six months.

The positive manifestation of disenchantment, as seen in the CND movement has been accompanied in Britain by one that is negative. With the established parties impotent in the face of the nation's problems, the Social Democratic Party emerged. Born in response to public disillusionment, it was weaned on public ignorance: when it neared the peak of its rise, an opinion poll showed that more than half of its supporters believed that it favoured abandonment of the European Communities, to which all of its leaders were devoted. Its advantage lay not in the record of its founders, but in the fact that it was not among parties that had already failed. The prevailing public mood was such that in October 1981 the Liberal–SDP alliance was able to wrest Croydon from the Conservatives, although the SDP did not even pretend to have specific policies. In a period of social decline, when the creativity of the minority has petered out, people are easily seduced by vague promises. But the sequence of hope and disappointment is not endless. The SDP is probably the last new straw to which the British people will be invited to clutch within the present political framework.

Since social violence has been intermittent throughout history, it is not easy to say when it symptomatizes decline. But there is a difference that may be significant between upsurge today and that of other times. In the past workers struggled for better conditions. They are still doing so; but now their more savage and indicative actions are aimed at preserving their very jobs. In the first quarter of 1982 Belgian steel workers became increasingly violent when faced with the threatened closure of their plants. On 16 March several thousand (estimated by the BBC at 10,000) fought with security police when advancing on the houses of parliament in Brussels. Squads of rioters threw paving stones and railway bolts. Among the

180 casualties eight police, insufficiently protected by their shields and helmets, were seriously injured; two police horses had to be destroyed. In the first half of the nineteenth century Luddites in England and their counterparts in Switzerland and Germany tried to save their jobs by wrecking machines. This was a reaction against new textile techniques that rendered handicrafts obsolete. But while it was rebellious in its expression it was conservative in content and the cause was soon lost in an expanding economy. Today's outbreaks arise not from underlying social dynamism but from chronic stagnation. The Luddites won little mass support because their action contradicted an evident trend. They were, in fact, reactionary. But the Belgian steel workers, like many others, are faced with a dead end. A process that was dynamic has come to a full stop. As masses of people lose their jobs the number of vacancies is insufficient to absorb all but a handful of them, whether or not they are retrained.

In France, while there have been a number of sit-ins by workers whose factories were closing, the most primitive response to threatened livelihood has been in the country. Spanish vegetables have been pulled from lorries and destroyed soon after crossing the frontier. In March 1982 French grape-growers went berserk and used explosives to blow holes in two huge wine tanks, which stood out against the sky like gasometers. They destroyed 5 million litres of what they thought was Italian wine. But it turned out to be all French. While police did not intervene, the episode was filmed and shown on television. About the same time white-uniformed hospital doctors were parading in the streets to express their grievances. It is hard to imagine that a civilization in which such incidents are becoming more frequent has a high survival value.

By the end of 1982 the current social and economic dislocation had not produced in the United Kingdom violence equal to that across the Channel – leaving aside sheer hooliganism, which is a symptom in its own right, and riots with a racial component. But at both Brixton and Toxteth rioters showed the ultimate in disillusionment with the entire political complex: they rebuffed the good offices of extreme leftist agitators, whom they saw as only wishing to exploit them for political purposes. Similarly, unemployed on Merseyside formed their own organization, outside the TUC framework. A member of a Community Education Training Unit said:[7] 'I think the unemployed are fed up with people organizing them; they want to organize themselves.'

For Toynbee social schism in a disintegrating society was

superficial; beyond the social expressions of disintegration lay 'the personal crises of behaviour and feeling and life which are the true essence and origin of the visible manifestations of social collapse'.[8] This many-sided syndrome, with examples from the Sumeric, Greek, Roman and other societies, whose deaths it ushered in, takes up 367 pages in volumes 4 and 5 of Toynbee's major study. The disorder occurs when the response to challenge is polarized into two alternatives – one passive and the other active, but neither of them creative.[9] Thus an individual may seek to regain lost creativity by means of spurious modes of self-expression, such as the drug culture[10] and abandon, 'in which the Soul "lets itself go" '.[11] The active counterpart, equally sterile, is an effort at self-control through a regime of spiritual exercises. This is what we see today. Alongside the growing drug culture, morbid cults are devoted to what their initiates see as spiritual discipline.

Arising from spiritual impotence, Toynbee says, are the twin movements of archaism, in which people try to revive the ethos of their ancestors, and futurism, which looks for salvation in a wild leap into an imagined paradise. Perpetrators of both – and this is the very important point – seek to avoid the arduous spiritual challenge that confronts them. One of the 'principal impulses towards the archaistic form of utopianism is the virus of nationalism, which we see at work in the contemporary world'.[12] At its worst this is marked by a people's attempt to recapture the mythical purity of a past age. Toynbee gives Nazism as the most striking modern example; more recent fascist–racist movements throughout Europe would also qualify. Nationalism, though not in its most vicious form, has shattered attempts to unify Europe by means of the European Communities (better known by the more realistic title of Common Market); increasing parochialism has blocked consideration of European problems as a whole. Faced with economic difficulties, individual countries have raised the cry: 'We must become more competitive.' But this is no answer; for if each country achieved that goal to the same extent all would remain as they were in relation to one another, and if one or two were considerably more competitive than the others, the failures would import less from the successful, as Germany has already found. While this blind, nationalistic groping for economic survival does not constitute archaism in ideas as seen by Toynbee, it certainly fits his definition that nationalism is what makes people think of a part of a society as if it were the whole.[13]

Akin to archaism is attachment to ancestral ideas that are no longer applicable. This infatuation with the past,[14] as Toynbee calls it, does not in itself constitute so profound a spiritual malady as archaism at its worst, but it breeds 'a fatuous passivity' towards present challenge, which can be fatal. While most people accept that the British Empire is gone forever, there is none the less a streak of nostalgia for the aggressive attitudes that made it possible. Such feelings are reflected in a mystical belief that Britain's problems – the product of an environmental challenge that has yet to be met – could be solved by a revival of the old spirit of private enterprise. The failure of ultra-conservatives to arouse significant enthusiasm for this slogan arises partly from public realization that it is pointless; in the days when commercial and industrial initiative were almost certain to yield rewards no appeals were necessary.

The rise from feudalism and the development of vast overseas European possessions were at once the consequence of enterprise and the creator of opportunity. During this period of unprecedented socio-economic dynamism the Western middle classes, in scarcely one hundred years, 'created more massive and more colossal productive forces than . . . all preceding generations together'.[15] To that brief tribute from Marx and Engels we may add Toynbee's observation:[16]

The 'man power' of no less than ten disintegrating civilizations has been conscripted, wholesale, into the Western body social within the last four hundred years. . . . Nor has the monster been content just to prey upon his own kind. Within the same four centuries he has hunted down and swallowed up almost all the primitive societies that had not become the prey of other predatory civilizations before the beginning of the sixteenth century.

The ten civilizations to which Toynbee refers include the Russian Orthodox Christian. It may seem at first sight too much to say that its manpower was conscripted wholesale. But there is no doubt that the partial Westernization of Russia put workers on Western payrolls and, even today, diverts part of their product to Western banks. The cost to Russia includes considerable cultural dislocation, the consequence of which cannot be predicted.

The point is that most of this expansion, destructive or not, is coming to an end and maxims evolved during the rise of capitalism are no longer applicable. The situation is greatly different from what it was when cheap cotton, provided by slave labour, helped to accelerate the industrial revolution.[17] After this feather-bedding had become superfluous the West benefited from cheap oil, bought under military and political pressure at what turned out to be far below the true market price. This prop has also been removed. Now a third is tottering – the neo-colonialism that succeeded colonialism. It is sometimes argued that Europe made little or no profit from its colonies; John Strachey, for instance, said that Britain gained no net financial benefit from India. But this debate is irrelevant here. What matters in the present context is that the colonies made possible a rapid growth that could not otherwise have taken place. Now, for cultural and demographic reasons, which will be dealt with in the next chapter, Western expansion in what has become the Third World is near a dead end.

Having approached the limit of its economic living-space, a creative society would not attempt to fall back on slogans that assume there is still plenty of room for manoeuvre. Western Europe would see that, apart from the United States, to which Europeans migrated, Japan is the only sizeable country that has convincingly adapted the Western capitalist model, and in doing so has become a rival. Economically the Third World is near enough to a desert furnished with bazaars. In these confining circumstances what is needed is not commercial enterprise but a new, rational approach to the present complex challenge, arising from a specific spirit. As Max Weber has shown, it was such a development that made modern capitalism possible in the first place: 'One of the fundamental elements of the spirit of modern capitalism, and not only of that but of all modern culture . . . was born . . . from the spirit of Christian asceticism.' A different spirit is required for the historic task of our time. The old spirit is not only irrelevant; it has been vitiated by the system that it helped to create. Weber wrote as long ago as 1904:[18]

> Since asceticism undertook to remodel the world and to work out its ideals in the world, material goods have gained . . . an inexorable power over the lives of men as at no previous period in history. . . . The rosy blush of its laughing heir, the Enlightenment, seems also to be irretrievably fading. . . . No one knows . . . whether at the end of this tremendous development entirely new prophets will arise, or [whether] there will be a great rebirth of old ideas and ideals, or, if neither, mechanized petrification, embellished with a sort of convulsive self-importance. For of the last stage of this cultural development, it might well be truly said: 'Specialists without spirit, sensualists without heart; this nullity

imagines that it has attained a level of civilization never before achieved.'

This, written more than three-quarters of a century ago, is a picture of decline. Weber did not foresee that the spiritual degeneration that he diagnosed would be followed by chronic economic illness. Mechanized petrification is with us, but even this is threatened. It is not old ideas, but new prophets, that are needed now.

Reversing the growth in rationality that has taken place since the seventeenth century, more people are turning to astrology. In the United States this regression has gone so far that astrology has 'become a growth industry'.[19] Many businessmen and politicians employ astrologers in timing political campaigns, appraising potential employees, deciding which employees to group together, making merger or investment decisions and determining the compatibility or trustworthiness of partners. In Brussels the President of the European Communities Commission, Gaston Thorn, gave a not unsympathetic hearing to an astrologer's predictions of the communities' future. Related to reliance on astrology is deference paid to luck. Such passivity in the face of personal and social challenge, which, as Toynbee says, is the common mood of believers in chance and fate alike, characterizes disintegrating civilizations.

Futurism – a strong symptom of decline – is hideously conspicuous today in the shape of organizations like the so-called red brigades. As Toynbee says, whereas archaism substitutes mimesis of ancestors for mimesis of creative leaders, futurism imitates nothing that has ever created anything. Those whose passion is to murder present-day leaders in the belief that this will bring about a just society are almost by definition pathological killers; at other times they would find different outlets, such as war. But they can only exist in their present form within a sick society, in which there is at least some sneaking sympathy with them. It can be no accident that they are mostly to be found in Germany and Italy, the two former fascist states; though the malady of European discontent is widespread, it is more likely to erupt violently in a community that has experienced large-scale, organized brutality than in one that has not. Akin to terrorism are the housing riots of Berlin and Amsterdam, which express contempt for the ruling minority no less than a desire for accommodation. All this violence is an early warning sign of greater troubles to come. As the growing spiritual and economic crisis accentuates, more and more people will turn away from present leaders. Some will be violent, some not, depending on their temperaments and vulnerability to psycho-social illness. Whether order or disintegration is to be the outcome will depend on the quality of new leaders, who can be expected to emerge. These will not arise from the red brigades or from any political revolutionaries, if a truly regenerated society is to be established; for, as Toynbee points out, all revolutionaries observed today are futurists who abuse from the beginning 'a leadership's obligation to carry the mass of society with it'.[20] They claim falsely that 'the intermediate stage between misery and potential happiness may be leap-frogged with one massive stride far into the future'.

The spiritual malaise of decline is inevitably apparent in art. Toynbee saw the adoption of African forms by Western artists as evidence of aesthetic impotence. The native Western genius had already been sterilized for centuries by the conseqences of a Hellenizing renaissance. But in this century, reacting against the 'fatuousness of the "chocolate-box style" ', the West had fled from vulgarity to seek inspiration in West Africa:[21]

> West African music and dancing, as well as West African sculp-ture, have been imported into the heart of the Western World on the lips and in the limbs of African conscript-immigrants . . . and the effect upon the ethos of our Western dominant minority has been . . . swiftly and . . . deeply demoralizing.

Sculptors with nothing to say turned, indeed, not only to Africa, but to the Far East and South Sea islands; some sought fulfilment in the styles of dead civilizations – Egypt, Babylonia and ancient Greece. That the West should resort to Africa is especially significant. It has been said that Western sculpture is either a dreary imitation of Greek representationalism or a self-conscious attempt to avoid it.[22] Africans have no such problem; their art at its best is religious; it comes straight from the spirit; it is timeless, and untroubled by what is modern and what is not. The spirit finds the form. But a spirit is part of an ethnic personality; it cannot be plundered along with the slaves, palm oil and minerals. Only a society with no spirit, with a shrivelled soul, would have acclaimed attempts to find inspiration in forms that expressed feelings of which it was incapable. This, to my mind, is one of the most striking signs that Western society is spiritually bankrupt. It is part of the cultural promiscuity that Toynbee found to 'pervade every sphere of social activity' in dis-integrating civilizations:[23]

The personal sense of drift has a social counterpart in the feeling of cultural anomie – a total loss of all sense of particularized form and style which is the inverse of the process of differentiation of civilizations through growth. In the sphere of social intercourse it results in a blending of incongruous traditions and in a compounding of incompatible values.

That is an exact description of marked tendencies in West European society – and other societies – today.

Two important present-day social symptoms – the moral defeat of the minority and its susceptibility to influence by an undisciplined majority – are reflected in music. With the aid of transistor radios a variety of unseemly dins has swept the West. Their insidious quality was noted in the 1960s by Ernst Roth, who, as Chairman of Boosey & Hawkes, the London music publishers, knew most of the leading European composers of the first half of this century. Recalling the 1950s, he said that the 'howling, frightening abandon' of Rock 'n' Roll had a 'shattering effect on the young and sent them into paroxysms of destruction'.[24] Dance halls were wrecked and heads broken. Police had to intervene not only in the United States but in London, Rome, Paris and Berlin. 'Beat' music soon took over, but the effect was the same. Roth says:

> It is pop music with a sinister undertone: it does not aim to please or to entertain but to excite, to stir up. It is a temptation and a lure into an inexplicable freedom, into an imaginary wilderness untouched by rule or order such as cannot be found in cities or countryside, life or work.

In other words, it is like a drug. Any of us can submit to it; but it is as well to know what is happening. It is, above all, the antithesis of creativity. The author first saw the link between modern pop and decline when in Aden during the British withdrawal in the late 1960s. A middle-aged British diplomat, taking part in the liquidation of one of the British Empire's last outposts, smiled youthfully over his gin while praising the Beatles. Spurious excitement was compensating for the loss of glory.

It is not the first time that Europe has been plagued by rhythmic banality. In the eighteenth century C. P. E. Bach, son of Johann Sebastian, condemned the growing keyboard practice of 'thumping away at a drum base', which was mostly 'devoid of expression', and required 'little mental effort'.[25] But in those days there were sufficient men and women of character in the minority to protect the culture; C. P. E. Bach led the orchestra of Frederick the Great, a fairly accomplished flautist, who would have been unlikely to countenance musical degeneration. Today the minority connives in and is degraded by every plebeian inroad; uncouth wailing is broadcast by national radio stations with adulation previously reserved for trained voices. Even the innocent are in danger of being corrupted by an inescapable bombardment of low-grade music in shops, restaurants, aeroplanes and coaches; for, as Plato said in the fourth century BC and Boethius in the sixth century AD, music has the power to uplift or debase character. Inversely, spiritual disorientation is bound to find expression in music. During the social decline associated with the downfall of Athens in the Peloponnesian War (431–404 BC) certain Athenians lamented musical vulgarization. In this century the wounds suffered by Western civilization include the dethroning of a tonal system that has been the means of its highest musical expression. Traditional tonality had long been modified. But it was not until the 1920s that Arnold Schönberg virtually delivered the *coup de grâce* to its authority with his note-row. This formula rapidly became a fad; it was seized upon by sterile composers, just as sculptors devoid of inspiration latched on to African art. At the same time, according to the innovative German composer, Paul Hindemith (1895–1963), who resisted Schönberg's theory, there was a general deterioration of craftsmanship. Expressing a similar view, Robert Simpson, composer of eight symphonies, said (in a letter to the author):

This is the first time in history when it is possible to be regarded as a composer without being a musician. Craftsmanship is suspect in a throwaway age. This may have something to do with a dark inner feeling that craftsmanship is a waste of time if it is going to be annihilated anyway. [Dr Simpson did not know that the author was writing about, or had any views on, the atomic bomb.]

By the 1980s musical anarchy had become grotesque; Britain's Arts Council gave a grant to a man to experiment with making instruments from old car parts. The rich tonal system that Schönberg shattered had been developed solely by Western society to satisfy its spiritual and emotional needs. It is not without respect for Schönberg's fifteen years of dedicated work on his own method that one asks what the overthrow of the civilization's characteristic tonality signifies for its future – even though Michael Tippett maintains that concern for harmony is essentially a German phenomenon.

Toynbee writes lengthily of the 'proletarianization', 'vulgarization' and 'barbarization' of dominant minorities during disintegration.[26] This takes us to Plato.

2 **Plato:** A democratic society that is in difficulty could find it instructive to recall Plato's description of life in the last days of a democracy. Without attempting to define it precisely, what we are referring to is a politically democratic state; we are not dealing with the economic democracy imagined by communists or with traditions that some writers call village democracy, as in Java, where despots did not interfere with the ancient custom of *musyawarah* and *mufakat* (consultation and consensus) on local affairs. Democracy as Western Europe knows it today is of recent origin. If we were to accept voting rights as the sole criterion, the United Kingdom would only have been a full parliamentary democracy since 1928, when for the first time women under thirty were allowed to vote. If this were considered to be a quibble, we could not go back farther than 1918. In that year, threatened by 'dangers on the home front' although the war was 'still raging',[27] Parliament was obliged to relax the residential qualifications for men and give the vote to women who were married or aged thirty and more. This measure, the Fourth Reform Bill, added nearly 13 million voters to the register. The process of enfranchisement had been slow. Miners and agricultural workers could not vote until the Third Reform Bill was passed in 1884 – and then, like others, they had to be householders; voters in England and Wales in 1885 totalled only 4,391,000 in an adult population (twenty years and over) of 13,958,900 (1881) – about one-third. Household suffrage in the boroughs had been accorded by the Second Reform Bill in 1867. The First Reform Bill, in 1832, had merely reinstated and strengthened middle-class power over the House of Commons. In France, despite the Declaration of the Rights of Man and the Citizen issued by the Constituent Assembly during the revolution of 1789, there was a certain caution about how far the suffrage should extend. Class interests aside, it was not considered that all people were endowed with the same political wisdom. Universal suffrage for men was not introduced until 1848, and then rather impulsively; women were not given a vote until 1945.

None of these measures went as far as Athenian democracy, in which the smallness of the city-state made it possible for all free men (as opposed to slaves) to vote directly on all legislation. This procedure required no elected parliamentary representatives; the principle is preserved to some extent in Switzerland, where referenda are held on matters that in other democracies are the prerogative of parliament. Like the rival systems of oligarchy and dictatorship, democracies in ancient Europe did not last long. Plato knew of their rise and fall, not only from history; in his own day democratic Syracuse came under despotism. A time comes, Plato says, when if the leaders of a democracy do not permit unstinted freedom they will be cursed as oligarchs; law-abiding citizens will be insulted as non-entities; and honour will be bestowed on 'rulers who behave like subjects and subjects who behave like rulers'. He continues:[28]

> In such a state the spirit of liberty is bound to go to all lengths. . . . It will make its way into the home, until at last the very animals catch the infection of anarchy. The parent falls into the habit of behaving like the child, and the child like the parent; the father is afraid of his sons, and they show no fear or respect for their parents, in order to assert their freedom. Citizens, resident aliens, and strangers from abroad are all on an equal footing. To descend to smaller matters, the schoolmaster timidly flatters his pupils, and the pupils make light of their masters as well as of their attendants. Generally speaking, the young copy their elders, argue with them, and will not do as they are told; while the old, anxious not to be thought disagreeable tyrants, imitate the young and condescend to enter into their jokes and amusements. . . . I had almost forgotten to mention the spirit of freedom and equality in the mutual relations of men and women . . . The whole place is simply bursting with the spirit of liberty.

All these signs seem to be present today. Governments have consistently spent more than they can afford to satisfy popular demand, often against their better judgment. Mass pressure and demagogy have threatened the rule of the law by contemptuous rejection of court decisions on trade union affairs. Governments are increasingly less thought of as rulers, although they are elected to rule, no less than elected European kings in the Middle Ages or African kings who became divine upon election; once this concept is lost anarchy is inevitable. Plato's reference to the indiscipline of children and weakness of parents is too evident in Britain to require illustration. In Italy an official inquiry revealed widespread violence against teachers, one of whom was thrown from a window; a group of youths demanded an automatic pass in examinations; and extreme left pupils in Rome subjected a woman communist teacher to a trial because she had telephoned a pupil's parents.[29]

The question is whether, in fact, Plato's description of a declining democracy was satisfactory, and, if it was, whether the symptoms he observed have the same significance today. If Plato does apply, it would be erroneous to think that such a fundamental problem could be solved by superficial measures such as stricter discipline of children, more dignified behaviour by those bearing responsibility, laws against pornography, the banning of sex shops, stricter measures against trade unions or racial discrimination. In the light of what Toynbee has shown us, the degeneration described by Plato is merely a symptom of an underlying malaise, which can only be cured by a radical change in spirit. Plato found that a democracy was always succeeded by a dictatorship, equally short-lived. A society that felt democracy was on the wane might do well to begin thinking of an acceptable alternative or modification.

Excessive freedom leads to disruption, in which people may accept any rule that restores security and ensures a regular livelihood. That such a development could occur in Britain is already evident. An unsuccessful, poorly disciplined and badly led society first began to turn hopefully to the SDP, but was soon disillusioned. It only required such an irrelevant event as the Falklands affair to trigger strong but subsequently reduced support for a leader who showed the ruthless single-mindedness that makes people feel more secure in troubled times. While her policies had cost more jobs than would have otherwise been lost, the Iron Lady was seen as a protector of what could be saved in an uncertain world. At the same time fear of unemployment bridled the exercise of what had been cherished as democratic rights; workers were less unrealistic in their demands, strikes diminished and union demagogues lost much of their power. The Iron Lady has, in fact, gone close to presiding over a dictatorship of circumstance, caused to some extent by her economic policy. As the elections of 9 June 1983 showed, it is possible to perform such a function with the support of a mere 30.8 per cent of registered voters (42.4 per cent of the 72.7 per cent turnout). The Conservative vote was weaker than in the 1979 elections, when it was 43.9 per cent of 76 per cent, or 33.4 per cent. That this feeble result could be widely hailed as a landslide victory, attributed to the Iron Lady's dynamism, exposes the irrationality of the British electoral system in particular and reflects the illusory nature of Western parliamentary democracy in general. Despite strong press support, the Conservatives won fewer than five percentage points more than Communists in Czechoslovakia, who topped the poll with 38 per cent of votes in the last free and competitive elections in 1946. Throughout Western Europe democracy is confused or in disarray. Italy, where dissatisfaction with the corrupt and incompetent mandarin class is growing, has had forty-four governments since the Second World War. In Western Germany it was possible for Chancellor Helmut Schmidt to be overthrown solely by intrigue within the political élite in October 1982, while his successor felt obliged to go through the constitutionally Gilbertian process of getting himself voted out of office by his parliamentary supporters, in order to hold general elections on 6 March 1983. In Denmark the government approved the installation of American missiles in Europe, although a parliamentary majority opposed it. Demonstrations against the French Socialist–Communist government by students, doctors, workers and shopkeepers in May 1983 were followed by a challenge to authority when a section of the police demonstrated in June.

Although it is impossible to say when Western Europe's decline began, Toynbee did not rule out that it could have originated in the wars of religion in the sixteenth century, which cracked the foundations of Western Christian civilization; John Stuart Mill made the important point, in another context, that no system of values had been developed since feudalism. It is values, not technological achievement, that keep a civilization alive. Toynbee says:[30]

> Since the vulgar estimates of human prosperity are reckoned in terms of power and wealth, it thus often happens that the opening chapters in the history of a society's decline are popularly hailed as the culminating chapters of a magnificent growth; and this ironic misconception may even persist for centuries.

It was by the criterion of values that Weber judged the present civilization to be a nullity. But even by lesser criteria the present age lacks the creativity of those ancestors who introduced rationality into science and developed institutions associated with the radically new economic system of modern capitalism. Present-day Western Europe is lethargically carried on by momentum created in the past. It is content to tinker with ancient, creaking economic machinery and has failed to adapt political institutions to a new situation.

To those concerned with the survival of the civilization the worship of technology can only be disquieting; for in the past technical advance has been the handmaiden of disintegration. After discussing several examples Toynbee recalls:[31]

> In the history of the successive improvements in the Hellenic [including Roman] art of war, we have a clear case in which it is not the growth of a civilization, but its arrest and breakdown and disintegration, that goes hand in hand with the improvements in its military technique; and the histories of the Babylonian and Sinic civilizations offer us equally good illustrations of the same phenomenon.

If rapid technological advance can mask disintegration, that taking place in Western Europe and its cultural offshoots in Eastern Europe and across the Atlantic is all the more disturbing, since for the first time in history it provides the means of total destruction. It is clear that drastically new thinking on fundamental issues will have to be done if a catastrophe is to be averted. History suggests that such a switch of heart and mind cannot be expected of a civilization in decline. Radical moral change is the only hope. That is the relevance of this chapter to the issue of nuclear disarmament.

3 Marx: Nor could a declining civilization be expected to solve its economic problem. This will be discussed in the next chapter.

Chapter 5

Economic débâcle and nuclear danger

Unemployment

If there were doubt about the significance of evidence outlined in the previous chapter, the sheer incompetence of Western civilization in the face of its economic ills would be enough in itself to suggest the onset of disintegration. Unemployment – a disgrace and a threat to any society – continues to rise. Bankruptcies have increased, shops close and big companies that seemed invulnerable are struggling to survive. Even banks are in danger; as a Dutch banker said (to the author) it only needs one to tumble in Europe and others will follow. It is now being recognized that large-scale unemployment has become part of the economic structure – an entirely new predicament. Yet governments blindly attempt to deal with it as if it were merely cyclical, or the consequence of wrong policies, when what is needed is radical structural change. We have here another example of anachronistic thinking, of failure to develop a new vision in the face of problems that unquestionably constitute a historic challenge to the very existence of the civilization. As M. W. Thring, former Professor of Mechanical Engineering at Queen Mary College, London, and of Fuel Technology and Chemical Engineering at the University of Sheffield, says:[1] 'There is an ever increasing gap between the common sense of ordinary people (which is aware that our civilization is degenerating towards disaster) on the one hand and the short term palliative promises of the power possessing beings on the other.'

In a chapter entitled 'The Disintegrating Industrial Jalopy' Giles Merritt, of the *Financial Times*, likens the 'collapse of manufacturing industry in the world's wealthiest countries' to a Mack Sennett comedy, in which a battered Model-T Ford, losing one part after another, slowly breaks up and settles in the dust.[2] He finds that in Europe the first wheel flew off about twenty years ago, almost unnoticed. We may add that this wobbling economic crock is usually portrayed as a limousine, temporarily out of order. It is represented as vastly superior to the economy of the Eastern bloc and is among the complex of Western structures that nuclear weapons are supposed to defend. But it may be found that the long-term difference is minimal; or even that the alien model, which is less capable of self-destructive acceleration, is more durable. In that event defence of the jalopy would hardly justify the risk entailed by possessing nuclear weapons, although there could, of course, be other grounds for retaining them, which will be discussed in subsequent chapters. We shall, therefore, take up a little time in examining the economic débâcle.

Of all the evils of unemployment the worst is the demoralization of young people who leave school to face a sterile future. Adults who are thrown out of jobs have had at least the irreplaceable social experience of work and have satisfied what is probably an instinctual need to be convinced that, except in impossible circumstances, they can fend for themselves. The loss of a job is demoralizing, but while the psychological consequences may be illness or suicide,[3] most people can cope with it, though often with great difficulty; such is the productivity of the capitalist system, even when it is failing, that they can be housed, fed and even to some extent entertained. But for those who have no prospect of work it is immeasurably worse. I would go so far as to say that any economic system, whatever its disadvantages, that rid society of the cancer of unemployment would be better than one that did not; for, humanitarian considerations apart, the social disinheritance of a substantial number of the rising generation must deepen the general feeling of helplessness and thus vitiate further the creativity of the entire community. The gloom that pervades households as children near the school-leaving age may be good for the discipline of those employed; but it is bad for social growth in any proper sense of the term and is ultimately fatal to stability.

These thoughts are obvious enough and they have been put down only to give human meaning to the figures that follow. In 1982 only one-third of British school leavers were expected to find jobs; this pattern is expected to prevail in the nine countries of the European Communities in the first half of the decade, when 8 million will leave school.[4] Already nearly 40 per cent of British jobless are aged less than twenty-five, while teenage unemployment is rising at three times the national rate. By the middle of the 1980s nearly half of the unemployed in the European Economic Community (EEC) could consist of people under twenty-eight who had never or scarcely known work. The Department of Applied Economics at Cambridge University estimated in April 1982 that British unemployment would rise steadily to well over 4 million by 1990;[5] Merritt cites other forecasts that it could be close to 5 million by the middle of the decade.[6] Unemployment in the twenty-five countries of the OECD is expected to increase by 50 per cent to 35 million by 1990. These are conservative estimates. European trade union economists warn that unemployment in the EEC, which was more than 12 million at the beginning of 1983, could reach 18 million in 1985.

Three points need to be made about these figures. The first is that official unemployment records always understate. We may dismiss the charge that scroungers inflate the statistics. There are certainly scroungers, and not a few, but in the rise of the number of registered jobless in Britain from 281,000 in 1966 to the present staggering total scrounging cannot be more than an insignificant factor. People, in fact, like work; in 1978 National Opinion Polls found that 82 per cent of a sample of British workers close to retirement said they would prefer not to give up working, even if they received full pay. The official figures understate because many unemployed do not register. Unfortunately for governments, as a French inquiry established, it is often these people who fill jobs created at great expense to relieve unemployment, with the result that the number of registered jobless is not reduced by the number of new vacancies; Merritt maintains that, at a most conservative estimate, if there are 3 million registered unemployed in Britain there are 4 million who would work if they could.[7] The second point is that so far forecasts of unemployment have generally been too low. In August 1980 the National Institute for Economic and Social Research warned that 2,190,000 would be jobless in Britain by the end of 1981, but this figure was attained about five months after the report was issued; similarly Warwick University's Manpower Group forecast that unemployment would touch 3 million two years later than it did. The third point is that the longer-term forecasts do not take into account the widespread introduction of micro-technology, including word processors, which is expected to slash employment in offices and to reduce it further in factories when it gets under way later in the decade. Some people maintain that the new technology will create as many jobs as it destroys. But since micro-chip devices can be produced cheaply by unskilled labour directed by a handful of highly qualified technicians in the Third World, this argument is dubious. Whether or not jobs will be replaced, their destruction is certain. Analysts on the UK's Central Policy Review Staff are among specialists who agree with a forecast made for the West German Government that micro-chip technology could halve employment. It is of little comfort that an OECD team has arrived at a lower figure, a loss of 32 per cent; this is equivalent to 35 million jobs in the present EEC labour force.

That something is radically wrong was seen, though dimly, by *The Times* on 27 January 1982:

> After making every allowance for economic principle and political prudence, the nagging doubt remains that the present economic reality in Britain simply does not make sense. With three million out of work, output at below the level of 1974, large chunks of our industry disappearing, our cities crumbling, services deteriorating, the education and training of our children being hacked away, and the financial costs of the recession actually raising government expenditure and interest rates, it is not clear that the kind of budget which is being previewed and indeed heralded as a new dawn is appropriate to the daunting task which faces our rulers.

For *The Times* the solution was 'massive investment, private and public', to restore Britain's competitive strength. But the economic malaise infects all industrialized countries, not only Britain. As was pointed out in the last chapter, if all became equally more competitive, all would remain in the same position in relation to one another. This is a crisis of Western civilization and its offshoots, not merely of the British economy. The Conservatives have certainly accelerated the slide in Britain, just as the Socialists have done, by other means, in France, where an abortive attempt to reflate the economy was inevitably transformed into an unintended policy of stop-go, beginning with a period of austerity that was not mentioned in election promises. But the Conservatives are not responsible for the fact that unemployment is of the same order of magnitude in both the EEC and the United States, which have labour forces of approximately the same size; nothing they did would have much effect on that fundamental and inexorable situation. Nor can Thatcher, Mitterrand or even, solely, Reagan's high interest rates be blamed for a rise of 44 per cent in American bankruptcies in January–June 1982 compared with the corresponding period in the previous year. And it was certainly not Thatcher, Mitterrand or Reagan who brought down the German giant, AEG-Telefunken, ran America's chemical company, Du

Pont, into difficulties and piled up the huge losses of International Harvester, which was unable to pay $4,200 million owing to 200 banks. AEG had not paid a dividend since 1973. In August 1982 it appealed to its creditors, mainly 25 banks that had bailed it out in 1979, to write off 60 per cent of their loans. In return it promised a new AEG, which would cease its consumer production and concentrate on power engineering and, ominously, radar, which was sure to be in good demand in a world that is preparing to destroy itself. Small businesses are in a similar plight; in May 1982 the British Government's loan-guarantee scheme, devised to help them, was reported to be 'in jeopardy', with the government worried about the cost of a 'high level of failure'.[8]

The economic rot is too widespread to be given any important national significance, although initial vulnerability has varied from people to people. Whether we look at Britain, Europe as a whole, the United States or Japan, the same fundamental symptoms are apparent. By 1981 nearly three-quarters of a million jobs in British manufacturing industries had disappeared; the Manpower Services Commission, without taking much account of the effects of micro-chip technology, which are hard to predict, expects that by 1985 Britain will have lost a further 1,200,000 manufacturing jobs.[9] A major collapse is possible. Britain's shaky car industry remains the largest generator of skilled employment in the country, even though its production is only about half of what it was ten years ago. BL (British Leyland) only employs 160,000 workers, but estimates of those directly dependent on it range from 600,000 to 1 million. Its failure would have incalculably serious effects on the lives of others more remotely linked with it – shopkeepers and those supplying them, for example. Such a catastrophe cannot be ruled out; according to one prediction, the only European car firms destined to survive are Volkswagen, Fiat, Renault and Peugeot-Citroën.[10] The fate of all companies will be determined by their productivity, which, in turn, depends on replacing men with machines.

The European steel industry, now working at only 55 per cent capacity, is also faced with further rationalization. By 1985, if present plans are carried out, governments will withdraw subsidies that offset operating losses of nearly $3,000 million a year. The consequent adjustments could cost about 250,000 jobs. At the end of 1982 the British Steel Corporation had cut its work force from 166,000 to fewer than 90,000, with 15,000 more redundancies planned. Since 1972 shipyard employment in the EEC has dropped by 42 per cent, with further cuts in the offing.

In Japan the crisis that precipitated urgent government measures in September 1982 was already looming in the 1970s, when production of steel, non-ferrous metals, chemicals, lumber and, even more, textiles, fell seriously. Workers in manufacturing industries dropped from nearly 14,500,000 to about 13 million; it is officially forecast that by the late 1980s the figure will be only 10 million in a total work force that will have risen from the present 54 million to 60 million.

The rise of unemployment in the United States, whose economic performance is important to the entire capitalist world, has been spectacular. With dismissals soaring at a record rate, 550,000 lost their jobs in October 1981 alone, bringing the total to 9 million in November; by January 1983 the number had swollen to more than 13 million. The unemployed do not consist largely of people incapable or barely capable of work. Nearly one in four of those who experienced unemployment in 1980 belonged to families with annual incomes of $20,000 or more.[11] Suffering is widespread. In May 1982 considerably fewer than half of the jobless were receiving unemployment benefit.[12] Social security is complex in the United States because responsibility is divided between the federal and state governments; but the principle of eligibility is that a worker must have been employed for three of the previous twelve months. Normally entitlement only lasts six months. But Congress granted a thirteen-week extension in the thirty-three states hardest hit by unemployment and in May 1982 a move was well under way to concede a further thirteen weeks. On the other hand, one of Reagan's financial restrictions forced the state of Michigan, which is afflicted by some of the worst unemployment in the country, to suspend the first thirteen-week extension; and states that had exhausted their reserves were obliged from 1 April 1982 to pay 10 per cent interest on loans from the federal unemployment fund, which until then had been interest-free. In the middle of 1982 the number of those who had exhausted their rights because of time limitation was expected to increase steadily even after recovery began, assuming that it did. Americans generally are becoming less well off; in 1981 the average family income fell by 3.5 per cent.[13] Net American farm income fell by 30 per cent in real terms in 1979–81, with a further 30 per cent drop expected in 1982 to the lowest level since 1934. Since farmers cut capital investment by 14 per cent in 1981, with tractor sales falling 40 per cent, it appears that the trend will continue.

In the United States the inept efforts at economic recovery that characterize the West took the exceptionally bizarre form of Reaganomics. Reagan cannot be given all the blame for this, since his short-lived policy was supported by influential people inside and outside the administration. Adopting supply-side theory, Reagan took the view that America's economic decline was caused more by governmental crippling of the productive process than by lack of purchasing power. Once taxes and other constraints were lifted the economy would spring up like the head of a Jack-in-the-box. More hours would be worked, savings would increase, investors would take more risks and large numbers of the unemployed would be swept up in a productive drive. With the entire nation responding to a surge of prosperity, the national income was to rise at such a rate that Reagan would be able to cut taxes heavily while at the same time increasing expenditure on war weapons to record levels. Reagan ignored warnings that even if a boom could be generated by those means, it would not come fast enough for him to achieve his two objectives in the near future. There was, in fact, little to distinguish Reaganomics from the millenarian dreams to which more primitive societies succumb in times of trouble. Reagan's critics saw no reason to believe that the tax windfall would either increase capital accumulation or induce people to work harder. They found it more likely that taxpayers would spend most of the gain, just as if it were a rise in salary; instead of working longer hours people would simply reduce overtime and moonlighting. There might have been a surge of small business. But tax reduction and less restrictive regulation could not solve the problems of key industries such as car and steel manufacture, which are caused by surplus productive capacity in relation to the world market, or improve the badly run-down transport system, which is itself an obstacle to recovery. The end of Reaganomics was sealed by a reversal of tax policy. In the words of a Senator: 'Congress passed the largest tax cut in history, which led to the largest budget deficit, which led to the largest tax increase.' About three-quarters of Reagan's tax cuts remained after the Senate had finished with Reagan's measures. But the problem of a huge budget deficit, which has mounted since Reagan began trying to reduce it, remains. *The Economist* said that figures in a budget worked out by the President and Congress could not be believed. It predicted that American deficits would continue to increase and that Reagan would 'preside over a supply-side disaster'.[14]

Just as forecasts of unemployment have been consistently low, those of an economic upturn have been repeatedly invalidated by events. This unseeing hopefulness has not been confined to politicians purveying diverse and contradictory economic doctrines, such as Reagan and Thatcher on the one hand and Mitterrand on the other. In an article entitled 'The recovery that never comes' *The Economist* said on 10 July 1982:

> In each of its past two bi-annual examinations of the 24 big industrial countries who are its members it [the OECD] has suggested that economic recovery is just around the corner. Each time that tempting corner keeps slipping out of reach. The OECD soothsayers now think that the real growth of members' gross national products this year will be only ½%. Last year they were predicting 1¼% for 1982; a year ago, 2%. Recovery's new corner, around which lies gnp growth of 2½ per cent, is now postponed until 1983. Prepare for it to recede again, like Tantalus's grapes.

On 7 August 1982 *The Economist* published an article headlined 'Help! Has anyone seen our recovery?' It said that in what amounted to a 'dreadful message' a survey made by the Confederation of British Industries had found a collapse in general business confidence, an unexpected fall in output in the previous four months, continued destocking and continued redundancies. *The Economist* commented: 'Be it noted that, for the past six CBI surveys at least, the forecasts, though mostly gloomy, have been outdone in gloom by the realities reported in the next edition.'

The Third World chimera

There was a time when some Westerners felt that the slave trade was not only good for their economy, but benefited the pagan negroes, to whom it brought Christian enlightenment. This blend of selfishness and imagined altruism now takes another form – the view that North and South are inter-dependent and that by helping what are tactfully called the less developed countries the more developed will also help themselves. Stripped of their idealistic veneer, the bare bones of this thinking were starkly revealed by James Callaghan, then Prime Minister, on the eve of his visit to India in January 1978: 'What I am deeply worried about is the impact [of trade recession] on the poorer countries, because of their indebtedness. I am talking about the need to keep those developing

countries moving ahead in order to keep our own moving ahead.'
Similarly, François Mitterrand said in an interview published in *Le Monde* on 24 October 1981 that France must solidify and liberalize its relations with the Third World. He explained: 'I believe . . . that development corresponds to our fundamental interest, because we could not survive the collapse of the Third World, and because the North needs the South to get out of the crisis.'

Just as the sufferings of the uprooted slaves were ignored, so, in statements like these, are the destruction and misery in the Third World caused by Western-style development. Vast, useless industrial and other projects are sold; huge ecological damage is done; the slightly better off peasant improves his lot at the expense of the poorest; and even such an apparent bounty as the introduction of cash crops can so disturb a society that witchcraft is increasingly sought to ease the pains of maladjustment. Details of this dislocation are provided in *The Third World Calamity*,[15] and need not be repeated here. What matters in the present context is that, although there is still good money to be picked up in the Third World, the West's endeavour to extricate itself from its economic morass by expansion in that direction is approaching a dead end, the defence of which is not worth the risk of nuclear war. Instead of offering unlimited scope for investment, the Third World has become a repository of unpayable debts, while Western firms have lost large sums in enterprises launched there, including car assembly plants; instead of providing an advantageous market for exports, it has embarrassed the West with manufactured exports of its own, which are cheaply produced by a small fraction of its large, mostly destitute population. People in the West can buy Third World goods, which are not infrequently shoddy, at prices lower than they would otherwise be; but the added cost is jobs. The methodology of this subject is difficult and estimates of the net job loss vary. After making 'very rough adjustments' of studies carried out in Germany, the Netherlands, Belgium and the USA, the OECD found that the ratios of jobs 'created' by exports of manufactures to the entire Third World to those 'lost' by imports were 'something like 0.65–0.80 for the direct and 0.75–0.95 for the total (i.e. direct plus indirect)'.[16] That jobs have been created in the Third World does not mean that the basis of a sound economy has been established there. The 1982 report of the United Nations Conference on Trade and Development (UNCTAD) says:[17]

The developing world is facing its gravest economic crisis since the Great Depression [when, in passing, neither most of the nations involved nor the concept of the developing world existed]. As in that earlier period, the crisis is the product of the malfunctioning of the economies of developed market-economy countries, and has been intensified by the growing disarray of the trade and financing systems.

On that analysis alone – and there is more to be said – there is little chance of the West curing its economic ills by exercise in an area that it has so gravely infected. Aid is certainly not the answer to the problems of either region; judiciously applied as charity, it can help in the Third World, but it cannot transform. Nigeria, for example, receives oil revenue on a scale that Third World countries could never expect in aid. Oil accounts for 80 per cent of total government receipts, which in 1977 were 8,042 million naira (£6,700 million at the official rate of 1.2 naira to £1). When Nigeria became independent on 1 October 1960 its economy was similar to those of most Third World countries – subsistence agriculture and cash crops, which provided the bulk of its exports. If its windfall had come, not as oil, but as aid, the result would have been the same. The old economy has been seriously damaged, perhaps permanently; corruption has soared; simple people have been lured from their villages to engage in construction work that is often uneconomic; and businessmen, who are not noted for their industry in Nigeria, have been debased by easy money. Agriculture has been dislocated and it is cheaper to import than to grow all rural products that were exported before the oil period, except cocoa. Until the oil money began to pour in, Nigeria was the world's biggest producer of groundnuts; within a decade the exports declined to virtually nothing. More serious, in the long term, is the great exodus from farms. According to an Oyo State survey the departure of youth was almost total. Only 0.6 per cent of farmers were aged between eighteen and twenty-four, 12 per cent between twenty-five and thirty-four and 24 per cent between thirty-five and forty-four.[18] Hence 63.4 per cent were older than forty-four. The prospect is fearful. When the oil runs out, Nigerians will not have the currency to import food and will have lost the difficult skills of producing it; and they will have no competitive industry. It is the same in the Middle East, where Arabs have already forgotten the art of living in the desert, without having acquired the attitudes and values that will be needed for their survival when the oil wells dry up.

In this respect the Indians are better off. Although their plots are dwindling as the population rises, they at least remain on the land and extract subsistence from it. But this largely primitive economy, despite the publicity given to India's Western-style enclave, offers little opportunity for Western expansion. The limitation may be seen in the relatively small number of factory workers. In 1975–6 this number rose by 328,000 to 6,381,000, in a total labour force estimated in 1974 at 183,000,000, of whom 152,000,000 were male.[19] If factory employment rose by 100 per cent in ten years the total would only be of the order of 13 million. While greater industrial production would provide additional work in other fields, we are still dealing in relatively small figures. Any increase in employment arising from industrial growth would be small compared with that in the labour force of 5 million a year.

India provides a good example of fallacies in the Brandt Commission's report. Since the incomes of most Indians are negligible and their farm plots diminutive, there is no chance of their forming a substantial market. This situation is unchangeable. Transfers of Western wealth, as proposed by the commission, could never be on a sufficient scale to create a significant number of productive jobs in India, let alone the entire Third World. Added to this, new factories being established in India, as elsewhere, are increasingly capital intensive. Even if these obstacles were overcome by unforeseeable means, a corps of teachers, larger and more competent than any yet dreamed of, would have to be trained and paid to educate the labour force in literacy and techniques. The immensity of this insoluble problem may be measured by the fact that the amount of money spent per head in education alone in the United States is about four times the Gross Domestic Product (GDP) per head in India. Lack of skilled labour and management is one of the reasons why large amounts of agreed aid remain unused throughout the Third World. At one point the Wilson Government warned India that aid commitment would be reduced if the funds offered were not used; a European diplomat in New Delhi told the author that if a Western ambassador had a project accepted he sent a triumphant message to his capital. Much aid is no more than subsidized exports.

From the entire Third World the OECD has only been able to choose six countries that can be classed with Greece, Portugal, Spain and Yugoslavia as what it calls Newly Industrializing Countries (NICs).[20] They are (with Gross Domestic Product per head in 1976 measured by an index in which that of the USA is 100): Singapore (42.4), Hong Kong (34.9), Brazil (31.1), Mexico (25.4), Taiwan (23.7) and South Korea (19.9). These account for only 231 million of the 3,000 million people said to be living in the poorer countries. At most only three of them, small islands with a strong concentration of Western capital and influence, may be considered dependable. They are Singapore, where oil refining accounts for 40 per cent of industrial output, Hong Kong (although its future political status is in doubt) and Taiwan, which could be swallowed up by China; their populations total only about 23,100,000. South Korea is always unpredictable; and neither Brazil nor Mexico has escaped the economic ills of Latin America, where, according to *The Economist*, inflation ran out of control in 1982. Latin America contains the world's largest and most vulnerable borrowers, who owe more than 60 per cent of the Third World's foreign bank debt. Mexico had to be rescued from default. Its export earnings, like those of Brazil, are less than is needed to service debts to the West. About two-thirds of Brazil's exports come from agriculture and mining. This means that farmers, mostly poor, are shouldering a large part of the amortization and interest paid to foreign banks – to keep the West moving ahead, as Callaghan put it.

We may now add a few words to the UNCTAD report. It is true that the Western economic malaise has spread to Third World economies. But the cause of the development impasse lies deeper. Development is impeded by the persistence of cultural constraints that kept Afro–Asian countries stagnant for centuries and made them vulnerable to imperialism. Japan is an exception that is being increasingly understood; taking Max Weber as a starting point, Michio Morishima, the Japanese economist, argues that Japan's economic rise was made possible by cultural traits not to be found elsewhere in Asia, including China.[21] The view that cultural barriers impede Third World development is elaborated and illustrated in *The Third World Calamity*[22] and will not be pursued here. It is enough to have indicated that the Third World should be written off as a way out of the Western crisis. The West cannot move the Third World ahead; it has to find a means of moving itself.

If the economic crisis in the South reflects that in the North, it is also rebounding and striking at the heart of the international financial system. The first big shock came in August 1982, when Mexico's threatened default required a large rescue operation. At that time a record number of twenty-six countries were late with external debt payments. Then Brazil, now the world's largest debtor, opened 1983 by announcing that it was only able to pay interest, not repay principal. The prospect is such that on 11 December 1982 *The Economist* said that every banker was frightened. As a proportion of export earnings Argentina's debt servicing requirement shot up from about 65 per cent in 1978 to 170 per cent (estimated) in 1982, Mexico's from about 120 per cent to 130 per cent and Brazil's from about 70 per cent to 120 per cent.[23] It appears that the only way the West can get some of its money back is to go on lending on a scale that Latin America's export prospects cannot justify. When the Mexican crack appeared in the financial edifice, *The Economist* asked: 'How long can bankers pull rabbits out of the sombrero?' The answer seems to be that they should be able to do so for a considerable time. Western economies, even though in grave difficulty, can afford to shed a good deal of their surplus, while still providing better material standards, even for the unemployed, than the previous generation imagined possible. Yet there is probably some limit. It does not seem likely that the exponential fiasco, in which loans are used to pay off loans, rather than to finance the production that enables debts to be honoured and interest paid, can go on indefinitely. More than 40 per cent of big banks' international deposits are redeposited with other international banks. It would not take many failures to bring about a major banking collapse. *International Reports*, a newsletter that circulates among bankers and businessmen, has gone as far as to forecast the consequences of writing off debts of $100,000 million to $200,000 million.[24] One prospect is that governments will nationalize banks that have lost their capital; shareholders will lose their equity, but the banking system will carry on. Meanwhile in 1982 twenty-seven American banks had failed by the third quarter, while Chase-Manhattan, a key bank, reported its first quarterly loss in its history.[25]

Marx and the future

Bankers have been blamed by commentators for careless lending. This is not altogether hindsight, since some bankers were, for example, too shrewd to lend to Poland. All are now cautious about credits to the Third World, whose public and private non-guaranteed debts totalled more than $420,000 million in 1980, after large sums had been written off or rescheduled on inflation-eroding terms by Western governments. But the point is less that the money was lent than that it had piled up in the first place, and that under the existing economic system there was nothing else that could have been done with it profitably. This brings us to Karl Marx (1818–83), who, in spite of his protest, 'All I know is that I am not a Marxist',[26] has been seized upon by many futurists as a prophet. Marx sought to demonstrate that the last days of capitalism would be characterized by what stands out today – a vast accumulation of capital (such as the money lent by the banks), high unemployment and a falling profit rate. Corporate profits in the USA declined by 3 per cent in 1980, a further 4¾ per cent in 1981 and were estimated to fall 15 per cent in 1982; in Germany profits fell 15 per cent in the first half of 1981. Merritt says:[27] 'If the average industrial share in Britain were to have yielded a reasonably healthy profit over the past ten years, it has been reckoned that the FT index would now be about 1,300 instead of stagnating around the 500 [700 in 1983] mark.'

It is true that the money available for loans has been swollen by the recycling of petrodollars from OPEC countries. But this is none the less capital accumulation produced by the system; and if the money had not been paid to oil producers, much of it would still have been placed in international banks. The accumulation was substantial before oil prices rose. Early in the 1960s a European ambassador, justifying his government's support of the Indonesian junta, said (to the author) that Indonesia was needed as an investment outlet. In the 1970s, as James Morgan, a BBC financial correspondent, has noted, banks had big deposits from exports and had to lend them somewhere.[28] At the beginning of the same decade Bernard Bell, World Bank representative in Jakarta, reprimanded an American bank for encouraging the Indonesian national oil company to borrow excessively. Britain's General Electric Company had more than £1,000 million waiting to be invested in 1982, while in Western Germany Siemens was unable to put DM 8,500 million of cash and securities to productive use. It may be asked why this capital is not used to provide employment. The answer is that if the companies sitting on funds could invest them profitably, they would do so. This would apply whether the company were private or run by a co-operative or autonomous socialist enterprise in any market or partially market system so far conceived. Not to invest profitably could ruin the shareholders, who might well be trade union pension organizations.

This contradiction of abundant capital alongside unemployed workers was one of the puzzles that Marx set out to solve. Unfortunately his reasoning has been proved wrong. This does not mean that his inquiries in economics and his impressive sociological work are not of continuing interest. Howard and King say that his elaborate theory of cyclical economic crises was well in advance of its time; the view has been taken that he initiated growth theory and that models devised independently in the late 1930s were less refined than his; and the Russian-born American Nobel prize winner, Wassily Leontif, derived his input–output matrix from Marx.[29] Howard and King maintain that Marx's abstract models show that although balanced growth is possible in a capitalist mode of economic organization, it is extremely unlikely. But Marx failed to achieve one of his main goals – a proof that capitalism will collapse when it cannot employ a socially acceptable proportion of the work force. His argument fails on several counts. He showed that, with advancing technology, investment in machinery increases at a greater rate than that in labour. But the inference that this aggravates unemployment is invalid, since the rates are only relative and there is no reason why jobs should not increase, even though investment in them is slower than in capital goods. Marx's 'absolute general law of capitalist accumulation' rests on premises that no longer exist. It entails rapid population growth and regular transfer from the pre-capitalist to the capitalist economy, which was taking place in Europe in his time. Marx recognizes, but does not satisfactorily dispose of, economic forces that operate to make capital-saving innovations more profitable than those that save labour; one such force is the reserve army of workers, which can keep wages down. Howard and King end their analysis of Marx's section on capital accumulation with: 'Marx provides no proof that technical progress will have a labour-saving bias sufficiently strong to produce an increasing reserve army [of unemployed].'[30]

The *coup de grâce* to those of Marx's theories that involve value magnitudes appears to have been delivered by Ian Steedman, who analysed them along lines devised by Pierro Sraffa in his critique of neo-classical economics. Steedman retains respect for Marx; but at the end of his book, he declares that he has 'proved that Marx's value reasoning is often internally inconsistent, completely failing to find the explanations which Marx sought for certain central features of the capitalist economy'.[31] What is left is a great deal that is untouched by the Sraffa-type analysis. But there is nothing with which to forecast the future of capitalism with any certainty. Nevertheless we are still faced with the periodic recurrence of the huge capital accumulation, high unemployment and falling profits, which Marx saw as a fatal weakness in the system.

Perhaps ominously, the present crisis differs from its predecessors in that the co-existence of stagnation and inflation appears for the first time, while those who lose their jobs now tend to stay out of work. Related to this is that robots have become cheaper than humans. While we have no means of proving that the capitalist economy is self-destructive, it is obviously working very badly. It could be doomed, even though the reason is not understood, or only dimly seen. No major progress in understanding economic fundamentals has been made since Marx. Howard and King attribute this failure to concentration on trivia and to the inherent complexity of the problem.[32] But this is another way of saying that Western civilization has given birth to a monster that it cannot understand, just as it has created a horrific weapon that is out of control. The two are not unrelated. War has ended unemployment in the past and is the only solution in sight for the future; recognition of this grim fact caused a senior official in the French Prime Minister's office to say in 1981 that policies aimed at solving unemployment, however much of a gamble, were necessary as 'the only way to avoid a world war'.[33] A society in such a predicament could well ask whether it should trust itself with the means of total destruction.

Part 2

Threats, risks and prospects

Chapter 6

Helsinki, Afghanistan, Poland and morality

While dealing with the Russians may always be hard, because of cultural differences, dealing with the Americans has already proved virtually impossible. Reagan's caricature of American rawness in international affairs may have done Europe – the whole of it – a good turn. The need for some kind of West European accommodation with the USSR is again being felt, and the Ost-politik initiated by Willy Brandt when he was Chancellor could well come to embrace more than German interests. Obstacles are said to be Moscow's failure to honour clauses in the Helsinki Agreement (1975), its intervention in Afghanistan and its influence in the affairs of Poland.

Helsinki: The 'basket 3' provisions of the Final Act of the Conference on Security and Co-operation in Europe (the Helsinki Agreement) are often referred to as if they were intended to establish the beginnings of Western-style democracy in the Soviet Union. This is not so. Moscow had a great deal to do with the draft, and made sure that vital clauses were flexible enough to be interpreted in its own way. For instance, the right of an individual to practise his religion is respected in the agreement, but nothing is said about the teaching of his children. The signatories undertake to promote the effective exercise of civil and political rights and other freedoms 'which derive from the inherent dignity of the human person and are essential to his free will and development'. But this provision needs to be read in conjunction with the first article, which affirms the right of each state to 'choose and develop its political, social, economic and cultural systems as well as its right to determine its own laws and regulations'. The agreement stipulates that every citizen has the right to know what his rights are and to act upon them. On this point the Kremlin says it has distributed 25 million copies of the agreement; as for a person's acting on his rights, it claims the right to be the final arbiter of what they are.

When the agreement gets down to specific details an important phrase is 'human contacts', which the signatory states agreed to facilitate for the purposes of contacts and regular meetings on the basis of family ties, reunification of families, marriages between citizens of different states, travel for personal or professional reasons, improvement of conditions of tourism and meetings among young people. Another provision is for greater dissemination of foreign publications. Several pages are devoted to cultural exchanges, of which an increasing number has taken place. Discretion is clearly left to the signatories; one clause says that if an application for family reunification is not granted, it will be reconsidered at reasonably short intervals.

Moscow has produced a booklet intended to show that it has observed the agreement.[1] It says that when exit visas are not granted they are reconsidered every six months, free of additional charge, if the applicant requests it. Emphasizing that the agreement aims to improve relations between people, it produces some impressive figures on the cultural side. Twice as many American films are screened in the USSR as Soviet films in the United States. In 1980 the Soviet Union staged 130 plays by present-day Western writers. It has more teachers of Western languages than there are students of Russian in the United States. Works by more than 200 foreign authors have been published in the USSR in editions of more than 1 million copies each. After the Helsinki conference the USSR put out a three-volume multi-language collection of European poetry. Less impressive is the 'tenfold increase in Western newspapers and magazines' sold at news stands since the Helsinki conference; the number available is still minute. On the fate of individuals, which is of more concern in the West, the Kremlin is evasive. It says that 'in recent years thousands of Soviet citizens married to foreigners have taken up residence in 110 countries'. A request to the Novosti Press Agency, which published the booklet, for a breakdown of this and other figures produced no reply. Similarly, while Moscow says that 3 million Soviet citizens travelled abroad in 1978, it does not reveal how many got farther than the satellite borders. Nor, while detailing the increase in foreign tourists in the USSR, does it mention that their movements are severely restricted.

Nevertheless nobody familiar with the uninterrupted streams of Russian history would have expected the Soviet Union to see the

Helsinki Agreement through Western eyes. That an attempt should have been made to oblige it to do so amounts to either incompetence or a cynical ploy to force Moscow into a politically embarrassing corner. The traditionally bizarre nature of Russian domestic repression indicates psychic traits that lie deeper than political purpose and sometimes appear to reflect a puritanical fear of alien contamination, similar to what we have seen in Iran. Combined with evidence of historical continuity given in chapter 3, some additional examples of the Russian mentality may help to make Soviet behaviour more comprehensible, if not more acceptable. The Old Believers, the substantial sect that broke away from the Muscovite church in the seventeenth century and persisted in spite of cruel persecution, protested against the use of Western weaponry, even when it was vital to defence, on the ground that Holy Russia, seen as the Third Rome (after Constantinople) would be tainted; they preferred to rely on God. Because of a puritanical objection to instrumental music in churches, no Russian Orthodox church has ever possessed an organ. In a country rich in folk music, some tsars banned folk singing.[2] After the revolution certain musicians proposed to destroy all pianos, in order to abolish the compromise of equal temperament and restore pure intervals. In 1906 censors, zealously guarding the Russian soul, struck out passages in letters written by musicians to the *Musical Courier*, in the United States.[3] Yet great composers emerged even in the most dictatorial post-revolutionary period; possibly, as Antony Hopkins suggested of Prokofiev in a BBC broadcast, they were stimulated by the restrictions imposed upon them. Be that as it may, the West would find negotiations with the Russians more profitable if it thought of them less as communist and more as Russian, whatever they may think of themselves. None of this means that the Russian psyche cannot change. But if the West wants to see a transformation, or modification, it should realize that any official statement it makes about Soviet internal behaviour will be counterproductive; for it will be resented not only by the Kremlin, but by the whole of society, with the exception of a few dissidents. In general Soviet citizens distrust the West. Criticism of sub-standard practices, such as the incarceration of dissidents in mental hospitals, should never be used as a political weapon, but should be left to impartial bodies, such as Amnesty International. The expulsion of the Soviet Union from the international organization of psychiatrists, with the implication of barbarism, was a humiliation that would have certainly been felt by many educated Russians who would disdain the strictures of Western politicians and leader writers.

It could be argued that while the Soviets may be expected to behave as they do in their own country, the West cannot tolerate their intervention in others. But if this argument is a moral one, it is evident, as we shall see later in this chapter, that the West is morally disqualified from advancing it.

Afghanistan: Probably more than anything else, it was the West's intemperate and disproportionate response to the Soviet intervention in Afghanistan that generated some of the thoughts that have crystallized in this book. The representation of Russia's action as a threat to the Middle Eastern oilfields seemed so obviously false that, not for the first time, one was impelled to ask whether the West was being led by people whose imprudence would steer it into a nuclear war. The Soviet Union's strategic gain was infinitesimal. If Moscow had intended to strike at the oilfields it would not have been likely to pause in troublesome Afghanistan, when it needed only to drive across the border with Iran. Missiles in Soviet territory were already within range of the Gulf; but, as against that, the USSR was vulnerable to US nuclear-armed submarines in the Indian Ocean – a long way from home. The alarm seemed as unreal as the now discredited scare about the tsarist threat to India in the last century, when Britain attributed to Moscow ambitions that were far beyond its technological, financial and military resources; the 'great game', in fact, was no more than a melodrama.[4]

When the author was in Kabul towards the end of 1973 the Russians were already established there; a British diplomat said that they totalled about 5,000, some of whom were training the Afghan Air Force. Asked how he knew the number, the diplomat replied: 'We asked the Russians.' He did not share fears expressed by a West European diplomat in Islamabad, that the Russians were planning a thrust through Pakistan's province of Baluchistan to establish a warm-water port on the Arabian Sea, but considered that their interest was to consolidate relations with a neighbour whose geographic position was important to them. In other words, they wanted stability on their southern flank. In the 1960s the Afghan monarchy was already dependent on the USSR for most of its trade and nearly all its military assistance. The United States, loath to displease its preferred ally, Pakistan, neglected Afghanistan, which was trying to engineer a Pathan–Baluchi secessionist movement. The close Afghan–Soviet relationship continued after

Mohammed Daud had overthrown the king, who was his cousin and brother-in-law, on 17 July 1973. Soviet training and education of scores of military officers and civilians, both in the USSR and in Afghanistan itself, led to the spreading of a half-baked kind of Marxism, which had no application by any standards in so backward a country. These men provided the roots of a coup in which Daud was killed on 27 April 1978.

The new President, Nur Mohammad Taraki, and Hafizullah Amin, who became Premier on 27 March 1979, were members of the People's Democratic Party of Afghanistan (PDPA), a faction-riven, pro-Soviet, communist organization. But there was no evident reason why Moscow should have sought their advent; its relations with the monarchy and Daud had been sufficient for its purposes. No sooner did Taraki take over than Amin began to edge him out of office, while faction fighting intensified in the PDPA. Moscow was powerless to influence these bitter and complex power struggles. Amin appears to have seen to it that Taraki was murdered, and became President on 16 September 1979. Meanwhile he had been sufficiently powerful to launch social changes enforced by terror, in which many thousands were imprisoned and tortured. At first Moscow supported him, probably because it had little choice; but when hatred of Amin destabilized the entire country, it decided to get rid of him. In December 1979 the Russians moved in their troops and, despite their denials, put Babrak Karmal in power. Amin was killed in the process. Since then Karmal has tried to win support by various moves, including the restoration of Islamic green in the national flag and the opening of a clergy-controlled Islamic information office. But not the least obstacle to establishment of his legitimacy is the problem of dividing government and party posts between the two PDPA factions.

Although more details of the series of coups are available than have been recalled here, the full story has yet to be told and probably never will be.[5] But, combined with what has happened in Afghanistan since the intervention of 1979, enough has been said to show that the Russian action was not aimed at the West nor, obviously, at annexation, but stabilization. It cannot be entirely ruled out that Moscow encouraged the coup against Daud when he became too friendly with the Shah, who was close to the United States, and was very ambitious in the region. If this were so, it would indicate the depth of Russian fears of encirclement, to which we shall return later; for nobody in the Kremlin could have relished the risk of being drawn into the chaotic politics of Afghanistan, with its tribal rivalries and insensate private feuds. Doubtless the Soviets would be glad to pull out. But they will not do so unless they are sure there is no danger that an anti-Soviet government will be set up in Kabul. The Kremlin's intervention in Afghanistan was a great blunder, on a par with the West's misinterpretation of it. The difficulty of the terrain was known and the intractability of the people and the unfavourable reaction throughout the world were predictable. The possibility that either the West or China would gain some kind of foothold in the country if instability continued was too remote to justify the expense of men and material and the odium that the operation was sure to incur.

While the Soviet operation in Afghanistan is easy to explain, it cannot be justified morally. Rebellious tribesmen had been bombed by Afghan planes in Amin's time, when Soviet troops were already stationed in Afghanistan, doubtless at his request. But the Russians, as far as is known, did no shooting until they took part in the ousting of Amin in December 1979. Many Afghans favoured the reforms introduced by the communists after the overthrowing of Daud, particularly measures to break the mullahs' hold on education, which had helped to keep more than 90 per cent of the people illiterate, compared with almost total literacy in bordering Soviet Tadzhikistan. But villagers fought to preserve customs, which, although they are archaic and barbarous, are what most tribesmen cherish. Instead of stabilizing the country, the Russians and the Afghan forces that they support have forced 2 million people, or 15 per cent of the population, to flee into Pakistan; the price of such order as has been achieved is the inexcusable desolation of bombed villages.

Yet it is not for Western governments to pass moral judgment; their own record of violence in the Third World, and of their connivance in massacres, is too black for that. Well known though it is, the example of Vietnam must be cited, because it is the most horrific. Those who feel that any slaughter is justified in any war against communists of any kind anywhere, may prefer other examples. In the 1960s, when the British were withdrawing from South Arabia, they continued to strafe backward tribesmen from the air. Their aim was to protect the South Arabian Federation, a puppet government of petty sheikhs and sultans that was set up to maintain British influence in the region. The rulers were toppled one by one in a matter of weeks in August 1967 soon after British forces had withdrawn to Aden, on their way home. Brigadier Jack Dye, Commander of Britain's Arab force, the Federal Army, attributed their fall to a 'people's revolution of great depth' (in a conversation with the author). Communists had nothing to do with it. Unwilling to leave the country in a state of civil war between two rival revolutionary organizations – the National Liberation Front and the Front for the Liberation of South Yemen – Britain threw its weight behind the NLF and staged an air strike in its favour on 9 November. As the British left Aden, sector by sector, in 1967, black-bordered photographs of young townsmen, described as heroes who had died when fighting them, appeared on walls in the streets. The tribesmen and urban youth killed by British troops may have been fewer than the Russians' victims in Afghanistan; but the bereaved would have felt no gratitude for this mercy in an operation that was no more morally justifiable than that of the USSR – and not justifiable at all on national security grounds.

More recent has been the West's connivance – to say the least – in the annexation of the former Portuguese colony of East Timor by the Indonesian junta, the massacre and starvation to death of nearly half of its inhabitants and the imprisonment and torturing of others. Indonesian troops invaded East Timor and overthrew its native government, described as leftist, in so far as this term has any meaning in the Third World, in December 1975, after the Portuguese had withdrawn. Adam Malik, then Indonesian Foreign Minister, admitted that 50,000, perhaps 80,000, Timorese had been killed; but the Portuguese Foreign Minister, Futsher Pereira, said on 11 November 1982 that the total who were slaughtered, or died in the famine that followed the invasion, was 200,000 to 300,000 in a population of 600,000.[6] There is no space here for details of this much under-publicized operation, the effects of which are still being felt by the people. The point being made is that, in contrast with its protests over Afghanistan, the West was far from unhappy about this intrusion. In a letter to *The Times* on 3 November 1981 Lord Avebury said:

> Evidence indicating that Britain and her allies, while making the right noises in public about the right of the people of East Timor to self-determination, were at the same time secretly encouraging the Indonesians in their aggression against that country has been available for some time. That such charges have now been made on Portuguese television (*The Times*, October 13) therefore comes as no surprise.

Each year when the annexation is brought before the United

Nations General Assembly the West, in effect, sides with Indonesia. On 24 December 1981 the assembly carried its usual resolution affirming the right of the East Timorese to self-determination. The United States opposed it and West European governments, including the United Kingdom, hypocritically abstained. The West, British Labour Party leaders included, strongly supports the junta, despite its grim record in Timor, Irian Jaya (formerly Dutch New Guinea) and at home. It sees Indonesia, which Queen Elizabeth II visited in March 1974, as a market, a field of investment, a source of raw materials and a strategic asset; Britain has been pushing the sale to the junta of the Hawk ground-attack jet, described by the Government as a trainer plane, but claimed by Mrs Thatcher during a visit to the Middle East in April 1981 as a 'good buy', because it could be easily converted by adding bomb and rocket pads. In a letter cited by Lord Avebury and never denied, the British Ambassador advised the Foreign Office on 21 July 1975, when Indonesia was already intervening in East Timor: 'If it comes to a crunch and there is a row in the UN, we should keep our heads down and avoid siding against Indonesia.'

In the late 1960s, when the author asked a British civil servant in Jakarta why the British Council was spending so much money on a new, large establishment there, he replied: 'We are a bit fed up with the Commonwealth countries. We are looking for other countries, a bit authoritarian, to share their development with them.' At that time 'a bit authoritarian' meant among other things the detention of political prisoners, officially stated to number 69,000 in 1969, although estimated by Amnesty International to total 117,000, including ethnic rebels. Almost all of them had been held without trial since 1965, when the junta fomented the massacre of 160,000 people, according to Malik's estimate, or 400,000, in the opinion of a *Life* magazine correspondent, who made a village to village investigation. This field operation, which exploited a mixture of religious and political conflict, was part of the army's campaign to liquidate the Communist Party and overthrow Sukarno, whom the communists supported.[7] Most of those killed, like most of those imprisoned or sent to inhospitable Buru Island, were ignorant peasants from areas where the Communist Party, which was pro-Chinese, had been strong. In his four years in Jakarta the author did not meet one diplomat from a major Western country who regretted the fate of those wretched people or one who did not admire what was seen as the junta's pragmatism. It was the same with attitudes to Irian Jaya, where the junta has killed thousands of

Papuan rebels. The Act of Free Choice – on whether or not the territory was to become an Indonesian province – was rigged in Indonesia's favour after brutal intimidation, with the complicity of a United Nations team;[8] but the Western bloc endorsed the team's report in the General Assembly on 19 November 1969, despite a tactfully worded Ghanaian proposal that the referendum be held again. The Soviets, anxious to improve their relations in the Indian Ocean, also voted in favour of Indonesia; similarly, they were the first to congratulate the junta's political party after its victory in the Indonesian elections of 3 July 1971, when rigging, threats, beatings and occasionally murder were employed as and when required. Like the West, the Soviets were able to hide behind the United Nations team's report on Irian Jaya; but on the East Timor issue, despite their concern to remain on good terms with the Indonesian junta, they voted for the Portuguese resolution, perhaps with an eye to Third World opinion.

Indonesia's political prisoners have been released progressively, but subjected to harsh impediments in their attempts to resume a normal life. Among them is Pramoedya Ananta Toer, a writer considered by some to be worthy of consideration for the Nobel prize, who was allowed to leave Buru Island after having been held there, separated from his wife and children, for fourteen years without trial. The junta condemned Pramoedya because during the Sukarno period he was conspicuous in a cultural organization sponsored by communists. But his stories contain no trace of communist propaganda. All are banned in Indonesia. Pramoedya says of himself: 'My books are an expression of my innermost feelings, and my innermost feelings are in no way directed towards communism.' One of his novels, *This Earth of Mankind*,[9] has been published in English; it was one of two works, 10,000 copies of which were burned by the junta when they were published after his release.[10] In Indonesia the West is more fortunate than the Soviets are in Afghanistan. It has a common interest with a well organized, experienced military client, who requires no direct armed support, although in the 1970s the Indonesians had to be bailed out of a financial catastrophe, with the state oil company's debts equal to two-thirds of the annual gross national product, brought about by mismanagement and huge corruption.[11] There is no rule of the law, and trade union pressure that could be disadvantageous to investors is out of the question. Arrests continue of Moslem leaders, Aceh secessionists, Papuans, Timorese and students likely to disturb the existing order.

In Africa the West sits less comfortably, and the French have found it necessary to send their own men into battle. French military action was decisive in the overthrow of Jean Bedel Bokassa, the crazed dictator of the Central African Republic, whom France had propped up for years. In 1978 French military advisers or trainers were working in eleven African countries; French toops had a combat role in Zaire, Mauritania and Chad, where France unsuccessfully backed one of the eternally warring factions. In May 1978 French and Chadian troops, supported by supersonic Jaguar fighter-bombers of the French Air Force, wiped out a band of rebel guerrillas in three days; 278 bodies were counted in a palm grove.[12] Russians in Afghanistan could hardly have done better.

Poland: Since moral scruples and humanitarian considerations play no serious part in the foreign policy of Western governments, the question arises as to why they have moralized so much about events in Poland. The answer is complex. First, Western spokesmen can gratify themselves by expressing liberal sentiments on issues in which the West has little or nothing to lose by their doing so; second, moral sanction is a useful weapon against the Soviet Union. The second factor possibly issues from a third – a surging of irrational fear and animosity, characteristic of tribal emotions, which persist in more advanced countries no less than in others. Whatever the cause, the practice of throwing stones from inside glass houses endangers peace, and a civilization capable of averting war would examine its motives carefully. Poland, like other potential sources of conflict, needs more mature consideration than it has received. In the first place, it would be a mistake to assume that the Poles are more suited than the Russians or people of the Third World to a style of democracy that evolved in the West from particular ethnic roots. Serfdom continued in Poland well into the nineteenth century. The peasants and not a few of the urban people are much motived by belief in a particularly superstitious form of Mariolatry, which is taken to its polytheistic extreme; their psychology, looked at from a Jungian point of view, has more in common with what is found in the Third World than with the relative rationality that played a vital part in the emergence of Protestantism and Western institutions. There is no reason to believe that Polish society is much more likely than, say Turkish, to develop a Western-type democracy.

The Poles have always been given to internecine strife at all levels

and their intense patriotism and renowned valour are disproportionate to their ability to govern themselves successfully. Early in
the seventeenth century they were sufficiently powerful to plant a
Polish tsar in Moscow; but after their subsequent internal decline,
marked at times by corruption on a scale worth mentioning in
history books and by the betrayal of honest men, their territory was
carved up by Russia, Prussia and Austria under treaties beginning
in 1772. The restoration of Poland towards the end of the First
World War led to destructive political wrangling, which precipitated the retirement in 1923 of Marshal Joseph Pilsudski, both as
head of state and from the army, of which he was Commander-in-
Chief; he could not abide the politicians' selfishness, and under the
existing constitution was unable to handle it. But in 1926, with the
country heading for serious disorder, Pilsudski brought off a *coup
d'état*. When the right moved in parliament to prevent him from
reassuming his army post, he suddenly appeared in Warsaw at the
head of an armed force and gained control of the capital after two
days of heavy fighting. Ruling as premier, he set up a veiled dictatorship by means of a new constitution, which, though less authoritarian than that of Mussolini, gave strong powers to the executive
while reducing those of parliament. Decrees severely restricted
political discussion and press freedom; many issues of state organization over which the politicians had argued were settled by regulation. In the autumn of 1930 socialist leaders were imprisoned and
brutally treated. On 23 April 1935 a constitutional change considerably strengthened the executive at the expense of the legis-
lature. After Pilsudski's death in the following month, this form of
government continued with little change until the Second World
War.

There was no reason to expect that the state which was to emerge
in Poland after the war would be more democratic than the one that
preceded it. In fact, it was less so, in that the Poles found themselves
again under Russian domination. Stalin had liquidated the Polish
communists during the war and was obliged to set up a new party led
by opportunists who had no genuine interest in communism. Nevertheless, while the Russians withdrew increasingly into the background, Poles asserted their independence in various ways. As early
as 1958 the author saw an enthusiastically received comedy in
Warsaw, well produced with state money, which pointedly satirized
a police state. Among changes after the Poznan riots of 1956 was the
appearance of abstract paintings, which had been kept in a cellar,
on the walls of the national gallery, although such an exhibition

could not have been held in Russia. By the 1980s Andrzej Wajda was making *Man of Marble*, a profound film, which recalled the sinister cruelty of the Stalin period, satirized ideological humbug and exposed the hollowness of a materialist society. Meanwhile Moscow had not intervened when the Polish Government decided against collectivizing agriculture, negotiated with Western banks and took substantial measures to encourage small private enterprise. Poles were free to emigrate.

The Russian influence was not intrusive and may be dismissed as an important, early factor in the ferment that led to the formation of Solidarity. Similarly, while there had long been resentment at the privileges and corruption of the communists and their bureaucracy, this had no serious consequences as long as the considerably improved living standards were maintained. Improbity, however, cannot be blamed entirely on the rulers. Polish society has a streak of corruption, such as pervades those in which the more superstitious forms of religion are found; a certain moral weakness, extending beyond the state apparatus, was strongly suggested in *Man of Marble*. In 1958 the author was told in Warsaw that the only person who could not be bribed was Copernicus – a statue in a public square.

It was not corruption, but the incompetence that goes with it, which brought the Government down and led to its virtual replacement by the Committee of National Salvation and the imposition of martial law. Aided and abetted by Western bankers, who had more money than they could safely and profitably lend, the Government set about industrialization on a scale that was beyond its managerial ability and Poland's economic potential. Huge loans pouring into the country helped to create an artificial living standard, from which some workers benefited more than others. Food was lavishly subsidized. Expectations were raised far above the desire of the people to work and – in view of widespread alcoholism, a long-standing handicap in Poland no less than in Russia – their capacity to do so. When the crash occurred and belts had to be severely tightened, the Russians became a popular scapegoat for what was, in fact, a national failure. On the whole it remains true that people get the governments they deserve, even, relatively speaking, when there is pressure from outside. The Hungarians, with their experience of capable government in association with the Austrians, got Kadar, who made Hungary a reasonable, even pleasant, place to live in; the Poles got what might have been expected from their chronic lack of social cohesion. Poles have difficulty in uniting, even in acute crises.

A major factor, for instance, in the failure of the 1830 rising against the Tsar, in which 110,000 Polish troops were mobilized against 114,000 Russians, was party strife in the insurrectionary Government in Warsaw, accompanied by an outbreak of irresponsible mob violence at the height of the fighting and conflict between politicians and peasants.

The Supreme Court's order for the registration of Solidarity as a trade union on 10 November 1980, following a threatened general strike, represented a radical institutional change. After such an achievement, the movement might have been expected to pause and consolidate. But workers immediately embarked on a series of strikes, the most crucial of which aimed at abolishing Saturday work. Poland needed to increase production to provide the workers' needs and to create exports that would enable it to service its foreign debt, with a view to obtaining further financial help. That the workers and their leaders could have made shorter hours an issue at such a critical time showed inability to understand cause and effect, more marked than in the West, where it is apparent enough. But the Government gave in, rather than have no production at all, and work was abolished on three Saturdays in four. On 6 May 1981 parliament approved the registration of an independent trade union of private farmers.

The most drastic change of all took place in July, when the Polish United Workers' Party (communist party) introduced a secret ballot in the election of its Central Committee – a reform that a few months earlier would have been considered impossible anywhere in the Eastern bloc. With the communist structure in a state of flux, Solidarity began to make a bid for power. At its first conference, held in Gdansk in September, it demanded a referendum on self-management of enterprises and 'free elections'. Apparently unaware that it was regarded by many people in the Eastern bloc as an example of Polish hot-headedness, it directly confronted the Soviet Union by expressing sympathy for workers seeking free trade unions in the other satellite countries. At a further meeting from 26 September–7 October the Solidarity leader, Lech Walesa, was under fire for having accepted Parliament's watering down of self-management, but fought back and was elected President. Soon afterwards Solidarity won the Government's agreement to hold down prices temporarily, a measure that the exchequer could ill afford.

With disturbances continuing throughout the country, General Wojciech Jaruzelski, former Defence Minister, who had been

Prime Minister since February, also became Party First Secretary, in mid-October. Army detachments were sent to various regions. Solidarity retaliated with a general strike of one hour against the repression of its activists and to bring about what it called social control over the economy. At a meeting with Jaruzelski and Archbishop Glemp on 4 November Walesa put up Solidarity's plan for a 'social council for the national economy', but, it was reported, rejected Jaruzelski's proposal for an advisory body. A sign of serious anarchy emerged on 18 November, when students at the fire brigade officers' school in Warsaw occupied the building to enforce a demand that the institution be controlled by the Ministry of Higher Education, instead of the Ministry of the Interior. When security forces finally drove them out on 2 December Walesa ordered an 'immediate alert' for a general strike. On 7 December Polish radio broadcast a recording of a statement made by Walesa at a closed Solidarity meeting: 'No change in the system can be made without losses. The essential is to be victorious.' On 13 December Jaruzelski declared martial law; Walesa was interned and several thousand of his supporters were imprisoned.

It is easier to applaud the popular struggle than to see what benefit it could have produced in the prevailing circumstances. According to the Government, production had fallen by 25 per cent, with coal output declining by 30 million tons, since the birth of Solidarity in August 1980; shops that had been well stocked were empty and food was in short supply. If such an economic crisis had existed in the United Kingdom a national government would almost certainly have been formed. But it could not be said that Walesa's proposal for shared economic management amounted to the equiv-alent of such a measure. The church was not equipped to make a useful contribution, and showed no signs of wishing to attempt it; and Solidarity, which was made up of several factions, lacked both the unity and the experience needed for the purpose. The joint body proposed by Walesa, who was handicapped in his judgment by having been built into a folk figure, would have been a mere wrangling society, subject to diverse and often irrational pressures, such as the disturbances in March 1981, which were provoked by an increase in the tobacco price. As Richard Portes says in his study of the Polish debt problem, published by the Royal Institute of Inter-national Affairs before the declaration of martial law:[13]

The mood of Solidarity vacillates widely, there too partly because of uneasy relations between the leadership and the rank and file, exacerbated by the absence of clear hierarchical relationships in the organization, such as it is. Some of this confusion reflects the lack of any clear government programme to discuss. . . . Some of Solidarity's economic advisers surely perceive the pressing need for consumer-price increases . . . yet the union's leaders may fear losing their members' support by appearing to collaborate with the Government on anything, much less on such unpleasant measures.

Without decision, the economy would have deteriorated catastrophically and, with a bankrupt state unable to pay its security forces, civil war, already a danger, would have been almost a certainty. While there was widespread opposition to the Government, there was also a core of strong support for it as the only available instrument that could save Poland from disaster. On 16 December 1981 the BBC World Service reported that Dutch journalists in Gdansk had seen students scraping Solidarity posters from a wall; it said on 24 December that the public attitude to soldiers patrolling the streets varied from hospitality to shooting some of them in the back. If the situation had been allowed to drift, it would have been bad for the Poles, bad for the Russians and bad for the West, in so far as it had any chance of getting its loans repaid. A firm grip was needed from somewhere; only Jaruzelski was able to provide it. Jaruzelski, described by Pope John Paul II as more a patriot than a communist, remained under constant attack from both the West and intransigent Party men, one of whom, Tadeusz Grabski, was still openly criticizing him in October 1982. In his attempts to conciliate the people he was helped by the Catholic hierarchy, which appealed to youth, who comprised most of the demonstrators in 1982, not to allow themselves to be exploited for political purposes. In November, following the failure of a strike appeal by Solidarity, then underground, Jaruzelski was able to release Lech Walesa. By this time his entourage had worked out economic reforms and training programmes intended to overcome Poland's inefficiency. Martial law was suspended on 12 December 1982, but the military remained predominant in government.

When martial law was declared, bankers in London and New York were pleased, according to the BBC World Service's economics correspondent (14 December 1981). He said the view was that 'if a few people got shot' this would be a small price for getting the country running again. One banker was quoted as declaring that it would be impossible to help Poland if 'human rights' became the main issue. It follows that what would have been good for the bankers, had it not been for subsequent Western sanctions, would also have been to the material benefit of the Polish people; for without tightly controlled economic rationalization and financial help, there was no way of arresting and reversing the fall in their living standards. The initial judgment of the bankers was subsequently confirmed by a World Council of Churches mission, which found on visiting Poland that martial law was 'generally accepted as a painful necessity – the lesser evil'.[14] The team condemned Western sanctions as having 'immediately and directly affected the people in the further shortage of consumer articles, including food'.

In the period leading up to the declaration of martial law the Soviets repeatedly and by various means, including troop manoeuvres, threatened Solidarity and put pressure on the weak, divided and corrupt Polish government. But in the absence of direct evidence to the contrary it is difficult to reject the statement of Mieczyslaw Rakowski, Polish Deputy Prime Minister, in a gruelling interview with the Italian journalist, Oriana Fallaci, that Moscow, while expressing concern, gave no specific instructions.[15] Indeed, military rule would have been ideologically distasteful in the Kremlin, which allows only one military man, the Defence Minister, a seat in the Politburo. What Moscow wanted was that the disrupted party should unite and assert its authority, not that it should be virtually displaced by a general, Party member though he was, who discredited it by arresting several of its leaders, including Edward Gierek, former First Secretary. Whatever happened behind the scenes, the Soviets, though loath to send in troops, would certainly have done so the moment there was imminent danger of a coup that could open Poland to Western political influence. Jaruzelski must have known this. Whether the Russians gave him orders or dropped him a strong hint, or whether he read the signs at home, in Moscow, and other Eastern bloc capitals and acted independently in Poland's interests as he saw them, Western security – which is what we are discussing – was unaffected. Moscow broke no new ground, and attempts to construe its cajoling of Poland as part of some generally expansive drive cannot be substantiated. Its aim was to maintain the *status quo* in Europe by ensuring the reliability of its *cordon sanitaire* (see chapter 7). In so far as its relations with the West are concerned, its policy contained no element of aggression.

The same cannot be said of the West in relation to Russia.

Without borrowing, Poland was unable to service its $21,100 million foreign debt, owed mostly to Western banks, of which $8,109 million was due in 1980 and $4,274 million in 1981. When the Poles could not pay their interest the Soviets were reported to have sold 9 tons of gold and helped them with a soft loan of $4,000 million repayable in roubles. Portes's paper, cited above, provided a sound basis for tackling the debts question in collaboration with the Russians, which could have had valuable consequences for world peace. Western governments, which had guaranteed a substantial part of the loans, might well have grasped this exceptional opportunity for East–West co-operation; instead, they devoted themselves to the principle of self-determination, which they had cynically ignored in Papua, Timor and, until recently, Palestine. Disregarding the self-righteous posturing, important though it is in any international situation, the underlying reason seems to be that the West, led by the United States, subordinated the problem of the debts to the larger issue of confronting the Soviet Union; as a *Financial Times* correspondent said on the BBC World Service (23 December 1981), the banks could stand the loss. West European governments followed the American line with varying degrees of enthusiasm, but their reserve had little effect on their actions. At one stage Helmut Schmidt cited George Kennan, former US Ambassador to Moscow, who warned that the West was pushing the Soviet Union against a closed door; if the West wanted evolution in Europe, Kennan said, it must not give the Russians the impression that at the same time it was trying to undermine their security.[16] This is precisely what the American-led West did. With public declarations and a radio campaign based on reports that were frequently wild,[17] it tried to influence the course of events to the detriment of the Soviet Union and thus to gain a political advantage inside the Eastern bloc. The Soviet Union's strategic interest in Poland is well understood in the West. As Malcolm Mackintosh, consultant to the International Institute for Strategic Studies (IISS), London, says:[18]

> Poland is . . . the vital country astride the main route and axis from Russia to Western Europe. The Soviet Union therefore has to work to achieve the dominance of Poland – which it needs – while warily taking account of traditional Polish pride, independence, and unanimous suspicion and even contempt for the Russians.

There is no reason why the West should sympathize with the Russians in their difficult task. But its pointless attempt to foster a change in the *status quo* of a Europe threatened by nuclear war created a danger where none had existed. This showed that the Western dominant minority lacked restraint and common sense even on the very issue of survival.

The right of the Poles, like the Afghans, Timorese and Papuans, to full self-determination, wherever it might lead them, cannot be disputed. But, as we have seen, the West is in no position to moralize. Looking at the economic side, the Poles will never within the foreseeable future be as prosperous as when they were spending money borrowed from the West while accepting a measure of Eastern bloc discipline. Action along the lines of the Portes report could, however, help to bring them nearer to that condition.

Chapter 7

Soviet contraction

It is not a coincidence that a surge of anti-Soviet hostility has occurred at a time of despair about the economy, when Western leaders have been reduced to declaring that salvation depends on Third World development. Despite the mountain of unrepayable debts and the disappointment of firms that have established factories in the Third World, including South Korea, a fear is abroad that if this last resort is lost to the Soviet Union, the West will perish. This feeling is reflected in a report on Western security produced jointly by the Royal Institute of International Affairs and equivalent bodies in New York, Bonn and Paris.[1] Warning against 'enhanced Soviet military threats', the report emphasizes on its first page that the West faces 'an increasingly unstable and volatile Third World, upon which it will depend more and more for its economic survival', and forecasts 'a prolonged economic crisis worldwide' in the 1980s 'characterized in the West by very low growth rates combined with high inflation and high unemployment rates'. A limited attempt has been made in chapter 5 to show that the Third World affords no solution of Western economic difficulties. Since defence of wrongly assessed Western interests in that region is one of the main reasons advanced in justification of nuclear weapons, the subject is one of the highest importance. It would be history's greatest irony to date if a nuclear war were fought over what is no more than a chimera.

Leaving aside the question of resources, which will be discussed in the next chapter, the Soviets would be doing their adversaries a service if they tried to dominate the Third World; for the cultural, political, demographic and environmental problems are so complex that they would be sure to bury themselves there. So far there are no signs of their doing so, except in Afghanistan. Suspicion (one might say primitive suspicion), which characterizes both Eastern and Western blocs, leads the West to accuse Moscow of expansionism.

In fact the Soviets have not expanded in the past twenty years, but have undergone a spectacular contraction. This point has been well made by John Kenneth Galbraith, the American economist and former Ambassador to India. Galbraith points to the Russian setback in China, once described by Dean Rusk, US Secretary of State, as a 'Soviet Manchukuo', but now 'the greatest power in Asia'; to the loss of influence in Indonesia following the fall of Sukarno, when Western-backed generals killed off communists (and inspired the killing of scores of thousands who were not communists) 'with a cruelty that no one anywhere could condone'; to the reverses in Algeria and Ghana, resulting from the overthrow of Ben Bella and Kwame Nkrumah; and to the expulsion of Soviet experts from Egypt by Anwar Sadat in the 1970s. In Eastern Europe the satellite states show a tendency to pursue their own policies, while in the West communist parties, once instruments of Moscow, have proclaimed their independence. Galbraith adds:[2]

> Against all this has been the Communist expansion – in Afghanistan to rescue a falling Marxist regime, a country as inhospitable to imperialism in the last two centuries as any in the world. And in Angola, where the MPLA regime is sustained by Cuban soldiers and, in a possibly much more practical way, by revenues from . . . oil. And in Ethiopia, where, as Evelyn Waugh once observed, the writ of government has never run reliably very much beyond the airport, in his day the railway station. Such is the 20-year record of the Soviet Empire [an ironical reference to a term advocated by Reagan]. Expansionism indeed!

To Galbraith's list of reverses may be added those in Iraq and Sudan, where communists in the governments were murdered, and Syria, where they were reduced to unimportance; and in addition to ousting Russian experts, Sadat broke off relations with Moscow and repudiated a debt of $7,000 million. Having lost its foothold in Egypt, the USSR is now faced with a further weakening of its relations with Iraq, which, as the International Institute for Strategic Studies says, 'has been seeking to broaden her contacts with the West, particularly with France and Italy, and to establish herself as a non-aligned country'.[3] It was to avert the spreading of this tendency, while providing a counter to increasing Israeli, hence American, power that Moscow obliged Syria by installing advanced missiles on its territory early in 1983. The missiles, aimed at Israel, which the USSR does not seek to destroy, were kept under Soviet control. Despite euphoric moments, Moscow's relations with Libya have never been stable, and in October 1981 Qaddafi went to Beijing to court China. In Ethiopia the rulers have refused to buy Russian aeroplanes.

A point of significance for the future is that while American machinations played some part in the decline of Soviet influence, the internal factor was always stronger than the external, which in China made no contribution at all to Beijing's assertion of independence. Similarly, Soviet activity was not responsible for the ejection of the Portuguese from what became Angola, nor for the overthrow of Haile Selassie. In one respect the Third World's weakness is its strength; the cultural traits that obstruct all but superficial Western-style development, combined with the large size of its backward population, also make it impregnable against any kind of alien penetration at depth. Some awareness of this seems to have developed in the USSR, where the same kind of obstacle exists in certain areas, such as Azerbaijan, which borders Iran;[4] while in the 1950s Moscow justified its support for nationalist military governments in the Middle East on the doctrinal ground that they were heading for socialism by means of what was called non-capitalist development, Russian scholars have since begun to note the effect of bribery, corruption and family networks in the Third World.[5]

Although, as Galbraith has shown, the citing of Afghanistan, Angola and Ethiopia as evidence of Russian expansionism becomes absurd when put into perspective, some people find sinister intent in the naval build-up. At a conference in Fiji in October 1982 Asian and Pacific Commonwealth leaders expressed alarm at the increasing naval strength of great powers in the Indian Ocean and committed themselves to trying to establish a nuclear-free zone there. The Australian Prime Minister, Malcolm Fraser, went farther and said that Moscow was looking for a base in the Pacific and had tried to make a deal with Tonga. But in a BBC interview Robert O'Neill, Director of the International Institute for Strategic Studies, London, said the talks had only been about fishing rights. He did not think that the Russians were looking for strategic bases in the South Pacific, which was too far away to be of interest to them. Nor did he think that there was a serious possibility that Moscow would try to cut the Western bloc's sea lanes, unless a war had already broken out. There is, indeed, no evidence that in increasing their naval strength the Russians are not motived by a feeling of insecurity and a foolish desire to match their rival, as befits a great power.[6]

The Russians' influence is certainly low in proportion to their military strength. They possess nothing to compare with the European Communities' Lomé Convention, which groups more than seventy African, Caribbean and Pacific countries. If we apply, with detachment, the conventional concepts of power relations – although these concepts will have to be dispensed with if the world is to survive – it would be hardly seemly of the weaker part of Europe to make too much fuss if the stronger part took a nibble or two at this vast Western imperial residue. As it is, even Angola and Mozambique are slipping from Russia's loose grip. Both have said they want to join the Lomé Convention, to take advantage of aid and trading arrangements; if they fail it will not be Moscow that stops them. While the Russians have lost heavily in the Middle East, the United States is now voiceless in Iran, which is uncompromisingly hostile to both camps. But Washington has gained Egypt and retains Israel as a strong bastion that could not exist either militarily or economically, except at a very low living standard, without its heavy American subsidy. The tail sometimes causes embarrassment by wagging the dog, but Israel has embarked on no military action, the outcome of which did not fit Washington's conception of its interests. Wealth acquired by the Arabs when they raised their oil prices has compelled Western Europe and, to some extent, the United States to modify their policies on Israel. Since the oil states are obliged to support the Palestinian cause, along with that of annexed Jerusalem, while the West needs to win favours from the Arabs, particularly in the sale of arms to them, oil has brought some advantage to the Palestinians. But sentimental prejudices apart, Israel's strategic value, as perceived, would ensure that the West would never acquiesce in the foundation of a Palestinian state that could rival her, no matter how just the Arab claims might be.

A balance sheet of the numerous military aid and training agreements made by both blocs with the Third World cannot be undertaken here, but a list of bases and other facilities reflects the fact that whether or not the Soviet Union is expanding the West has already expanded:[7] **Asia and Australasia:** The United States has major bases in Japan, South Korea and the Philippines, and B-52 bomber and naval refuelling facilities in north and west Australia. A joint US–UK base was established in Diego Garcia, in the Chagos Archipelago, after Britain had bought the archipelago from Mauritius in 1965. The USSR has forces in Afghanistan under an agreement signed in April 1980. It has access to naval facilities at Cam Ranh Bay and Da Nang, in Vietnam. **Middle East and North**

Africa: The United States has two staging bases in Oman and its navy has the use of port facilities in Bahrein. British military men are serving with Oman's forces. Soviet warships use Aden's facilities. **Sub-Saharan Africa:** Agreements provide 'limited US access to naval and air facilities' in Somalia and Kenya. After the loss of its facilities in Somalia, the USSR transferred its operations to Dahlak Island, Ethiopia. Britain has overflying, training and defence agreements with Kenya. **Latin America:** Under treaties negotiated in 1977 about 40 per cent of the former Panama Canal Zone, including three of fourteen bases, remains under US control until 31 December 1999. The United States retains jurisdiction and control over Guantanamo Bay, southeast Cuba, under an agreement with pre-communist Cuba, which, Washington says, will not be modified or abrogated. The Soviet Union 'has no formal defence agreements with any of the states in the area, although she has supplied military equipment to Cuba and Peru'.[8]

The four-institutes report, which is cited earlier in this chapter, expresses concern at 'the impact of Soviet actions in the Third World regions', and particularly emphasizes the need to link 'offensive Soviet behaviour' in the Middle East with East–West relations in Europe.[9] But compared with that of the United States, Soviet activity in the Middle East has been limited. Moscow has launched no venture comparable to that in Iran, where the United States heavily armed the Shah with a view to making him their policeman in the region, financed and set up his internal security organization, SAVAK, and trained it with the help of Israeli intelligence men.[10] Following the murder of President Anwar Sadat, the United States carried out a large-scale, ten-day military exercise in Egypt in November 1981. Four thousand US troops and an equivalent number of Egyptians took part in the largest operation ever carried out by American and Arab forces. B-52 bombers that flew direct from the USA dropped bombs on an imaginary enemy; about 100 tanks went into simulated action. In the autumn of 1982 US marines were engaged in manoeuvres in Morocco. Before the middle of 1983 Washington had assumed a dominant role in Lebanon.

It was not a communist but an Islamic threat that provoked the American exercise in Egypt. After Sadat's murder by fundamentalists, Washington warned that it would never allow a repetition in Egypt of what had happened in Iran. This declaration reflects America's willingness to push to the limit its view that it should decide what is good for the world. If Moscow had launched such a military operation, in conjunction with a client state governed by an autocracy, it would have been accused of 'offensive behaviour' in the Middle East. That the West takes its own actions for granted shows that it has yet to shake off its imperialist attitudes. The Soviets, though mistakenly, would undoubtedly like to be much more influential in the Third World than they are. But, as is indicated by the American operations in Egypt and Morocco and the French military actions in Zaire, Chad and the Sahara in 1978, the West is more belligerent in retaining its advantage than the Soviet Union is in trying to reduce it. It is probably not simply a desire to avoid war that accounts for the Soviets' relative restraint. Doubtless they realize that the more the West intrudes in the Third World the more it is likely to precipitate revolts such as the one that took place in Iran, where the United States is loathed for having backed the Shah; but the fundamental reason appears to be that Moscow, unlike the West, does not see itself in such a desperate economic state that it depends on the Third World for its survival.

In the Middle East the Russians have clearly been at pains to avoid conflict in an area that they find all too close to their southern flank. Their restraint to this end accounts to some extent for their loss of influence, which, however, was inevitable, in view of the wealthy Arab élite's fear of revolution and the West's greater capacity to satisfy the bazaar appetite. The Soviets have been more responsible than opportunist. They have refused Arab requests for nuclear arms and have annoyed the militant states by repeatedly urging them to recognize Israel's right to exist. While the West charges them with expansionism, the Arabs accuse them of being lukewarm in their cause. In the 1950s Moscow proposed that neither superpower should sell arms to Middle East countries. In 1967 it tried to prevent war between the Arabs and Israelis. After the Egyptians had closed the Straits of Tiran to Israeli shipping, an official Soviet Government statement issued on 24 May emphasized that Soviet support for the Arabs was neither unlimited nor unconditional and that the USSR could not condone an attempt at a military solution of the crisis.[11] The statement said: 'It is the firm belief of the Soviet Government that the people have no interest in a military conflict in the Middle East.' When the Egyptian Defence Minister was in Moscow from 25 to 28 May, Kosygin told him: 'We are going to back you. But you have achieved your point of view. You have won a political victory. So now is the time to compromise, to work politically.' In October 1977 Moscow quickly took up Carter's proposal that the USSR and USA should be co-chairmen of a conference on Middle Eastern problems. A substantial improvement in relations between the two powers then seemed possible; but in the following month Washington dropped the idea and launched its Camp David process. In February 1980 the Soviets suggested an international conference aimed at assuring the access of all countries to the Gulf. Leonid Brezhnev, General Secretary of the Communist Party of the Soviet Union, reiterated this offer in an address to the Indian parliament on 10 December 1980 and in his speech at the Twenty-Sixth Congress of the CPSU on 23 February 1981. But the West did not respond.

A sign of the Soviet Union's desire to maintain peace in regions from which conflict could spread and create instability on its southern flank is to be found in South Yemen. During the wave of anti-Soviet feeling a good deal has been made of the Soviet presence in that territory, which, apart from the port of Aden, consists largely of desert. Early in 1968, when the British left South Arabia, the Soviets made contact with the National Liberation Front, which formed a government. At that time the author asked the US Ambassador in Aden why Washington did not step in and offer financial aid, which the South Yemenis badly needed to maintain the administration. He replied that Aden was not strategically important, because the Soviets were already well served in Somalia, while the Americans were more interested in Ethiopia. The switching of African allegiances since that time has not changed the strategic balance. Yet the long-standing Soviet presence in South Yemen is now being seized upon as evidence of some far-reaching conspiracy to deprive the West of its oil. In fact, when the South Yemenis were engaged in clashes with the pro-Western oil state of Oman in February 1979, the Soviets persuaded them to desist.[12] And on 27 October 1982 it was announced that Oman and South Yemen had signed a treaty resolving their differences. Two alternative deductions follow from that event: either the USSR has no effective influence in Aden or, if it has, it may be credited with having contributed to a measure of peace in an area in which it is being accused of trying to foment trouble.

Although I should prefer not to pillory individuals in what is essentially an account of a declining civilization failing to face up to itself, it is convenient to cite the four-institutes report as an example of the dominant minority's dangerous prejudices. In the light of the facts that have been recalled in this chapter, the report's melodramatic reference to 'offensive Soviet behaviour' in the Middle East is so far removed from the truth that it demands an explanation of how it came to be made by institutes normally devoted to objective study. Financed by an American-controlled fund and distributed gratis, the report was plainly intended by someone as propaganda in academic dress. Some of the four directors who prepared it appear to have been dissatisfied with certain aspects; the preface says that 'not every member of the group endorses everything in the paper'. The report was distributed in America by the Book of the Month Club. Pamphlets of this kind are fed to newspapers, which pass the message on to the public through editorials and by a slanting of news, which is usually unconscious. In the present international climate, if a serious misstatement or miscalculation is made, nobody's career is in danger as long as it is the Soviets who are hit; the same, in the opposite direction, applies in the USSR. What is endangered is the survival of the entire civilization.

While Western Europe has its own contributors to misinformation about Soviet activities, the chief source is the United States. So far no leading European politician has equalled Reagan's declaration that the Soviet Union was behind 'all the unrest that is going on' and that if it were not for Moscow 'there wouldn't be any hotspots in the world'. Reagan represents the view that if only the communists could be annihilated and all doors opened – to the United States, with the help of friendly juntas – the entire world would leap into an era of prosperity. This delusion is accompanied by fantasies concocted to make the image of the Soviets fit the concept. Richard Helms, former CIA Director, saw a Soviet hand in the Iranian revolution, a suspicion shared in England by Lord Chalfont. Ayatollah Khomeini's sustained anti-Soviet vehemence would make it difficult to advance such a theory today, but in April 1979, when the author visited Iran just after the revolution, it was already obvious that no Soviet intrigue was needed to rouse the mullah-led people against the Shah.[13] In February 1979 a false picture of a Soviet threat in South Arabia, sent to Washington by the US Embassy in Sanaa, North Yemen, to suit a transient political purpose, led President Carter to promise the immediate despatch of military supplies, including tanks and planes, worth nearly $400 million, to be paid for by Saudi Arabia. As it turned out, the measure aborted when the Saudis declined to pay for the equipment following a regional political change. Subsequently a US military attaché, Lieutenant-Colonel John Ruszkiewicz, discovered the embassy's falsification and protested to higher authorities. He was told: 'If Yemen had not happened at that particular time, it would have been invented.' Ruszkiewicz wrote later:[14]

It seems to me we disastrously escalated our involvement in Vietnam as a result of an attack on an American warship in the Gulf of Tonkin which never occurred. I cannot help but view what happened in Yemen as a Middle East version of the Gulf of Tonkin incident.

The Soviet Union is unsurpassed in the manufacture of falsehoods. However, it is less important to compare productivity in that industry than to identify a factor that could be dangerous. If Moscow tended to miscalculate on the basis of its lies, it would be all the more desirable that the West should not miscalculate on the basis of its own.

Whether or not it is agreed that the Soviet Union has not been aggressive, but relatively restrained, in the Third World, the West is certainly more powerful there. That is why it has rejected offers to negotiate. Its main concern is to cling to its strategic advantages. Since it is stronger in all regions, there can be no negotiation as long as this attitude is maintained. The West would be found to lose in any neutralization agreement, such as that sought by the Russians in the Indian Ocean, from which patrolling US submarines could fire nuclear weapons into Soviet territory at any moment, while the USSR has no base there; but this loss would be a small price for a major step towards peace.

There are some who believe that Moscow's policy is to impose communism on the whole of Europe, while others think that it is simply tsarist imperialism in communist dress and yet others that it is both. The first seems to be out of the question. Doctrine remains important in the Kremlin, which sees communist parties as having a historical role. The faith persists that capitalism will collapse for reasons given by Marx, who adapted the dialectical process seen in history by the philosopher, Hegel; just as the feudal system contained contradictions that led to the emergence of capitalism, so the contradictions of capitalism, which Marx analysed, will cause it to break down; when that time comes, and not before, there will be communist revolutions; meanwhile it would be futile to try to force the pace of history. After the Russian revolution the Bolshevik Party believed that uprisings would quickly follow throughout Europe, first in Germany, where, indeed, there was a possibility. Russia, Lenin said, would then be again backward, and the more industrially advanced countries would take the lead. Meanwhile the Russian Party inevitably supported those in other countries and created the Third International (Comintern). But when it became clear that world revolution was not imminent after all, the Kremlin turned inwards. The Comintern was dissolved in 1943; its replacement was short-lived. When Russia became a great power, it succumbed to false pride and sought spheres of influence, as all powers have habitually done, even though this pursuit unfailingly played a part in their eventual downfall. But its interest in spreading communism remains Marxist, not adventurist; that is to say, it awaits the historical conditions for revolution, the prerequisites for which were laid down by Lenin in '*Left-wing' Communism: an Infantile Disorder*, written partly in an attempt to cure the chronic immaturity of the British Communist Party. Lenin said that what he saw as the historic, proletarian revolution in capitalist countries could not take place until (a) the workers wanted change and were ready to sacrifice their lives for it and (b) the economic system was in such a state of collapse that the rulers would be unable to keep it running. Since Lenin's word is sacred in the Soviet Union, there is no reason to believe that the Kremlin now sees history differently. As for the tsars, their imperialist drive, like those of other European powers, was east, not west, if we exclude the Baltic states, which were ethnically mixed and always an object of rival incursions, and Slavonic areas.

There has not been one Soviet westward move that has been inconsistent with Moscow's conception, right or wrong, of the need to protect itself against aggression. Assuming this premise, Russia may be seen to have used its power with the prudence that often marked the foreign policy of the tsars. When Stalin was bargaining with the Allies during and after the war he was unconcerned either with spreading communism or with territorial gain as such; what he wanted was a *cordon sanitaire*, which reduced the risk of invasion, such as Russia had suffered so many times in its history. He did not believe that communism would suit Poland and declared that it would fit Germany as a saddle fitted a cow.[15] But he was determined to ensure that Poland did not ally itself with the West; this required the establishment of a communist government. That the degree of Russian intervention in Europe has been proportionate to what it considers to be its security needs, not to a desire to expand westward or to impose communism, may be seen from its acts. This was already apparent in the closing stages of the war when, on the other hand, Britain, oblivious to the imminent dissolution of its empire, still harboured far-reaching aims. In May 1944 Washington rejected a British proposal that Britain should be given a free hand in Greece in return for Russian overlordship of Rumania.[16] Four months later

Churchill went to see Stalin and, without informing the Americans, offered him a 75 per cent interest in Bulgaria, while Hungary and Yugoslavia would be split fifty-fifty. Balfour comments:[17] 'Although this was only to be "for immediate war-time purposes" (and nothing was said about Poland), he [Churchill] deprecated describing the deal as "dividing into spheres" for fear such language might shock the Americans.' But Churchill was looking beyond the war, certainly when it came to Greece; and Stalin, willing to meet him on this point, did not intervene when Britain put down a Greek communist uprising.

What emerges from this is that while Britain wanted to control remote territory of strategic importance to its empire, the USSR was only concerned to ensure the submission and support of its neighbours. Of these the most important was Poland, a buffer between the Soviet Union and Germany. Churchill, who at that time was trying to win Stalin's support for his own aims, proposed at Tehran in November 1943 that the Poles should be given German territory in return for a slice of Poland acquired by the USSR.[18] But Poles in Moscow wanted to move their frontier farther west than the Allies were willing to concede – to include virtually the whole of Silesia instead of about a third of it; the Soviets backed the Poles, conquered the area, and handed it over to them.

The limited, strategic nature of Soviet expansion is evident in the differential treatment of the Baltic states. As the Second World War loomed Moscow looked with increasing anxiety towards neighbouring Estonia, Latvia and Lithuania; these small states, with their long coastline, and Riga only 500 miles from Moscow, could have provided an invader with easy access. The Soviets occupied them in June 1940 and, after going through the motions of elections, incorporated them in the USSR. Finland was treated differently; its strategic importance, although not negligible, is less than that of the other three states. After the German invasion of Poland Stalin offered to hand over Karelian lands to Finland, to relinquish certain territory claimed by the Finns and to forgo garrison privileges on Hangoe in return for strategic islands near Leningrad. When the Finns refused to yield enough the Russians attacked. After 105 days of fighting Finland signed a treaty under which it ceded about 10 per cent of its territory. When the Germans invaded the USSR on 22 June 1941, the Finns joined in the attack. They were again defeated and on 4 September 1944 asked for and were granted an armistice. Subject to Finnish cession of the Petsamo area in the north and the granting of a fifty-year lease on the Porkkala peninsula to the

Soviets, who later renounced it, the 1940 borders were restored, while the Finns were forced to pay heavy reparations. I am not attempting to justify the USSR's aggression in the Baltic states, let alone to condone the transportation of large numbers of their inhabitants to distant regions, but to emphasize the defensive nature of its action in Europe; this should be a factor in any calculation of whether the risk of abandoning atomic weapons is greater than that of keeping them. With the Germans soundly defeated, the Soviets could have annexed Finland and exploited its valuable forests to win hard currency. Indeed, the euphoria of victory in a world war might well have led a less prudent government to do so. It would not have been the first time that Finland had been ruled from Moscow. After 1,700 years of Swedish domination Finland was ceded to Russia in 1809. While it enjoyed periods of semi-autonomy, it was unable to free itself until after the fall of Nicholas II, when its declaration of independence was approved by the Bolsheviks. Perhaps the Kremlin felt bound by this decision. Whether or not this was so, it is clear that Stalin's interest from the beginning was defensive.

It seems that in deciding to what extent to coerce a neighbour, in order to prevent it from falling under Western influence, the Soviets measure its strategic value against the trouble that their intervention might cause them. This would explain the immunity of Yugoslavia. Stalin was antagonistic to Tito, who wanted to dominate the Balkans. Disagreement began early when, after the Soviets had liberated Yugoslavia, Tito ignored Stalin's advice that he should form a coalition with King Peter's government. The Kremlin has long disapproved Yugoslavia's economic policy, under which worker enterprises are allowed freedom not unlike that of privately owned companies in the West. Probably Moscow feels that this system contains the same flaws as capitalism; and, in fact, 1982 saw 800,000 unemployed (13 per cent of the work force) in Yugoslavia and the collapse of a bank. The presence on its border of an economically unstable state, increasingly dependent on the International Monetary Fund, cannot please Russia; yet the Kremlin has launched no invasion. Doubtless it has calculated the difficulty of handling Yugoslavs and has not forgotten the resistance of mountain guerrillas against the Germans. As Tito's death approached, some Western commentators expected that when he died the Soviets would move in. When this did not happen, it was explained that Moscow was inhibited by its troubles in Poland. If that argument is correct, it follows that no West European state is in serious danger from the Soviets as long as the Poles remain in the Eastern bloc.

After the war the aggressive consequences of Soviet anxiety led to misunderstanding and a loss of the goodwill that its great sacrifices and military success had aroused in all sections of Western society. Averell Harriman, US Ambassador to Moscow, said that if it were accepted that the USSR had the right to penetrate its immediate neighbours, 'under the guise of security', penetration of the next immediate neighbour would become equally logical. Harriman's fears were widely shared. The Russians' actions so disturbed some observers, but not all, that Ernest Jones, the Freudian psychoanalyst, postulated that they suffered from an anxiety neurosis caused by unbelievably tight swaddling in infancy; because of this, Jones thought, they would never feel safe and would always be aggressive. To those who have seen Russian swaddling or read an account of it, and are familiar with Dick Read's work on the care of babies, this theory will seem by no means fantastic. But neither Harriman nor Jones took into account the immense trauma of the German invasion, in which 7,500,000 Russian servicemen – one-third of those mobilized – were killed or died of wounds, while an estimated 7,500,000 civilians were killed or died of injuries, to say nothing of widespread devastation. As it turned out, quite soon after the war, the Russians did stop expanding in Europe, once they had established their *cordon sanitaire* of satellite states. In 1955 they confounded some observers by agreeing to pull out of their zone in Austria, which they had occupied for ten years, on condition that the country remained neutral; accepting a Soviet proposal, made in April 1954, Britain, the United States and France also withdrew. If the Soviet Government had been motived by either a desire for territorial gain or an urge to impose communism, it would have maintained its foothold in Austria and occupied Finland and Yugoslavia as well.

While its present rulers probably never lose sight of Russia's traditional desire for seemly relations with Western Europe, it would be a miscalculation to imagine that their restraint arose from fear of Western military reprisals. The West did not intervene when the Russians invaded Hungary in 1956 and Czechoslovakia in 1968, to plug holes that were developing in their *cordon sanitaire*; had they swallowed up Finland and Yugoslavia and squatted in Austria, the West would not have behaved differently. If we are to make a useful estimate of Russian intentions, it is necessary to try and look at events through Moscow's eyes. In the West formation of the

North Atlantic Treaty Organization (NATO) in 1949 has always been seen as purely defensive, although, while there were genuine fears, it is hard to imagine that the USSR, ravaged by war and lacking a nuclear weapon, had the resources or the administrative capacity to constitute a threat at that time. Since the Russians must have been aware of their limitations, and, in view of their past experience of the West, they could hardly have been expected to assume that NATO's intentions were entirely innocent; it is a widely accepted fact that the setting up of the Warsaw Treaty Organization in 1955 was a direct response to the inclusion of the Federal Republic of Germany in NATO.

If we remove the factor of American global ambition, all we are left with in Europe itself as a likely cause of war is an unreasoning distrust on both sides, neither of which has shown signs of a desire to attack the other. These tribal misgivings are reflected in the four-institutes report. While the authors elaborate upon the requirements of nuclear defence, the closest they get to justifying such a horrific arsenal is to assert: 'A spillover into Europe of actions like the invasion of Afghanistan can never be excluded.'[19] There is no logic at all in this extrapolation, which is of a kind not usually found in academic works. Elsewhere the report tries to make the best of a bad case by saying:[20]

> The temporary diversion of Soviet military forces toward internal policing in the wake of the Polish crisis, accompanied by the possible unreliability of the Soviet Union's allies in joining any aggressive design against the West, may, for the time being, reduce the risk of a surprise attack on Western Europe. However, this situation is unlikely to modify the long-term military balance.

This comment lacks the objectivity that so grave a subject requires. There is no evidence that the Russians imagine they have anything to gain by a surprise attack (although surprise is part of Soviet military doctrine), which would increase their already strained policing commitment; and since the satellite countries show a growing tendency to express their individuality, both economically and politically, they would be even less likely to support a Soviet adventure in the future than they are now. The satellites will never be a sound springboard for a Soviet attack on the West. It is true that since they were set up they have become more than a mere buffer and are now a source of ideological comfort to Moscow, which without them would be ideologically isolated. But it should not be assumed that this is a predominant factor in Moscow's policy towards Eastern Europe.

Nor does Moscow's determination to preserve Party control in the satellites arise from fear that any change might spread to the Soviet Union; the Kremlin is in no way threatened internally in this respect. Its interest in Party control in the satellites derives almost entirely from the fact that it is only through this structure that the Soviets can protect their buffer against Western influence. It was not ideological but strategic considerations that caused Brezhnev to say that the Soviets had been prepared to invade Czechoslovakia in 1968, even at the risk of a world war.[21] Dubcek, who did not expect a Soviet invasion, admitted that he had not taken the strategic factor sufficiently into account. This is surprising; for, as C. G. Jacobsen, Adjunct Professor of Strategic Studies at the Institute of Soviet and East European Studies, Carleton University, Canada, says, the Soviets could not 'tolerate hostile control over the mountain ranges of Western Czechoslovakia (east of which the plains stretch flat, if marshy, to Moscow)'.[22] Early in the 1970s some people in Washington understood this; the 'Sonnenfeldt doctrine' (attributed to Helmut Sonnenfeldt, who served as a member of the National Security Council under Kissinger) recognized the Soviet Union's buffer interests. Earlier President Lyndon Johnson attached more importance to the Vietnam war than to Czechoslovakia. 'Indeed it has been repeatedly suggested that the USSR received more or less explicit signals from Washington' that intervention in Czechoslovakia would not provoke a military response from NATO.[23] If the invasion of Czechoslovakia was not seen as a threat to the West, what is the threat now?

Judging from their actions, Western leaders have become insufficiently careful in considering whether a given Soviet action is offensive or defensive. Nor do they take into account what fears their own statements and actions might arouse in the Kremlin. Western foreign policy, particularly American, is sometimes conducted as if its aim were to unify the Soviet leadership during its prolonged debates on crucial issues. The false assumption appears to be made that Moscow is monolithic, whereas it took six months of debate for it to decide what to do about Czechoslovakia in 1968, with Kosygin arguing against interference.[24] Such miscalculations increase tension. The most serious consequence of the Western reaction to events in Afghanistan and Poland was to increase Russia's fear of a tightening encirclement. On its southern flank it is vulnerable to nuclear-armed American submarines in the Indian Ocean; in the East it fears the Chinese; and in the West it faces NATO land forces backed by warships, including British, which could strike at the Baltic. At the end of his term in Moscow as correspondent of *The Times* Michael Binyon wrote on 17 July 1982: 'The Russians feel themselves encircled by enemies intent on challenging the Kremlin politically, economically and militarily.' After four and a half years in Russia it was this, rather than any aggressive propensity, which appears to have impressed him. Summing up Brezhnev's career, Binyon said: 'Brezhnev generally wanted the best for his country, to be remembered, as Chancellor Helmut Schmidt described him on his last visit to Bonn, as a man of peace.'

Poland and China constantly worry the Russians. Communication between the large number of Polish immigrants in the United States and their relatives in Poland provides Washington with opportunities for influence, if not infiltration. At the same time the Chinese have unnerved the Russians with claims to territory seized by the tsars. These were not confined to border areas, now inhabited by 4 million people, that Alexander II forced China to yield under treaties of 1858 and 1860. Tass said on 14 January 1983 that 1.5 million square kilometres, including the port of Vladivostok, Sakhalin island, the city of Khabarovsk, large areas of Soviet Kirgiz and Kazakhstan, Lake Balkhash and the whole of the Pamir Highlands, in Central Asia, are included in maps of China used in schools and universities.[25] The Chinese replied through a Beijing newspaper that they had no territorial claims and only sought a border settlement on the basis of existing treaties. But, with the maps and past claims in mind, the Soviets would need a great deal of convincing before they felt secure. In January 1982 Beijing forecast a new population explosion and said that family planning guidelines were not being observed. Already China is badly overcrowded. It is with this in mind, not with aggressive intent, that Russia keeps a costly force, said to number 2 million, on its border with China; it has no desire to increase its growing and sometimes burdensome Asian population. China already has a nuclear force, capable of striking at important Soviet targets, and has built underground shelters for its élite and not a few others. Its leaders, in the days of Chairman Mao, pointedly emphasized that it could afford to lose a large slice of its 1,000 million population in a nuclear war.

Russia sees itself as having been harassed by the West throughout much of its history. In this it has the concurrence of Toynbee:[26]

Then again, in the fourteenth century, the best part of Russia's original domain – almost the whole of White Russia and the Ukraine – was shorn away from Russian Orthodox Christendom and annexed to Western Christendom through being conquered by the Lithuanians and the Poles. (The fourteenth-century Polish conquests of originally Russian ground in Galicia were not recovered by Russia till the last phase of the War of 1939–45.)

In the seventeenth century, Polish invaders penetrated the hitherto unconquered part of Russia as far as Moscow and were driven out only by a supreme effort on the Russian side, while the Swedes shut Russia off from the Baltic by annexing the whole east coast down to the northern limits of Polish dominions. In 1812 Napoleon repeated the Poles' seventeenth-century exploit; and, after the turn of the nineteenth and twentieth centuries, blows from the West came raining down on Russia thick and fast. The Germans, invading her in the years 1915–18, overran the Ukraine and reached Transcaucasia. After the collapse of the Germans, it was the turn of the British, French, Americans, and Japanese to invade Russia from four different quarters in the years 1918–20. And then, in 1941, the Germans returned to the attack – more formidable and more ruthless than ever. It is true that, during the eighteenth and nineteenth centuries, Russian armies also marched and fought on Western ground, but they came in always as allies of one Western power against another in some Western family quarrel. In the annals of the centuries-long warfare between the two Christendoms, it would seem to be the fact that the Russians have been the victims of aggression, and the Westerners the aggressors, more often than not.

It is possible to present a different picture by showing a great expansion of the Muscovites. But if we are to do this we should ignore, for the present purpose, Russia's eastward drive at the expense of less advanced peoples, which was part of the general nineteenth-century European imperialism. Again, in so far as westward aggression is concerned, we should eliminate the small Baltic states, of mixed population, which changed hands a number of times. The important expansion was within Orthodox Christendom, which the Muscovites came to dominate, but this constituted no threat to the West. In attempting to assess the significance of present Soviet actions, it is essential to take the historical background into account. This has been done by, among others, Malcolm Mackintosh, consultant on Soviet affairs to the

International Institute for Strategic Studies, London, who says that invasions from the east, south and west have 'fostered in the Russians a deep sense of the need to amass military power' and an 'overriding suspicion of the aims, ambitions, and superiorities of other nations'.[27]

Objectively, that is to say, disregarding the subjective factor of individual intent, it appears that the trend of history remains unchanged and that Russia still has more to fear from the West than the West from Russia. It took a devastating war, and preparation for it, to resolve the West's economic crisis in the 1930s and get the unemployed back to work:[28]

> Only the massive military spending of World War II had ended the Great Depression of the 1930's. The 15 per cent unemployment rate [in the United States] . . . was cured only by the enormous increase in military spending from about $1,500,000,000 in 1940 to more than $81,000,000,000 in 1945.

After the early post-war boom US unemployment rose to nearly 6 per cent in 1949, was reduced to less than 3 per cent by large expenditure on the Korean War, then rose again. In the United Kingdom 2 million who were unemployed in 1938 were absorbed in jobs and the armed forces during the war. There is no unemployment in Russia. Even if it is argued that prisoners of various kinds are in effect a labour reserve, it is a minimal factor in so large a population and bears no relationship to the more than 13 million out of work in the United States; war is not required to eliminate it. While it is not suggested that any government would launch a war simply to solve its economic problems, although there are some people in the United States to whom such a thought would not be alien if America itself were not seriously endangered, the climate of economic crisis is one in which wars are more likely to break out.

There is, however, a subjective factor. Reagan's view of communism as a virus is shared by people in his entourage, and it is obvious that some of those closest to him would not be unhappy if what they see as its source vanished from the face of the earth. The CIA report (cited in chapter 3), that the Soviet economy is sound, can only exacerbate the frustration of those whose faith in the American system led them to believe that it was not. They must fear increasingly that the state of the US economy, described by Reagan, when speaking unknowingly before a live microphone, as in a 'hell of a mess',[29] will worsen, while that of the USSR seems likely to improve. This author shares the opinion of the Soviet dissident scientist, Zhores A. Medvedev, that opponents of détente are probably more concerned about the Soviet Union's influence, which, he thinks, is certain to increase, than the possibility of its aggression.[30] The more the American right proclaims that the Soviets are heading for the 'scrapheap of history', to quote Reagan, the more it is to be suspected of wishing, consciously or not, to ensure the fulfilment of its prophecy. American commentators have said that those on whom Reagan depended most for support in his election are opposed to any gesture towards the Soviet Union in arms reduction. The Pentagon admitted in January 1983 that it was planning to stage military confrontations aimed at draining the Soviet economy, and to make itself capable of waging an extended nuclear war, with missiles fired from outer space. This is not for the short term. But meanwhile such an event as the failure of American banks, following a large-scale Latin American default, could lead to widespread economic dislocation and the threat of popular rebellion. In those circumstances the judgment of influential Americans who, like Reagan, believe fanatically that Russia is the cause of all the world's troubles, could not be relied upon. Moscow must be aware of this danger; West Europeans should not overlook it.

In the early 1950s, when the United States was insisting on German rearmament as the price of its retaining a military presence in Europe, Lord Beaverbrook put up posters reading: 'Don't rearm Germany'. Germany now has the largest army in NATO; its political future is uncertain. If Beaverbrook feared a German resurgence, even when Germany was helplessly weak, the Kremlin would need strong nerves when Pershing and cruise missiles arrived on German soil. It would be bound to look at the future in the light of two German invasions and of the possibility that Western capitalism, perhaps heading for collapse, could become desperate in its death throes.

Chapter 8

The worst case

The worst conceivable consequence of unilateral nuclear disarmament would be that Western Europe's relationship with the Soviet Union would be similar to that of a member of the present Soviet bloc. It will be argued later in this chapter and in the next that such a contingency may be ruled out. But, assuming the possibility for the moment, we may ask what effect it could have on the lives of West Europeans. If we look first at the economic aspect, which appears to be what interests most people, it will be seen that the new situation would certainly not be disastrous enough to warrant risking nuclear destruction in order to avert it. At the end of 1981 Lester C. Thurow, professor of Economics and Management at the Massachusetts Institute of Technology, said:[1] 'Last year East Germany passed them [the British] in per capita GNP. The Germans can make communism work better than the British can make capitalism work.' It is unlikely that the more easy-going British would have achieved the East German result, had they been in a similar position. The point being made is that living in the Soviet shadow need not be economically catastrophic. In view of difficulties in the methodology of comparing Britain's Gross National Product with that of the German Democratic Republic (GDR), Thurow's statement may be questioned; but it is likely that the GNPs per head are not markedly different.[2] If this is not apparent in a visible comparison it is partly because for years the GDR, like other countries in the bloc, has been investing more than 30 per cent of its Net Material Product,[3] compared with 16 per cent of the GNP in the United Kingdom; the benefits should be felt later. Then, whatever the levels of wealth may be, that in the GDR is more evenly distributed. Although fewer East Germans than Britons own cars, all have much cheaper public transport, housing and holidays.

The East German economic achievement is as remarkable as it is under-publicized in the West. After the Second World War, while

Western Germany received the stimulus of Marshall Aid, the East was stripped of much of its industry by the Russians, as war reparations. Hundreds of factories, some of them newly rebuilt, were dismantled and transported to the Soviet Union, along with railway track, repair workshops and power plants. In some regions East Germans were reduced to pedalling bicycles to turn lathes. It has been estimated that the dismantling amounted to 53 per cent of industrial capacity, on top of 24 per cent destroyed or damaged during the war.[4] The Russians also took a slice of current production. Eastern Germany had no fuel resources except poor quality lignite. Before the war it had produced only 7 per cent of Germany's steel. As soon as it began to recover, the GDR, unrecognized as a country by any other, including the Soviet Union, was subjected to a tight Western economic boycott. But this was eased and by the 1960s Eastern Germany, with a population of fewer than 17 million had become Europe's fifth industrial producer and the eighth in the world; it has Europe's third largest output of electricity per head.

The GDR's economic expansion has been accompanied by a steady fall in the industrial accident rate. A West German Government report said in 1971 that only 4.1 per cent of East German workers were industrial casualties, compared with 8.8 per cent in the Federal Republic (FRG).[5] It explained:

A more comprehensive catalogue of labour safety regulations, coupled with factory instructions, the general factory-based health service, accident research and the trade unions' strong functions in control and participation have produced a system which is superior to that of the Federal Republic.

In 1980 the East German accident rate was reduced to 2.9 per cent – about one-third of the Western average.

While it is correct to say that East German trade unions are an instrument of the government, it would be misleading not to add that the rulers' aim is to improve the lives of the workers. Dogmatic, inflexible, and disliked though he was both in his own entourage and in Moscow, Walter Ulbricht, the GDR's first leader, surely meant it when he said in 1969: 'What are the simple ideals and aims which unite us [communists and Christians]? Peace and humanity and mutual respect, happiness and prosperity for honest working people, happy families and happy children, healthy in body and soul.' At the age of twenty-one, during the First World War, Ulbricht was distributing anti-war pamphlets in the street, not without risk. Communists who resisted the Nazis, many at the cost of their lives, were aiming to uplift the workers, not oppress them. While trade unions in the GDR are not free in the sense understood in the West, their role in society, rather than as a mere pressure group, is not negligible. On the other hand, the part played by Western trade unions in obtaining higher wages in real terms is greatly exaggerated. Wages are a function of productivity and the labour supply and demand. In an advanced, expanding economy they increase with production, not only absolutely, but as a share of the product. In Spain, under a dictatorship, 'compensation of employees' (wages and benefits paid by employers), in relation to 'domestic factor incomes' (revenue from production expressed as compensation of employees plus operating surplus), rose from 53 per cent in 1964 to 62.9 per cent in 1975, when Franco died; five years later, in 1980, the figure had only increased to 63.3 per cent.[6] Trade union militancy had nothing to do with this progression. In the Soviet Union a factory manager will sometimes pay a highly skilled worker more than he receives himself, to retain his services.[7]

The GDR has gone a long way towards achieving the communist goal for workers. Income has been drastically redistributed. A doctor receives only double, and the director of a *kombinat*, which groups similar industries, only up to three times the wages of a skilled artisan.[8] Although a director is only paid a fraction of what his equivalent receives in the West, he works hard and bears heavy responsibilities under the system of one-man management. While artisans work five days a week, managers, according to one survey, spend sixty to seventy hours on the job.[9] It appears not uncommon for a manager to begin work at 6 a.m., one and a half hours before his factory opens, and to leave ten hours later to read documents at home. In 1949 Workers' and Peasants' Faculties were established to enable promising children who had left school at the age of fourteen to qualify for university entrance. These have since been reduced to two, but the extension of educational opportunity led at one stage to the training of more people for highly skilled work than can be absorbed. In April 1974 the West German magazine, *Der Spiegel*, said that in proportion to the population the GDR had 70 per cent more teachers than the Federal Republic.[10] In 1972 more than half the students at technical colleges and more than a third at universities were women, compared with an overall figure of 25 per cent in the FRG. Jonathan Steele, formerly *The Guardian's* East European correspondent, finds that in what he describes as an unusually generous welfare state East German working mothers have more pre-school facilities for their children than any in Europe.[11] A mother receives full pay while on leave for six weeks before and twenty weeks after the birth of her baby; she retains the right to her job if she stays at home for the child's first year. Student mothers are allowed to extend their courses and defer their examinations. Although women are not given the highest responsibility in the bureaucracy and the professions, they are conspicuous in all walks of life; 36 per cent of judges were women in 1973. In a health service that continues to expand as national income increases, the number of doctors per 10,000 inhabitants increased from 7.7 in 1955 to 20.7 in 1981; patients choose their own physicians. The infant mortality rate was reduced from 72 per 1,000 live births (babies aged up to one year) in 1950 to 12.3 in 1980; the Government expects that measures to be taken under the five-year plan, 1981–86, will reduce the rate to 10 or 11.[12] Most workers have four and a half weeks of paid holidays, with five to ten additional days, depending on their occupations. Married women, single mothers and single women aged more than forty are allowed an additional month's paid leave for household work. The minimum annual holiday is eighteen days. Newly married couples aged not more than twenty-six are given an interest-free loan of 5,000 marks to furnish, put in order or help buy a flat or house. Workers are encouraged to join an innovators' movement. By 1980 membership had reached 32.2 per cent of the work force; a total of 513,000 workers' innovations had increased production by 4,819 million marks a year. The educational system has been widely praised, in spite of the emphasis on indoctrination. Hans Wassmund, a West German academic who occasionally lectures in American universities and is highly critical of the GDR, says:[13]

> Yet, if one takes as a starting point that any system of education has to fulfil the basic functions of transmitting norms and values, preparing young people for economic and political duties and to stand up for their country, the results in the GDR are rather impressive.

It is education in *esprit de corps* and, from an early age, in sport that has given the GDR its extraordinary success in the Olympic Games; in 1976, with forty gold, twenty-five silver, and twenty-five bronze medals, it gained more first places than any country except the USSR, which has more than thirteen times its population. Wassmund's dislike of the government does not prevent him from saying:[14]

Seeing that all roads to the West were blocked after 1961, and considering the GDR's advanced social system (medical care, social security, pensions) and high standard of living (GNP per capita is higher than in Great Britain and there are extremely low, State-subsidised costs for all basic needs, such as housing, food, transportation and even holidays), it becomes understandable that over the years a certain loyalty to the State and a feeling of pride in the socialist system has developed.

Steele quotes an East Berlin vicar as saying: 'Through their work and their social duties people are conscious that they are helping themselves. They actually feel "We are the state." '[15] But what about that blocking of roads – the Berlin wall? We shall come to that later.

As consumers of non-essentials East Germans are not as well off as West Germans – or British; however, in 1981 99 per cent of households had television sets and refrigerators, 89.2 per cent radio sets, 83.4 per cent washing machines and 39 per cent private cars. Rapid strides have been made in overcoming the housing shortage. Between 1971 and 1980 the construction or modernization of 1,400,000 dwellings provided accommodation for 4,250,000. It is planned to end the shortage completely by 1990. All dwellings built since 1975 have hot water and those with central heating rose from 90.9 per cent in 1976 to 97 per cent in 1981. The race between the two Germanies is not yet over. The FRG has a large number of unemployed, who contribute nothing to production; the GDR suffers from a labour shortage, and has engaged Belgian contractors to build factories, using their own workers, who were given the choice of going to Eastern Germany or joining Belgium's jobless. The economic outlook of the entire West is uncertain and its main problems are imponderable. In a totally irrational situation the price of gold, which reflects nervousness, fell to less than $300 an ounce in 1982, but had shot up to $460 by the end of the year. In the planned economies of the Soviet bloc difficulties are easier to diagnose and, given the will, can be resolved rationally.

While the GDR's economy is not as flexible as Hungary's, it has some latitude. The planners set guidelines, but individual enterprises are not expected to produce a given number of shirts or overcoats. Almost without exception, the managing director of a *kombinat* is solely responsible for determining the quantity and nature of the products, including innovations, which are manufactured either for the home marktet, where he must predict the demand, or for export. In an export drive aimed at ensuring that it can meet its foreign debt, the GDR achieved in 1981 its first trade surplus with the FRG since 1965. Small, private businesses play a bigger part in the economy than is usually realized in the West. Eighty-four thousand independent firms employing 247,000 artisans carry out building work, maintenance and various services. Ten thousand private shops and 29,000 small retail businesses have contracts with state wholesale organizations. Of 34,000 restaurants 2,000 are private and 8,000 under contract.

Western newspapers tend to make light of the East European economies, but each year the United Nations devotes a technical analysis of about 450 pages to them. The report for 1981 says that in their five-year plans from 1976–80 the Soviet Union and all other East European countries set their economic development in the framework of general social development, and provided for continuous cultural and material improvement.[16] The main orientation of the plans shifted from fast growth, which had been achieved, to balanced growth aimed at redressing structural imbalances that had accumulated during years of extensive progress. Further adjustments were made to cope with rapid changes in the world economic climate. Despite their slower growth, the Soviet bloc economies continued to grow faster than the world average, although by a smaller margin. The aggregate annual growth rate of the Net Material Product (see note 2) was 4.1 per cent for the five years, with the Soviet Union achieving 4.2 per cent and the GDR 4.1 per cent; if Poland were excluded the average would be 5 per cent. In the same period the FRG's Gross Domestic Product grew annually by an averge of 3.1 per cent and Britain's 1.1 per cent. The FRG and Britain recorded falls of 0.3 per cent (GDP) and 2.2 per cent (GNP) in 1981; the Swiss Bank Corporation estimated a fall of 0.9 per cent in the FRG and a rise of 1.2 per cent in the UK for 1982.[17] The planned annual rise in the GDR for 1981–5 is 5.1 per cent. Previous performances of the GDR, with the planned figure in brackets, were: 1966–70, 5.2 per cent per annum (5.4); 1971–5, 5.4 (4.9); 1976–80, 4.1 (5). Real wages rose at an annual rate of 4.4 per cent in 1976–80.[18]

The United Nations report found that the GDR's concentration on industry was surprisingly high during 1976–80 in relation to other sectors. The report's suggestion that this could indicate an underestimation of the role of agriculture in development appears to have been confirmed by the recurrence of food shortages in 1982, which, however, seem to have been exacerbated by the need to send supplies to Poland. In the same period the GDR was the only Soviet bloc country not to experience a progressive decline in economic growth. For the group as a whole the deceleration was continuous until broken by a sharp rise in the Soviet Union.[19] Neither the intrinsic difficulties of planning, nor bureaucratic muddle, although this is marked in the USSR, were mainly responsible for the deceleration, which is part of a long-term trend. Examining the causes, the report says there is no doubt that labour shortage plays a major part, although it varies from country to country. A second major cause is the increasing scarcity and cost of material inputs; while the Soviet Union is rich in resources, their exploitation often requires huge investment east of the Urals. The third main factor is the decline in investment, although it remains high in relation to that of Western countries. In other words, the consumerism of the West has infected the East, and governments have been obliged to modify more prudent, long-term policies to appease the growing public appetite. The United Nations report says that Eastern bloc management still 'gives priority to various quantitative indicators [which were useful at an earlier stage] rather than to qualitative net indicators'[20] – clearly a reference to the Soviet Union, rather than the GDR. On this point the report cites Brezhnev's criticism of what he called 'bottlenecks and disproportions in the national economy', some of them arising from uncontrollable factors, but most of them probably from 'inertia, conventions and habits from the period when the quantitative rather than the qualitative aspect of the work loomed the largest'.[21] Since then Yuri Andropov has taken measures to rectify the defect. Doubtless he will be confronted by cultural obstacles of the kind described in chapter 3, but in the GDR it can be expected that planning problems, difficult though they are, will be substanially overcome.

What emerges from any study of Soviet bloc economies is that they are fundamentally rational and relatively stable. People are not left wondering whether life will get better or worse. Small, independent businesses are certain of patronage, if not of supplies. Increased living standards, cultural and material, are included and achieved in every plan; there is no reason why this process should not continue, even though modestly, throughout the foreseeable future. Automation is not a curse, which throws people out of work, but a means of increasing leisure. The prospects of automation have led to speculative thinking on the subject of worker alienation. Marx's view that capitalism alienated the worker by depriving him of control over the products of his labour is more metaphysical and, to my mind, less satisfactory in the light of developments since his time, than is realized by those who use it merely as a psychological cliché. Professor Georg Klaus, who teaches cybernetics at the Humbolt University in the GDR, believes that while social alienation of the kind Marx had in mind is abolished under socialism, the worker still undergoes technical alienation through being obliged to submit himself to monotonous work and the pace of the assembly line.[22] Klaus argues that automation will abolish this condition. Eventually only two kinds of industrial labour will remain: control and maintenance of robots and the creative work of engineers and planners. Various social theories have been developed around this concept. How well they will work out remains to be seen. Meanwhile planned automation is well under way in the GDR, and it would be rash to assume that East German workers will not be considerably better off than British, materially and culturally, by the end of the century.

There is no space here to discuss the issue of freedom. Nor is the author equipped to undertake so complex a task. It was Lord Acton's hope to write a history of the theory and practice of freedom; but it has been said that the project, as he conceived it, would have taken more than a lifetime. All that will be said here is that freedom is never absolute and that the subject contains difficulties that seem to be unknown to slogan-makers. Germany has always leaned more to authoritarianism than Britain. Under Hitler, following the unsuccessful Weimar democracy, it became totalitarian. After the war vigorous brain-washing by the Allies and a strong dose of Marshall Aid promoted another period of democracy, the future of which is not completely certain. Communists in Eastern Germany, backed by the Soviet Union, claimed that they were the vanguard of the proletariat and set up a dictatorship in its name; this has evolved into what Professor Peter Ludz, a West German, has described as consultative authoritarianism.

Although opinion may differ on the nature and extent of the consultation, the GDR is not being governed by an iron dictatorship. Ultimate power is firmly in the hands of the Socialist Unity Party of Germany (SED), which was formed by the merging of the Communist and Social Democratic Parties in 1946, and is, in fact, communist. The SED is allotted 127 of the 500 seats in the People's Chamber. But there are four other parties, each with fifty-two seats: the Christian Democratic Union, the Liberal Democratic Party of Germany, the National Democratic Party of Germany and the Democratic German Farmers' Party. The remainder of the seats are occupied by the Federation of Free German Trade Unions (sixty-eight), Free German Youth (forty), the Democratic German League of Women (thirty-five) and the League of Culture (twenty-two). An obvious point that emerges from the names is that if the organizations were truly free and democratic, there would be no need to emphasize it; on the whole, it may be assumed that the more a government insists that it is democratic, the less likely it is to be so. All of the parties and mass organizations comprise the National Front, which offers a single list of candidates to the electors every five years.

Under the constitution the People's Chamber is the nation's highest organ of power, but the almost invariable unanimity of its decisions reflects the predominance of the SED. Nevertheless, the parties can exert influence in committee; the Christian Democratic Union, for example, brought about the redrafting of a family law on the ground that it made inadequate reference to the religious factor.[23] Wassmund says there seem to be three main reasons why the SED tolerates other political parties.[24] The first is that the parties give the appearance of a truly democratic society; the second is that integration of bourgeois groups into the system is facilitated by their having organizations of their own; and the third is that the ideological purity of the working-class party is less likely to be tainted if other elements are channelled outside it. Since the SED believes that it has a historic mission and that the other parties are historically doomed, this view of the political structure as a convenient façade is reasonable. But there is more to it than that. In the first place, the parties have not been wiped out; though emasculated, they are there, and it is not in the nature of things that they can exert no influence at all. Each of the four parties provides vice-presidents of the State Council and of the Council of Ministers, or Cabinet; their members also head ministries. Wassmund says that the parties and other National Front organizations are useful in making the SED's will known to people whom it could not otherwise reach. But there is also a feedback of information about the public temper, which, as Steele says of the trade unions, enables the government to assuage discontent before it becomes dangerous.[25]

Despite the regular allocation of responsibility to members of the Christian Democratic Union, practising Christians are at a disadvantage; Jehovah's Witnesses are harassed. The churches do not identify themselves with the Christian party, which, they feel, has gone too far in acknowledging the leading role of the SED. While there is no overt policy of discrimination at the centre, none except those who support the SED without reserve find themselves in senior positions in industry, the state administration, universities or schools. Yet the government shows a great deal of institutional religious tolerance. While its educational aim is atheistic, it probably takes the view that the decline in church attendance throughout Europe, including Eastern Germany, will eventually reduce organized religion to insignificance, and that meanwhile acceptance of the churches eliminates a possible source of tension and provides a useful army of charity workers. There are about 4,300 Lutheran pastors; the Catholic church, headed by a cardinal, has two bishoprics and 1,300 priests; forty-seven other communities of various faiths include eight Jewish. Christian literature comprises 12 per cent of works published in the GDR;[26] churches and other religious organizations produce thirty-one periodicals, while church publishing houses print Bibles and theological works. Religious programmes are broadcast by radio and television. The state finances the training of Protestant theologians at six universities. It pays subsidies amounting to 190 million marks a year to 1,800 church-run hospitals, convalescent homes, old people's homes, nursing stations and other charitable bodies. In 1980 Catholics were allowed to use building materials, which are much needed for other purposes, to construct a modern church at Neubrandenberg; and in 1976 the Government released 500,000 marks in hard currency to enable the Primate to import a West German organ, costing nearly 1 million marks, for St Hedwig's Cathedral in East Berlin. Within its own ideology the state teaches virtue to the young; Pioneers, the equivalent of boy scouts and girl guides, tidy the grounds of blocks of flats, collect waste paper and visit the old. While the exit from the GDR is for the most part closed, the entrance is not. In 1979 8 million West Germans visited the country. Neither their tales of greater prosperity nor life in the FRG, as seen on television in the GDR, has provoked discontent on a scale that disturbs political stability.

Authoritarianism of any kind, even if it could be described as consultative, would go against the British grain. Bloch, the French authority on feudalism, who was executed by the Nazis, titled a section of his classic work 'The exceptional case of England'.[27] He noted that while the land of English peasants in the Middle Ages was even more at the mercy of the aristocracy than elsewhere in Europe, the line between freemen and serfs was drawn lower and the ordinary freeman was scarcely distinguishable in law from the nobleman. This tendency towards a broader, but orderly, liberty eventually degenerated into considerable disrespect for the law, but, as we saw in chapter 3, a reaction has begun to set in with a move towards a dictatorship of circumstance. If one were to consider whether the defence of political liberty justified the risk of retaining nuclear weapons, an attempt should be made to gauge how much of the present freedom would be practicable if economic and social collapse demanded radical restructuring. The difference between political and economic liberty in the West and that in the Soviet bloc might then be much smaller than it is now.

Three blots spoil the picture of steadily improving living conditions in the GDR. These are, in inverse order of obliquity, the Berlin wall, the contradiction of collectivist doctrine by privilege, and intellectual repression. There is a good deal of hypocritical talk about the wall. After the Second World War the victorious Allies were not displeased about the division of Germany. Yet, because the eastern part was communist, the West did its best to prevent it from becoming viable. At the same time many East German technicians and professional men were leaving for Western Germany as soon as they were trained; in 1960, the year before the wall went up, 688 doctors, 296 dentists and 2,648 engineers followed others who had left the country. The hundreds of thousands of East Germans who went to Western Germany included many of the most capable and enterprising youth, attracted by the freer atmosphere and by greater opportunity than was possible in the struggling GDR – but not necessarily in that order of motive. If the GDR were to survive, the wall had to be built. Today it is not so much a lack of Western-style freedom as a material living standard lower than in the FRG that makes the wall necessary. If free emigration were allowed, doctors, who are only paid twice the wage of a skilled worker, would probably leave in large numbers. Directors of large, successful enterprises could also earn much more in the West. But if cars became plentiful and cheaper than in the FRG, it is unlikely that many ordinary citizens would forsake their security for the right to vote for this or that politician.

The lesson of the wall is that the GDR has yet to create the new morality of which it boasts. Too few people are sufficiently high-minded to avert the damaging exodus that would ensue if the wall were demolished. In this the small clique that rules the country has failed to set an example and its affluence, relative to that of the majority, has generated cynicism, which has lowered moral standards generally. Living in a ghetto of official residences, it enjoys privileges that include special shops, luxurious, chauffeur-driven cars, holiday villas, special clinics and *de facto* preference for its children in university places. Rudolf Bahro, the East German Marxist exile, says that 'corrupt elements' see to it that the spirit of corruption becomes general and obligatory: the honest functionary is despised, not only as stupid, but as lacking in *esprit de corps* and is suspected of striving for positions that 'the hyenas have already occupied'.[28] While enjoying their privacy, the few at the top impose on the majority a collectivist drill, even in leisure, which is often boring and frustrating for those who differ from the herd but lack the privileges of the rule-makers.

While the wall can be explained and privilege excused on the ground that it is inevitable in any society (Marx ruled out egalitarianism), intellectual repression in the Soviet bloc can only be condemned as an affront to the spirit of Europe, which at its worst is more restrictive in its effect and more monstrous in its cruelty than that inflicted by the Inquisition. Whereas the Inquisition was devised to defend an established religious authority, communist persecution arose from the need to legitimize new rulers. The despotic tsars were considered to be divinely ordained; Lenin saw the Bolshevik party as the vanguard of the proletariat, thrown into power by Marx's inexorable dialectic of history. Marxists attach great importance to historical inevitability; but if there was anything inevitable in Russian history it was that the culture would ensure that after a revolution the government would be changed in form, but not in psychological content. Lenin expounded his legitimizing doctrine in a polemic directed at Karl Kautsky, a German socialist who had learned Marxism from Marx. Kautsky was appalled by events in Russia and maintained that a revolution should not destroy democracy. Lenin cited both Marx and his collaborator, Friedrich Engels, to justify his concept of the dictatorship of the proletariat (in fact, the Bolshevik Party). Marx and Engels believed that the dictatorship would only be temporary; it would remain as long as the proletariat needed it for defence against the class enemy; after that it would be possible to speak of freedom.

What Lenin did was to incorporate in an all-embracing dogma, which was later to stifle philosophic and scientific thought, the Marxist concept of a transient instrument, based on the experience of the Paris Commune, which would defend the proletariat against purely politico-economic counter-revolution. Scientists, but not philosophers, were excluded from this constraint for a time, because Lenin needed them. But under Stalin bizarre ideas that appeared consistent with, or not inconsistent with, dialectical materialism won state honours for their exponents, while men who opposed them, not a few of whom were known internationally, were cast into prisons and camps, where many of them died. Defence of the dialectic was vital; for if the principle broke down in science it would be false in history, and the logical and moral justification for Stalin's totalitarianism, seen as serving the historic role of the proletariat, would be demolished with it. Stalin claimed to believe, and possibly did believe, that a Marxist could predict a major historical event as accurately as Galileo had calculated the acceleration of a falling body. He thought that T. D. Lysenko, now discredited in the USSR, had explained evolution and the main principles of biology by means of dialectics. Among theories accepted as proven were that protein crystals and viruses could be transformed (dialectically) into bacteria, that life could be prolonged by sodium carbonate baths, that non-cellular 'living substance' was the main structural element of all living systems and that by mutation rye could become wheat and pines birches. The claimed discovery of plants on Mars became the basis of a new proletarian science – cosmo-botany. Condemned as inconsistent with dialectical materialism were Einstein's theories (subjective idealism) and quantum physics (with its non-dialectical leap); also outlawed were cybernetics and psychiatry – now used as a weapon against dissidents.

Intellectual repression has abated since Stalin died, but more in science than in other disciplines. What Toynbee called zealotry has long subsided from its peak. The present state of science is well described by Zhores A. Medvedev, geneticist and biochemist, who was forbidden to return to the USSR in 1973, when he visited the National Institute for Medical Research, London, at which he now works. The fact that he was among dissidents incarcerated in psychiatric hospitals has not deprived him of his objectivity. After describing the ups and downs of Soviet science, with its very considerable achievements, he says:[29] 'The general forecast which I can provide for the reader is optimistic, if considered from the point of view of those who would like to see the USSR as a peaceful member of the international community.' Scientific exchanges between East and West are already considerable; Soviet scientists are on the editorial boards of several dozen Western journals. After the struggles of earlier years, the main source of dispute between scientists and the government is the right of emigration and travel. Purely theoretical research is pursued to a greater extent than in the West, and is more generously financed. Medvedev is sceptical about the effectiveness of measures to control scientists politically and ideologically. There is, he says, a limit to the conformity that they will stand. Hundreds of them united against Kruschev's support for Lysenko and refused to co-operate with him even when he proposed a resonable reorganization of the Academy of Sciences.[30] All Soviet thinkers have to reckon with dogma in one way or another and it is impossible to say how fast the trend described by Medvedev will grow; but the relative freedom of physicists and mathematicians should produce results that will eventually influence philosophy and, hence, all thought.

During the worst period of terror Soviet scientists kept the true spirit of inquiry alive, although some died for it. Tyranny does not prevent thought, and original thinkers can withhold their message, if necessary, until changed circumstances make its release possible. Descartes, when he heard of Galileo's condemnation by the Inquisition, suppressed publication of one of his own works and planned to present his arguments in a way that would make them progressively acceptable to Rome. Some Soviet thinkers are doing the same thing today. If the worst happened, and Soviet dogmas were imposed on the West, this would be the course to adopt. Fear that Soviet domination would cast a dark shadow over Western philosophic and scientific thought does not justify the retention of atomic weapons. No person genuinely concerned with an idea of value to mankind, or deeply imbued with genuine piety, would risk the annihilation of the human race to ensure its propagation. A Christian would prefer martyrdom. If the victims of the Inquisition had been able to defend their ideas and values with nuclear missiles, they would have been mistaken had they done so; for the world in which their thoughts survive would not exist.

After the Second World War legitimation was required for the new communist governments of Eastern Europe, which at first were no more than Soviet satellites. All of them depended on Soviet backing. Since none had come to power through the collapse of capitalism, they could not claim to be products of Marx's historical process. But this did not deter them from declaring themselves to be history's chosen leaders. Whatever Marx had in mind, he would not have approved the tyranny of a self-appointed vanguard, supported by an alien armed force, over the minds of many dedicated socialists in countries where there had been no revolution at all. Marx and Engels could not have envisioned the ironical situation in which workers rose against their vanguard in protest against higher work norms, as East Germans did on 17 June 1953. Bertolt Brecht, the East German playwright, wrote in verse that according to a leaflet the people had lost the government's trust and could only regain it by redoubled work. Would it not have been simpler, he asked, if the government had dissolved the people and elected another. Of all the rulers in the smaller East European countries, those of the GDR had the greatest need of legitimation; for they had to legitimize not only a government but a state. In control of the mere rump of Germany, they wanted to show that this was the true German state and that the FRG was only a historically doomed capitalist remnant, discredited by Nazism, from which it had failed to dissociate itself convincingly. This and the characteristic German desire for a *Weltanschauung* ensured the rigorous application of dialectical materialism to all aspects of inquiry. Among the victims of official bigotry was the scientist, Robert Havemann, a member of the SED, who had survived a Nazi concentration camp. During the winter term of 1963–4 he delivered a university lecture in which he expressed heretical views on the relationship between science and dialectical materialism. The authorities were displeased and dismissed him from his post. In the 1970s, when he supported other critical thinkers, he was placed under virtual house arrest until he died in 1982.

In Hungary, which had the experience of adapting itself to the requirements of Austria, life is more relaxed. As Kovrig says, 'ideological deviants are no longer expeditiously liquidated.'[31] Subject to currency restrictions, citizens are free to travel west and, almost without exception, they return. Foreign tourists can obtain visas at any consulate and unlike in the GDR, may enter the coutnry without having booked accommodation. Japanese cameras and lawn-mowers are in shop windows. Food is plentiful. Hungary is less prosperous than Eastern Germany, but that does not make the people less content. A Budapest hotel receptionist said (to the author): 'The Germans have more money than we have, but they don't know how to live.' In a restaurant the foreign tourist may run into a couple of American businessmen, satisfied with their transactions, or a New Zealand civil servant buying railway carriages. While their educational work is severely restricted, churches receive state subsidies and are not without influence. The Government, despite its drive to develop the tourist industry as a source of hard currency, heeded László Cardinal Lékai and quashed a proposal to permit foreigners to bathe in the nude near a chapel and cemetery on the shores of Lake Balaton.[32] A superb recording of Haydn's 'The Seven Last Words of Christ', with the text in German, Hungarian, Russian, French and English, is on sale in Budapest –

and London. Sociology is free from constraint. The myths of proletarian internationalism that dominated the teaching of history have been replaced by Hungarian nationalism. But in the 1970s the authorities banned a debate on ontology. Janos Kadar, First Secretary of the ruling Hungarian Socialist Workers' Party, has skilfully eliminated both dogmatists and reformists. At the 1975 party congress he made an understanding and well understood statement that would not have been uttered by any leader in the GDR. The dictatorship of the proletariat, he said, would remain in force, but eighteen years of experience had shown that it was 'not such a bad dictatorship after all'; one could 'live under it, create freely and gain honour'. Kovrig appears to put it well when he says:[33] 'Kadar's pragmatism [in relation to the USSR] is rewarded by an ideologically neutral public acceptance that is equally pragmatic.' One has the feeling that Hungarians are less offended by the authoritarianism than by the intellectual absurdities that it propagates. There is also much resentment at being obliged to learn Russian as a second language. But it would probably be hard to find many Hungarians who, if they were free from such pressures, would think it worth risking atomic destruction to avoid them. Conditions in Hungary are not as bad as that; in fact, with employment secure, education good and culture far from stagnant, life is pleasant enough, despite the housing shortage.

In Hungary's neighbour, Czechoslovakia, intellectual repression has often been fearsome. But here, as elsewhere in the bloc, it is not always easy to separate the dissident thinker's desire to pursue fundamental inquiry from merely political criticism. In the light of the issue under discussion – whether there is any threat to Western Europe that justifies the risk of retaining atomic weapons – the difference is important. Political systems come and go. When we think of Athens we do not ask whether at a given time it was under a democracy or an oligarchy so much as what were the ideas on fundamental issues that it has passed on to us. It could be argued that if inquiry is suppressed, the human race might just as well be annihilated. That is a good argument, which could lead to the question of whether the condition of both Eastern and Western Europe, each degraded in its own way, suggests, in any case, the imminence of nemesis. But the view taken here is simply that while there is life there is hope; it is, therefore, life that must be kept going.

Czechoslovakia's rulers cannot claim Marxist historical legitimation, since they took over in a coup in 1948, not in a revolution following the collapse of capitalism, which has yet to collapse anywhere; but they almost certainly enjoy the support of most of the working class. Czechoslovakia, like the other members of the Soviet bloc, can be reasonably designated as a workers' state, since its main purpose is to improve the workers' lot. That these states are less than civilized, in that they suppress inquiry and violate the rule of law, is another matter. In the last free and competitive elections, in 1946, the Communist Party won 38 per cent of the vote, double that of its closest rival, Eduard Benes's National Socialist Party. The reforms attempted by Alexander Dubcek in 1968 reflected the discontent of professional people, academics and artists, not workers. In the ensuing period, following Warsaw Pact intervention, the 'majority of the population [were] seemingly anaesthetised into materialistic introspection by stable prices and steadily rising wages.'[34]

But neither consultative authoritarianism, the East German dream of an automatous paradise, nor intellectual repression would befall Western Europe simply because it demolished its atomic weapons; for our initial, tentative assumption that if Western Europe disarmed unilaterally it would come to bear the same relationship to the USSR as that of Eastern Europe begins to break down as soon as it is examined. In the first place there is no such thing as a typical East European response to Soviet pressure. Each country reacts differently in accordance with its culture and history. We have seen the marked divergence between Eastern Germany and Hungary. It may be assumed that the responses in Western Europe would be even more different. Secondly, the COMECON (Council for Mutual Economic Assistance) countries have already provided the USSR with as many problems as it can handle and it is scarcely conceivable that the Kremlin would be anything but loath to increase the membership of its club – originally set up as a buffer, not merely against nations, but against a hostile civilization, long regarded as a menace.

The peoples under Soviet pressure have between them a history of foreign domination and dictatorship. Their populations are relatively small, Poland's (35,900,000) being by far the largest. Czechoslovakia has a weak national identity. It was not a nation at all until 1918. Tension between Czechs and Slovaks continues. Despite increased centralization in the 1970s, Slovaks increased both their prosperity and political influence; few Slovak names appeared among the 242 signatories of Charter 77, which called for a dialogue with the authorities on fundamental rights.[35] East

Germans passed directly from Hitler into the arms of the communists. At the beginning of the Second World War Rumania, torn by bloody conflict, was under a royal dictatorship. Bulgarians 'have traditionally accepted foreign rule [Turkish, German and Russian] without opposition' and the ordinary Bulgar feels respect and even friendship for the Russians.[36] In the 1930s Bulgaria's authoritarian government, characteristic of the Balkans, disbanded all political parties and suppressed their newspapers; a large number of high schools that were regarded as breeding grounds of opposition were closed. King Boris and his Government favoured the Nazis. Hungary, after the First World War, was a Soviet republic for 133 days; its leaders were in no sense Moscow's surrogates, but had gone to Russia to fight alongside the Bolsheviks when they were struggling for survival. When the Second World War broke out, Hungary was a pro-German fascist state, complete with anti-Semitic legislation, although it controlled the more extreme groups. The relevant essentials of Poland have been outlined in chapter 6.

If the whole of Western Europe lacked the spirit to make a much better showing against any Soviet pressure than, say, Hungary (population 10,740,000) it would not be unreasonable to ask whether it deserved to survive as an entity. However, the question does not arise, as may be seen if we consider the present relationships within COMECON. These have been the subject of an important, overdue study, *Soviet – East European Dilemmas*, sponsored by the Royal Institute of International Affairs. The point that we are now considering is implicit in the title of that work. If the Soviet Union faces dilemmas in the small states of Eastern Europe, with their pitiful history of weakness and civil conflict, how could it cope with the greater task of effective domination over the whole of Europe? A reading of the eleven specialists' contributions to the study makes it clear that the Soviet Union, although powerful enough to have the last say, is sufficiently prudent to maintain harmony by compromise, not without cost to itself; the 'picture of a Soviet-inspired monolith in Eastern Europe has always lacked credibility – and probably most of all in Moscow.'[37] In 1948 strains were already evident and Stalin felt obliged to rid the socialist group of Tito, who was striving to dominate the Balkans; Albania broke away in 1961 and supported China. 'Even before the upheavals in Poland and Hungary in 1956 several East European states had begun the transition from obedient satellite to junior ally' (a status that strengthens with the passage of time).

Two of the studies dispose in detail of the view that Moscow is running Eastern Europe as a colony. In the 1960s and 1970s Eastern Europe 'could be said to have enjoyed an advantageous economic relationship with the USSR'.[38] This situation arose not simply as a consequence of policy, but to some extent because other countries in the bloc brought superior skill and knowledge to bear during price negotiations. With the statistics against them, the Soviets sought to redress the unfavourable terms of trade, but even then felt it necessary to make 'implicit subsidies available to its . . . partners – several of whom have higher average living standards than their patron'.[39] Mongolia's complaint, published in Soviet journals, that, although it had a higher growth rate than other COMECON countries, the absolute gap between them was widening, led to a trebling of Soviet aid between 1974 and 1978. For many years the Soviet Union supplied the bloc with extremely cheap oil; the new sliding price, related to the world market, still entails a considerable subsidy.[40] There is no chorus of economic enterprise. Under the bloc's interested party principle countries are not obliged to take part in joint projects. Poland, Hungary, Rumania and Czechoslovakia joined GATT when it was still officially anathema to the Soviet Union. Rumania's absence from several joint investment projects makes it debatable whether its membership of COMECON is more *de jure* than *de facto*.[41] After having successfully resisted an attempt to maintain it as a COMECON market garden and supplier of raw materials, Rumania became in 1980 the only Warsaw Pact country to make an industrial agreement with the European Economic Community. Moscow has endorsed economic reforms once considered as 'revisionist'. In 1964 one of the contributors to the Chatham House study found a 'most businesslike atmosphere' when he was invited to lecture economic planners on reform in Moscow and Tashkent.[42] In December 1966 the Soviet delegation to a conference of economists in Prague supported a new Czech economic blueprint.

The Soviet Union has met with considerable resistance to its foreign policies. All of the other Warsaw Pact countries, including the GDR, have declined to extend their defence commitment to socialist borders outside Europe – that is to say, to the Sino-Soviet border – a region of great concern to Moscow. Hungary, Poland and Rumania have been unhelpful towards Soviet intervention in Afghanistan. Czechoslovakia has firmly objected to underwriting the reconstruction of Vietnam, while Rumania has refused to have anything to do with it. Rumania's intransigent gestures of independence are well enough known. It established diplomatic relations with the FRG before other Warsaw Pact countries had done so, maintained diplomatic relations with Israel after others had broken them off, and developed a special relationship with Yugoslavia and, more audaciously, China. Along with Western communist parties, it blocked Moscow's move to establish itself as the world leader of communism. While disagreeing with Dubcek's reforms, it defended Czechoslovakia's right to self-determination. It bought French helicopters and British aeroplanes, and refused to take part in Warsaw Pact manoeuvres or to commit itself to increased defence expenditure. The GDR has also created difficulties for the Soviet Union in international relations. When early in the 1970s Moscow began to respond to signals from Bonn for a *rapprochement*, the GDR annoyed the Soviet Union by trying to block the process. Moscow eventually pursued its course, but its path was 'far from smooth'.[43] This episode has a double significance: it illustrates both the potential strains in the Eastern bloc and the Soviet Union's willingness to risk intensifying them in the interests of peace with the West.

The burden of Moscow's buffer system is so obviously heavy that a Western academic has raised the question of whether it is worth while.[44] The diverse interests within the Warsaw Pact demand careful calculation. If, for instance, Moscow provides too much help to appease the Poles, it risks antagonizing the other members. Nationalism, of which the leaders claim to be the custodians, thus supplementing their bogus Marxist claim to legitimacy, causes tension. Every government, except that of Husak in Czechoslovakia, 'makes no bones about defending the national interest, even in competition with its "socialist allies" '.[45] In debates on pricing policy alignments against the Soviet Union's position switch in accordance with national needs. With so many pressures to contain, Moscow is hardly likely to welcome, let alone try to enforce, the adherence of new, industrially powerful members to its troublesome group; it is already sufficiently concerned about East German efficiency. If large nations of Western Europe were brought in the challenge to their dynamism would produce a reaction that would ensure their rapid ascendancy; the tendency of East European countries to look westwards in economic affairs would increase; and the Kremlin would be confronted with unmanageable problems – which it would be the first to foresee.

Chapter 9

The risks: an assessment

While Western rulers warn that it would be dangerous to renounce nuclear weapons, they only make a vague estimate of what the risk is and are therefore unable to weigh it against that of possessing them. Nor do they look at the question in the light of Western Europe's greatly diminished stature in the world. In September 1943 Roosevelt was already able to forecast the demise of West European power, and said that nothing could stop Russia from dominating Europe after the war.[1] At that time Roosevelt appears to have been influenced by the spectacle of the Russians driving out the Germans, after having recovered 185,000 square miles of territory in the carnage of the previous winter. By the following year, however, he had found the Russians to be 'perfectly friendly'; they were not 'trying to gobble up the rest of Europe or the world' and had no 'crazy ideas of conquest'.[2] But this restatement did not invalidate his prediction of Russia's rise, nor that of his chiefs of staff that the end of the war would 'produce a change in the pattern of military strength more comparable . . . with that occasioned by the fall of Rome than with any other change during the succeeding fifteen hundred years';[3] for Western Europe, when it comes to a point, has been reduced to not much more than a spectator in the dangerous and senseless power game being played by Moscow and Washington. As two leading American specialists in foreign policy put it:[4]

> Western Europe is no longer the center of world power, yet it is there that the key to the Cold War may be found. No geographical region of the world is more crucial to the political outcome of the U.S.-Soviet global rivalry.

It is mainly this historical fact that causes Washington to disdain European opinion when devising tactics in the struggle for world supremacy, although arrogance and ineptitude also play an important part. If Western Europe were realistically concerned with its survival, it would examine carefully whether or not it had any concern with Russo-American rivalry – any more than neutral countries had with the two world wars. It would not confuse itself with vainglorious utterances and acts which assume that it still possesses a power that it has lost. And it would not underestimate Soviet society by applying political criteria that have no place in Russian history and culture.

While no dominant minority is likely to examine at depth the causes of the decay over which it presides, it should be possible for at least some influential people to grasp the significance of events on the surface. After the Second World War Russia was confronted with the dual problem of backwardness and devastation. Although Roosevelt's forecast proved to be essentially correct, there was no obvious reason why Russia should rise to be more powerful than the rest of Europe combined, thus attaining a status previously unknown in modern European history. Stalin's ruthless leadership is an insufficient explanation of this astounding development, since the effort required the participation of more people than could be merely bullied into action. A large number of Soviet citizens believed that they were building a better type of society and their endeavours and attitudes were such that in the early 1930s Sidney and Beatrice Webb, the fabian socialists, after making observations in the USSR, published a work entitled *Soviet Communism: A New Civilization*? Whether or not the Russian idealists were mistaken in their hopes, their faith constituted a dynamic contribution to the USSR's growing strength. While many people were coerced during the industrial drive that followed the Second World War, others voluntarily sacrificed the present for the future. As we saw in chapter 3, some older Russians now lament that an easier life has weakened the spirit that made it possible. If willingness to deny oneself for the welfare and security of the next generation is a sign of moral strength, there was a strong moral streak in Soviet society, whatever else may have accompanied it. This, and the ever present fear of yet another attack from the West, was a big factor in the creation of Russia's industry and arsenal.

It was different in the post-war West. Instead of self-sacrifice, we find unprecedented self-indulgence; instead of discipline, permissiveness. Although Western Europe believed, or pretended to believe, that it was under some kind of Soviet threat, money that could have been used to train and equip conventional armed forces was spent on what the previous generation would have considered to be unheard-of luxuries. Appetites were whetted by imbecilic TV advertising, on which huge sums were squandered. Such was the obsession with newly-acquired purchasing power that the people expected their real incomes not only to be maintained but to rise even after the price of oil had been quadrupled. This unreasoning consumerism had two consequences that could prove disastrous. Outclassed by Russia's conventional forces, Western Europe increasingly relied on nuclear weapons to the point at which it rejected a Soviet challenge to declare, as the Russians had done, that it would not be the first to use them; unwilling to make the sacrifices essential to its independence, it leaned on the United States for its defence.

There was no good reason why Western Europe could not have united, disciplined itself, contained its personal spending, standardized its weapons and established a joint force under a unified command, which would have made it completely independent of the United States. But the nations comprising West European civilization preferred to indulge themselves and to defend national shibboleths. Instead of unifying their defence, they vied with one another to capture the Third World arms market. In other fields they vaguely saw the need for substantial integration, but confined their efforts in that direction to measures such as monetary stabilization and the harmonization of agricultural and other products, which has done more to create intra-European animosity than anything since the Second World War. Failure to take the bold action needed to achieve unity and avoid dependence on an ally on the other side of the Atlantic is not merely a sign of decline; it is, *ipso facto*, decline – in a very advanced stage. It need not have happened, but it did, and is irreversible. As Roosevelt predicted when the Russians were rolling back the Wehrmacht, the USSR has emerged as the only real power in Europe and the other nations are small in relation to it. It is necesary to look at this turn in history with the detachment of a future historian or an observer on another planet. Not to recognize the new pattern would be illogical, imprudent and even unaesthetic. To attempt to avoid the outcome by threatening to press the nuclear button invites more danger than the issues are worth. Slogans such as 'fighting for freedom' are irrelevant. A nuclear war would not be a fight but a holocaust.

Nor, as we saw in chapter 3, is comfort to be gained by imagining that the USSR is on the brink of economic collapse. While the technological balance lies in the West's favour, Soviet technology is considerable. The Tokamak experimental reactor, constructed at the I.V. Kurchatov Institute of Atomic Energy in Moscow in the late 1960s, led to a surge of Western research into the possibilities of providing energy from atomic fusion. Comparing current work in various countries, the European Communities' Fusion Review Panel describes the Soviet theoretical contributions as outstanding; the quality of European work is rated as good, but the panel finds that more co-ordination is required.[5] In a study sponsored by the Royal Institute of International Affairs Raymond Hutchings says that official Soviet doctrine aims at a more rapid advance in science than in technology. He believes that this approach results from (1) the view that fundamental discoveries will be useful for military and non-military purposes and (2) to some extent a desire for knowledge for its own sake, rather than the acquisition of wealth.[6] The Soviet agency, Licensintorg, sells industrial licences throughout the Western world. The agency says that since its formation in 1962 it has sold to the United States twice as many licences as it has bought from it. These include the purchase by J. Ray McDermott of a machine used to construct large-diameter tubes, in the installation and use of which American engineers underwent instruction in the USSR. Kaiser Aluminium uses a Soviet process. USSC manufactures Soviet instruments for stitching blood vessels. Nippon Steel bought a Soviet electrical process for making large metal bars. Salzgitter, in Western Germany, manufactures polyethylene by means of a revolutionary process developed by Soviet and East German engineers. According to Licensintorg, more than 80,000 inventions are registered in the Soviet Union each year.[7] Western specialists agree that the Soviet economy is impervious to serious damage by boycott. If Western Europe had fallen in with the United States and withdrawn from the gas pipeline project, the necessary resources would have been transferred from other sectors. What is significant is that the USSR has the financial and technological ability to construct the pipeline, despite formidable technical difficulties in the low temperatures of Siberia, while the West needs the venture to provide employment. When the pipleline is finished the hard currency earned by the gas will be a source of Soviet economic strength.

Some may say that in building its armed forces Russia has had the unfair advantage of an authoritarian government, which is not obliged to heed the whims of an electorate. There are two answers to that argument. The first is that the Russian people, in the light of past experience, are too afraid of the West to need forceful persuasion that the Soviet arsenal is indispensable; the second is that a political system in which consumerism is allowed to outweigh real needs has a low survival value and must be held to account by those who think of security in military terms. Whether one reasons within an orthodox framework or that of this book, Western Europe has failed. The view taken here is that armed defence against Russia is not necessary and that, if it were, it would not be in Western Europe's interests to engage in it, particularly if the war were nuclear. But when a society believes, as Western Europe does, that it should defend itself by military means and devotes large sums to that end without spending enough, and without taking the other essential measures already mentioned, then it is well on the way down; for it has neither the will to take adequate customary action nor the vision to see an alternative. Fortunately the decline provides a challenge, which, if properly met, could give Western Europe a fresh start. We shall come back to this in the next chapter. Meanwhile we shall keep within a conventional reference frame.

In assessing American nuclear intentions, the Russians are handicapped by Washington's confusion; this is all the more dangerous, because it creates the additional hazard of Russian misinterpretation. In an article written for *Foreign Affairs* Robert McNamara, who was Secretary of Defence during the Vietnam War, George Kennan, former American Ambassador in Moscow, McGeorge Bundy, President Lyndon Johnson's Special Assistant for National Security Affairs, and Gerard Smith, chief of the US SALT delegation in 1969–72, said doctrine had succeeded doctrine until today the 'disarray that currently besets the nuclear policy of the Alliance is obvious'.[8] Arguments on nuclear strategy are based on shifting premises, and the muddle has become so great that it is a subject of academic study. The only constant is the pressure of the arms lobby, to which Reagan appears to be particularly vulnerable. In an article entitled 'The Great Defense Deception' James Fallows wrote that Reagan's military proposals had little to do with defence, or even concepts, but with sheer quantities.[9] When the administration announced its huge leap in defence expenditure, it did not say what the money was to be spent on; it only revealed that it intended to spend during five years a sum that was nearly three times the total spent on the Vietnam War, in real terms. Little account appears to be taken of limitations in technical capacity. The Trident, a very large submarine, nuclear-powered and nuclear-armed, to which Britain is committed, was approved in the early 1970s. The first was to have gone into service no later than April 1979, but trials did not begin until the middle of 1981. One cause of the delay was the discovery that the manufacturer's stocks included steel with poor welding qualities and inferior crack-resistance, in bar sizes that could have been used in 126,000 places in the Trident. The company had no record of having inspected tens of thousands of welds in the submarine and other vessels. Re-inspection was ordered. When the company examined such welds in the Trident as were still accessible, 2,772, or one-third of those inspected, proved to be defective.

Soviet-American rivalry, bureaucratic momentum, imponderable factors and, in the United States, the greed of some for profits and the need of others for employment have contributed to creating a stupendous nuclear Juggernaut, which is out of control. All that stands in its way in ruling circles is the impossible and pointless argument about parity – impossible because the diversity and location of the weapons makes any definition of parity arbitrary, and pointless because it boils down to a question of overkill, of whether one side can go on firing missiles after it has wiped out all that matters in the other. Kennan has repeatedly emphasized his view that the Russians are not clearly superior in nuclear weapons. In this he has the support of certain American experts, including Paul Warnke, former US SALT II chief negotiator, who said that Reagan had been 'badly misinformed' when he declared that Russia had definite superiority. He explained:[10]

> If you look at 100 per cent of both forces, the respects in which we have the edge more than balance the respects in which the Soviets have the edge. We have the edge in the most important respect, which is survivability, because . . . over 50 per cent of our strategic warheads [are] on the least vulnerable part of the nuclear deterrent triad . . . ballistic-missile submarines.

In an interview published in *The Guardian* McNamara said that arguments that Moscow could get away with a first strike against the United States were absurd.[11] To destroy America's 1,000 Minuteman missiles Russia would have to land two warheads of one megaton each on every site. This amounted to 2,000 megatons, roughly 160,000 times the power of the Hiroshima bomb. America would certainly retaliate once such an operation began. McNamara added:

> The idea that the Soviets are today sitting in Moscow and thinking, 'We've got the Americans over a barrel because we're capable of putting 2,000 megatons of ground-burst on them and

in such a situation we know they will be scared to death and fearful of retaliation, therefore we are free to conduct political blackmail', is too incredible to warrant serious debate.

McNamara said that even if Moscow could destroy the 1,000 Minutemen, it would not have a first-strike capability; for it still had to reckon with nuclear-armed submarines and bombers. Even the strength of Warsaw Pact conventional forces relative to NATO's was exaggerated; while the Eastern bloc had more tanks, for instance, these had been countered by an expansion of anti-tank weapons. McNamara said he had tried to correct misrepresentation of the balance when he was Secretary of Defence; but it appeared 'to serve the interests of some to consciously or unconsciously overstate the Soviet strength and understate ours'. His assessment is confirmed by the International Institute for Strategic Studies, which says that although Western forces have defects that urgently need remedying, it cannot be concluded that NATO would be defeated in a conventional war.[12] McNamara recalled that in 1960 President John Kennedy was told that the Russians had nuclear superiority; but it had since become clear that this was not so. Within two years America had such an advantage that the air force was confident that it could succeed in a first strike. Moscow's response was to expand its own forces. America reacted in turn.

In the *Foreign Affairs* article McNamara, Kennan, Bundy and Smith said:[13] 'There is no current or prospective Soviet "superiority" that would tempt anyone in Moscow toward nuclear adventurism.' In the light of this judgment, the outcry at Russia's progressive replacement of its obsolete SS–4 and SS–5 missiles, which have been targeted on Western Europe since the early 1960s, with more advanced, triple-headed SS–20s needs examination. Even within the concept of effective deterrence – which this book rejects – there are more pertinent considerations than the modernization of these missiles. In a study of such issues, Gregory Treverton, of the IISS, says it could be considered less surprising that the old SS weapons, which take at least a day to prepare for firing, should be replaced than that Russia took so long to develop new models.[14] Treverton believes that the issue of nuclear weapons in Europe cannot be isolated from the general strategic balance; 'a "Eurostrategic balance" simply does not exist.' The defence of Western Europe certainly does 'not necessarily require Western capabilities in Europe somehow matched to, or "countering" given Soviet weapons'. Treverton says that 'despite all the changes, if

Western Europe is in some impressionistic way "hostage" to Soviet continental weapons, it is still only slightly more so than a decade ago.'

The four authors of the *Foreign Affairs* article go farther than Treverton. They are sceptical about Reagan's offer to cancel deployment of 572 cruise and Pershing II medium-range missiles in Europe if Russia dismantles all SS-20s. Their distrust arises from 'troubling' variations in arguments advanced to justify the deployment, which 'cast considerable doubt on the real purpose'.[15] They cite an argument, put forward by officials, that unless the United States can strike at Russia from Europe, there can be no confidence that US strategic forces will be committed to West European defence. The authors comment: 'This argument is logically distinct from any concern about the Soviet SS–20s, and it probably explains the ill-concealed hope of some planners that the Reagan proposal [zero option] will be rejected.' The four men, who are in a position to have inside knowledge of official American thinking, refer in their article to 'a seeming callousness in some quarters in Washington toward nuclear dangers'. If former high American officials such as these feel obliged to express misgivings about Washington's policy, the Russians cannot be expected to be less concerned.

It was German representations that led to NATO's decision in December 1979 to deploy the missiles. For some time the Americans had thought of developing new weapons, which could penetrate Russian electronic defence; Germany's raising of the SS–20 issue was seized upon as justification. Treverton says that the installation of the SS–20 'demonstrates a traditional objective of Soviet efforts: to deter NATO's resort to nuclear weapons in war, to deter escalation if NATO goes nuclear and to have some chance of avoiding destruction on Soviet territory.'[16] If this interpretation of the Soviet military mind is correct, NATO's decision to upset a *status quo* that had been established for two decades was a blunder. The old models were unquestionably due for replacement and the SS–20 posed no qualitatively new threat. What has happened, Treverton points out, is that the overall strategic balance has been changed by the emergence of 'something like strategic parity between the United States and the Soviet Union', which previously was at a disadvantage.[17] But it is not the SS–20s that have made the difference. Two points arise from Treverton's analysis. The first is that the arguments of West European politicians and newspapers along the lines of 'they can fire at us, so why shouldn't we be able to fire at them?' are a primitive reaction in the complex strategic situation that he describes. The second is that in excluding from the concept of parity the expanding French submarine force and Britain's sixty-four Polaris weapons, which it proposes to replace with more than 500 highly accurate Trident warheads, Western leaders must know that they are adopting an unreasonable stand that the Soviets cannot accept.

From the Soviet point of view, as Treverton says, the cruise and Pershing II missiles 'are an *additional* American strategic option against the Soviet Union, on top of America's strategic triad, and one which might allow the United States to wage a nuclear war against the Soviet Union without involving her own territory'.[18] Russian arguments assume approximate parity (in 1982) in medium-range weapons, including French and British. But according to the IISS, the Warsaw Pact has an advantage of 'about 1.57:1' in the number of Allied European medium-range warheads that could survive counter-attack and reach their targets. The nicety with which the ratio is taken to two decimal places, and then regarded as only an approximation, reflects the pseudo-scientific nature of much nuclear war analysis. Because of technical complexities and non-quantifiable variables, it is impossible to arrive at any precise figure. For example, the power of a warhead needed to destroy a target is proportional to the cube of the directional error. A smaller number of more accurate missiles, of lower megatonnage, could therefore be more effective than a large number that were more powerful; to what extent this was an advantage would depend on the nature of the target – a missile silo, military headquarters or a city, for instance. Then, among other elusive factors, is the question of whether or not the missiles would survive; the IISS estimates that because Soviet planes are more up to date 29 per cent of their air-delivered missiles would hit the target compared with 23 per cent for NATO; what would happen to the others is not clear.

But none of this matters. More useful than an approximation to two decimal places is the warning of the four authors of the *Foreign Affairs* article that the world is confronted with 'massive thermonuclear overkill'. In this situation it is of no importance whether the Russians or the IISS are nearer the truth, assuming that the truth could ever be computed. Nor does it matter that the SS–20 has three warheads and is more accurate than missiles launched from submarines. If the Russians fired their SS–20s, the submarines, accurate or not, could inflict fearful devastation. It is not like a game of chess. More serious for the Russians – and they make great point of it – is that the cruise, though slower than the swift Pershing II, can penetrate their defensive screen without being detected; this, as they say, increases the possibility of an attempt at a successful first strike. With their anxiety increasing, the Russians are certain to seek a riposte, the least dangerous of which will be a further escalation of the nuclear arms race. Much depends on what they think the Americans are up to. Their conclusions could be right or wrong, and their consequent action benign or disastrous. But a Western Europe bent on survival would consider whether or not it was necessary to force them to a point of decision. That could well have been what Moscow was trying to communicate when it warned on 30 November 1982 that the new deployment increased the danger of nuclear war. Commenting on this statement, Adam Roberts, of St Anthony's College Oxford, recognized in a BBC World Service broadcast that the Russians were genuinely anxious that the proposed installation of MX missiles in America and cruises and Pershing IIs in Europe, backed by the Stealth bomber, could constitute the possibility of a first strike.

It is significant that four leading Americans, three of them with experience of military matters and one a former ambassador to Moscow, should have become sufficiently alarmed by Washington's nuclear expansion to wage a campaign against it. In his interview (*The Guardian*) McNamara deprecated the fact that Americans were being increasingly told that they should be prepared to fight a limited nuclear war. Some people, he said, were talking about atomic bombs as if they were rifle bullets or artillery shells; the Russians, on the other hand, with their experience of casualties, were more sensitive to the impact of war on their people than Americans seemed to be in statements and strategic analyses. Three times in the interview McNamara emphasized that the Russians, whatever their aims, were 'not mad'. His denunciaiton of false information, wrong estimates and reckless policy, and his explanation of Russian fears, leave no doubt where he thought the madness lay. McNamara's interviewer asked him how it happened that 'madmen' were in charge. His answer was: 'Because the potential victims have not been brought into the debate, and it's about time we brought them in.'

We shall now consider the measures that a civilization could adopt to survive in the circumstances described in this and the previous chapters. These will be discussed in order of stages in a diplomatic process, not effectiveness in ensuring survival.

1 An immediate freezing of nuclear weapons, which Russia has proposed. This means that Western Europe would forbid the deployment of the cruise and Pershing II missiles on its soil and that Britain would abandon its purchase of the immensely expensive Trident. According to an opinion poll conducted in April 1982, before Reagan's decision to deploy the MX system, a freeze would have the support of 68 per cent of Americans.[19] Among leading proponents of this policy are Warnke (former US SALT II chief negotiator) and Roger Molander, former nuclear strategist in the National Security Council, who said: 'I have never met . . . a US military officer who would trade the strategic forces of the United States for those of the Soviet Union.'[20] The official trend was summed up by Edward Luttwak, a Pentagon consultant, who said that the importance of parity depended on 'whether you believe in limited nuclear war or not'. He explained:[21]

> If you think everybody is going to throw everything at each other, including the kitchen sink, then the difference in the over-all total hardly counts. However, if nuclear weapons are going to be used . . . in controlled doses, it makes a very big difference.

There is no space here to discuss the small-dose theory in detail; it is perhaps enough to cite the four authors of the *Foreign Affairs* article, who said:[22]

> It is time to recognize that no one has ever succeeded in advancing any persuasive reason to believe that any use of nuclear weapons, even on the smallest scale, could reliably be expected to remain limited. Every serious analysis and every military exercise, for over 25 years, has demonstrated that even the most restrained battlefield use would be enormously destructive to civilian life and property. There is no way for anyone to have any confidence that such a nuclear action will not lead to further and more devastating exchanges.

As Sir Martin Ryle, the Cambridge physicist, said, citing a designer who resigned in protest, the Trident was conceived not to deter but to strike first – a capability at which both America and Russia were aiming; whoever was the aggressor, mobile, medium-range missiles would ensure the destruction of any European nation holding nuclear weapons.[23] As the arms race escalates and political tensions increase, aggravated by economic crisis, the possession of nuclear weapons will make Western Europe not more but less secure; for, as Sir Martin said, one or other side is bound to try a surprise attack sooner or later. Apart from such considerations, it is useless to imagine that the West can gain a significant advantage. This point was emphasized by Senator Gary Hart, a member of the Senate Armed Services Committee; he said that because lack of political constraint enabled the Soviet leadership to use whatever resources it considered necessary for its armed forces, the United States could even lose the arms race in quantitative terms.[24] Since the West cannot win the race, and since mutual destruction is already assured if nuclear war breaks out, Western Europe has a chance to do something radically original for the first time in centuries – by simply putting an end to escalation. Not even loyalty to the United States need inhibit this measure; for while American territorial security does not require additional missiles in Europe – rather the opposite – the British Trident, according to Sir Martin, would only increase the destructive power of the United States by 1 per cent. The Americans are producing more than enough Tridents for themselves.

2 Western Europe could abolish the strategy of first nuclear strike, whether or not this doctrine was camouflaged by the term 'flexible response' or any other euphemism. It was mainly to advocate such a change that the four Americans wrote their article for *Foreign Affairs*. They point out that since NATO was formed in 1949 it has relied 'on the asserted readiness of the United States to use nuclear weapons if necessary'[25] to repel aggression, conventional or otherwise. Kennedy had misgivings about this policy. But when he promised that America would not strike first, there was, Field Marshal Lord Carver recalls, 'considerable concern in Nato'.[26] Kennedy then said that the United States might strike first at Soviet forces engaged in aggression beyond their borders, but not at Soviet territory. Lord Carver says that 'flexible response', in fact a first strike, emerged as a compromise. There are military objections to this strategy. The most obvious is that it could lead to the destruction of the people whom armed forces are supposed to defend. Another is that reliance on early use of nuclear weapons could have created an inconsistency between military plans and those that political leaders would be willing to adopt in a crisis. Field Marshal Lord Carver says that the only effective deterrent to aggression is a convincing conventional force; he deplores NATO's training of its forces around the concept of a first nuclear strike:

> That strategy has been incredible and irrational for over 20 years, ever since the Soviet Union gained the capability to answer back in kind at every level, as Liddell Hart pointed out in his book *Deterrence or Defence* in 1960. To initiate nuclear war would not redress or restore the situation: it would be an act of unredeemable folly.

The four Americans say that the profusion of nuclear systems makes it more difficult than ever to construct rational plans for the first use of these weapons by anyone; this could lead to an irrational first strike by either side. They argue that the gap between the two conventional forces has been exaggerated and that NATO countries could provide, without undue budgetary strain, the additional weapons and men that, in their view, abandonment of the first-strike strategy requires. What is needed, they maintain, is a plan for second use, which would leave the Soviet Union in no doubt that it should adhere to its declared policy of no first use; 'we already have in overflowing measure' the weapons needed for this purpose. The authors add:[27]

> A posture of effective conventional balance and survivable second-strike nuclear strength is vastly better for our own peoples and governments, in a deep sense more civilized, than one that forces the serious contemplation of 'limited' nuclear scenarios that are at once terrifying and implausible.

3   Western Europe could extricate itself from its risky and unpredictable alliance with the United States, no matter what financial sacrifice was needed to enable it to defend itself, assuming for the moment that defence were necessary. This is the minimum requirement for its security, to say nothing of its self-respect. America, because of its inexperience, ethnic division, irresponsible feuds in the administration, remoteness, interests that conflict with those of Europe and the very style of its diplomacy is unsuited to be a major ally, let alone Europe's leader, in a world threatened with a holocaust (see chapter 2). Western Europe has diminished itself to such a lowly status that it is not even present at Soviet-American wrangles, which could prove fatal to it, over strategic arms limitation and reduction. On the whole Western Europe's experience is

that of France, as described by its Foreign Minister, Claude Cheysson, who said on 6 December 1982 that Washington did not inform Paris of its decisions until hours before implementing them, and had not consulted the French on any important matter for seven months. With or without consultation, Western Europe is tied to the United States by a feeling of obligation and, despite occasional protests, a reluctance to offend what it sees as a protector. In these circumstances it is easily manoeuvred into supporting or accepting reckless statements and actions, which may have no larger purpose than that of winning an American election. The dangers inherent in this complaisance are increased by American diplomatic ineptitude. Washington's failure to ratify the SALT II agreement, which was made after years of negotiation, recalls the muddle over the Treaty of Versailles and the League of Nations. The dumping of the Russians within weeks of having proposed co-chairmanship of a conference on the Middle East unnecessarily exacerbated tension. On 16 October 1981 Reagan made a thoughtless and barely comprehensible remark, which was interpreted as meaning that the United States saw the possibility of fighting a limited nuclear war in Europe. Brezhnev, doubtless with Western opinion in mind, commented that 'it would be good if the President of the United States would make a clear and unambiguous statement rejecting the very idea of nuclear attack as criminal.' Contributing to a series of contradictory American statements, in which the administration's built-in power struggle played an inevitable part, Haig said on 4 November that Reagan had been 'precisely right'; he confirmed that there was an option that if the Russians attacked Western Europe with conventional arms, the West would fire a tactical nuclear weapon 'for demonstration purposes'. The next day the Defence Secretary, Caspar Weinberger, said there had been a suggestion to that effect in the 1960s, but that at present there was 'absolutely nothing, in any plan', which remotely resembled that doctrine. An official statement was then issued to resolve this contradiction. But at a press conference Reagan, under pressure from journalists, revived the controversy when he said there seemed to be some confuson about whether a limited nuclear strike was part of NATO strategy or not; he had yet to receive a reply on that issue. Rather than let the world think that the President was ignorant about such an important matter, the White House spokesman said immediately after the conference that Reagan knew the answer, but did not feel disposed to give it. Whatever he knew, Reagan's handling of the matter from the beginning suggested that he and his entourage could scarcely be trusted with the delicate task of dealing with the Russians.

The fact is, as Lord Carver pointed out, that NATO has long been determined to use nuclear weapons if the Russians launch a successful conventional attack. NATO leaders repeatedly emphasized this point after the Reagan blunder had accustomed the West European public to the idea; previously it had been kept rather dark. This so-called doctrine has further implications. In October 1981, just after Reagan had broached the subject, *Pravda* published a letter, which said that Jack Kangus, a member of the Hudson Institute, in a discussion with Soviet specialists in Moscow, had raised the possibility of a nuclear war limited to Europe. The institute, which advises the Pentagon on certain matters, was founded by Herman Kahn, who developed the idea of a successful first strike (see chapter 1). Kangus was the guest of the US Embassy, which said after the disclosure that he had not been speaking officially. Subsequently he told the author that although he had not been misreported, his remarks had been misinterpreted. He had only discussed doctrine and had not suggested that the USA and USSR should agree to confine nuclear war to territories not their own. Nevertheless there are influential Americans who obviously hold the view that war will inevitably break out between America and the Soviet Union sooner or later and that, when that happens, it would be desirable to confine it once again to that time-honoured battleground, Europe. Certainly, if the Russians fired their missiles westwards, the Americans would not risk annihilation of their own cities by retaliating from American territory.

As the differences over steel, farm products, the Soviet gas pipeline and, above all, the gains and losses of détente would suggest, there is a conflict of interest between the United States and Europe, which can never be more than patched up. The United States sees itself increasingly as having more to gain economically in Latin America than in Europe, although there its prospects are largely illusory, as is indicated by the rescue operation needed to save Mexico and Brazil from serious default in debt servicing. While Reagan supported Britain during the Falklands war, he was under strong pressure from pro-Latin American lobbyists to declare neutrality. At the height of the conflict, on 25 May 1982, Argentina's national day, he tried to extricate himself by sending a message to President Galtieri, reaffirming 'the common interests and values that unite Argentina [in which 15,000 people rounded up by death squads have disappeared] and the United States'. Galtieri bluntly replied that US support for Britain made the message 'incomprehensible'. It was not until 2 November that Washington got on course again, when it supported an Argentinian motion in the United Nations General Assembly calling for negotiations on sovereignty over the Falklands. This meant that Washington was leaning more towards Latin America than towards its closest partner in the Atlantic alliance – a stance that Mrs Thatcher, unwittingly echoing Galtieri, described as 'disappointing and incomprehensible'.

It would not be going too far to say that there is a streak of dislike of Europe in the United States. This is complex in its origin, but on the more obvious plane it is manifest in irritation that Europe's economic recovery from the war, set in motion by the Marshall plan, has gone much farther than Americans expected in the 1940s. Instead of remaining a grateful client, Western Europe has become an often aggressive competitor. Instead of toeing Washington's political line, it has come to demand being treated as an equal; one government, the French, included communists among its ministers, despite official American expressions of disapproval. When America is confronted, as it is sure to be, by continued and deepening failure in its attempts to solve its economic and social crises, this resentment will intensify, and Europe will appear increasingly to American eyes as a loss that can be written off, for example, in a nuclear war. De Gaulle had no doubt about American anti-European feelings. After his retirement in 1969 he told André Malraux:[28] 'Despite its power, I don't believe the United States has a long term policy. Its desire, and it will satisfy it one day, is to desert Europe. You will see.' Meanwhile Washington is oblivious to contradictions in its improvised policies. It tried to force its allies to break contracts and withhold equipment from the Soviet pipeline, on the ground that Europe must not become dependent on Soviet gas; at the same time it said that if martial law were lifted in Poland, the contracts could be honoured. Apart from this inconsistency, the sanctions had little point, since experts seemed to agree that they could only delay the construction for two or three years. As soon as the congressional elections were over on 2 November 1982 Washington began to negotiate other sanctions, which were less damaging to Europe; those directed against the pipeline were lifted on 12 November. This seemed to confirm the view that the pipeline sanctions were aimed largely at the substantial Polish-American vote, just as the attempt to sell the Soviets three times as much grain as it had bought in the previous year was a sop for the farmers; Moscow's response was to buy less.

That Western Europe should have placed its destiny in the hands of a nation that subjects foreign policy to the pressure of the parish pump is, as we have said, not a mere sign, but a fact, of decline. Nevertheless, fear that an economic crisis could eventually precipitate mass revolt has led Western rulers closer to recognizing that America is unfit to lead. The losses that would have resulted from obeying Washington's ukase on the pipeline finally provoked a show of independence; unemployment, bankruptcies and a naked American attack on national sovereignty achieved overnight what the greater danger of US foreign policy had failed to do in years. While it took the pipeline to bring about confrontation, the trend had already been apparent, particularly in Western Germany. Schmidt made it known that he found the Carter administration almost impossible to deal with. After Reagan's election he frequently complained that Washington's economic policy was harmful to the rest of the world and pointed out that the only trade sanction that could affect Russia would be a refusal to sell American grain. Dissent accelerated during the pipeline controversy. In October 1982 Francis Pym, British Foreign Secretary, spoke up in New York with a declaration that while Britain did not overlook issues such as Poland, a working relationship must be established with Russia; trade feelers in Moscow followed. But the most significant statement was made by Cheysson, who said on 21 July 1982 that Washington and Europe had begun a 'slow divorce'. He explained: 'We no longer speak the same language. There is a remarkable lack of understanding between Europe and the United States. The United States appears to be totally indifferent to our problems.' This under-reported statement was not an expression of pique, but of serious disillusionment. As The Economist has noted, President Mitterrand was much more enthusiastic about the Atlantic alliance than his predecessor, Giscard d'Estaing, and 'let no opportunity slip to reaffirm France's commitment' to it.[29] When he came to power he realized that the Americans 'were worried by his election and he set out to soothe them'. Casting prestige aside, he went so far as to take a Concorde day trip to Washington 'just to have a personal chat with President Reagan'. In the light of these efforts by the French President, the statement by his Foreign Minister on Washington's failure to understand Europe or show interest in its problems may well be a turning-point in European history. But little of consequence can be expected from it until more radical and widespread changes have taken place in West European thinking. If the divorce were made absolute it would not only benefit Europe but the United States, which would then be forced to assess the extent to which, with no advantage to its people, it has over-reached itself throughout the world.

A wiser Western Europe would also look at America's declining prospects. We have seen (in chapter 7) that its economy is in what Reagan called 'a hell of a mess', for which no end is convincingly in sight. Yet America cannot accept that its economic dominance, of which it seemed assured when Europe lay prostrate after the war, has gone forever; its Gross National Product fell from 50 per cent of the world's total in 1950 to 30 per cent in 1980 and is expected to be 20 per cent by the end of the century. In GNP per head it shares tenth place with France after Switzerland, Denmark, Sweden, Germany, Iceland, Norway, Belgium, Luxembourg and the Netherlands. Germans have twice as many paid holidays as Americans, whose males can expect to live four years less than Swiss. America's roads, bridges, sewers and water pipes have been described as 'all cracking up'.[30] The cost of repairing them has been estimated at $591,000 million, compared with the Government's plan to raise about $33,000 million for improvements spread over five years.

Like any ailing, or dying, giant, America could be dangerous. Military officers and military-minded civilians have great power. This is also true of the Soviet Union. But the difference is that in the United States sabre-rattling is linked to profits and employment, a factor that has ramifications throughout society; work-hungry districts vie with one another for military contracts. According to an American study, the outstanding historical trend inside the United States is the emergence of 'what could almost be seen as a new class, defined more by its relation to the means of total destruction than by a relation to means of production'.[31] Other research has shown that American business executives, together with military officers, 'provide the strongest support for Cold War positions'. Profits from war industries are used, as in other countries, to buy the allegiance of politicians by helping to finance their campaigns. After he had left the presidency General Dwight D. Eisenhower warned against the growing influence of the military complex, which wields great power through organizing and financing research, development, production and maintenance on a vast scale. Beer lists 152 private companies that employ a total of 1,500 retired or former military officers.[32] This reflects what one researcher calls a blurring and reduction of much of the distinction between public and private activities in an important branch of the American economy.[33]

This convergence of economic, military and political forces constitutes a risk that a Europe properly appraised of the needs of survival would not tolerate. If it did so, it could not complain if the consequence were a disaster. There is a tendency, even among the confused dominant minority, for Europeans to see this point. The feeling is most apparent in France, where there is some official thought of reviving the idea of a European defence community, but less in Britain, with its illusion of a special Anglo-American relationship, and in Western Germany, which fears being left undefended against its eastern neighbours. Germany, however, which is faced with the risk of becoming the world's next big battlefield, has sought a role of its own as what Schmidt called an interpreter between Russia and the United States – thus betraying a lack of confidence in American policy. Like Cheysson's statement that a slow divorce has begun between America and Western Europe, this could be an important sign.

But it is not seemly for West Europeans to blame the United States for a position in which they have placed themselves. Nor can they justly criticize America for pursuing what it seems to be its own interests, of which its concept is no more false than that of Western Europe. The Atlantic alliance is only part of America's total strategy. As a mere pawn, which can be sacrificed at any time for larger gains, Western Europe is always in danger of being removed from the board. Its alternative is to declare unequivocal neutrality in the pointless Soviet-American conflict and to seek a *rapprochement* with its East European neighbour on its own account. A slow divorce from the United States could be too late.

4 Unilateral nuclear disarmament. While any of the three measures already discussed would reduce tension, none, nor all taken together, would eliminate the risk of nuclear war. As the four Americans say, 'a destabilizing political change . . . might lead to panic or adventurism on either side.'[34] A nuclear-armed Western Europe, even though militarily independent of the United States, could easily be caught up in folly perpetrated by Americans or by some rash Soviet leader acting in a crisis that we cannot yet conceive. We have already noted in chapter 1 the abortive attempt to rescue hostages from Tehran, which, as planned, had little chance of success. Helicopters broke down, the commander was in tears and lives were lost. Miscalculation in a nuclear attack would be no less likely. Similarly, misjudgment of Russian intentions could precipitate a war that was unjustified by any criterion. The record of misinterpretation is well established. In the nineteenth century British governments spent large sums on military activities and an elaborate espionage network in Persia, and ruthlessly coerced the shahs, in the belief that Russia planned to invade India. Yet the threat to India is now known to have been a 'myth without substance' (see chapter 6, n. 4). In the same way, as we have noted earlier, the Russian intervention in Afghanistan was represented as a threat to the Gulf, although it obviously was not. In fact, predictable Afghan resistance serves to help protect the Gulf. It now seems that when the Kremlin was debating what to do about Afghanistan, the issue was whether the Red Army could control the rebellion. A Russian defector in Tehran said that the KGB had opposed the operation on the ground that Afghanistan would become Russia's Vietnam.

Since the West's dominant minority has so far been unable to discover what, Lord Carver says, has been obvious for more than twenty years – that a first strike can only bring disaster – it is unlikely to see the logical solution of the nuclear predicament, which, although it is easy to derive, involves a leap from the groove of habitual thinking and the purging of emotional impediments. A Western Europe that had a chance of coming to grips with this problem would first rid itself of a complex of prejudices, such as that by which Islamic fundamentalists who rose against the Shah and his American-created intelligence organization are branded as fanatics, while those who resist a Soviet-backed administration are hailed as patriots. It would not confuse dislike of the Soviet Government, or traditional aversion to the Russian culture in general, with a danger of aggression. It would see that to recover its lost dynamism it would have to stand on its own feet. It would not rely on an unsatisfactory trans-Atlantic ally, which had already warped its cultural personality, but would face up to its historical position and work from there. Here the fundamental fact is that for the first time in history a part of Europe, and a very considerable part, has declined to the level at which it has virtually no say in its destiny. Stepping aside for an objective view of current history, Western Europe would not mistake its wishes for reality; it would realize that it was in no position to challenge Russia in Europe and that it was maintaining an illusion of strength by an alliance that could lead to its destruction. Sobered by recognition of this fact, it would ask how deep was the malaise that led it to believe that it could compensate for such a fundamental weakness by threatening to press a nuclear button that would almost certainly annihilate itself as well as its enemy.

Such reflections could lead a morally improved Western Europe to examine more carefully the dangers confronting it. Having rejected the Atlantic alliance, it would have to look towards Russia afresh, and measure the risks of retaining nuclear weapons against those of abandoning them. It would need to postulate a range of possible Russian moves, from the least to the most harmful, that could follow unilateral nuclear disarmament, and estimate their probability. Important though such a task is, the present ruling minority is unlikely to undertake it; for in a disintegrating society the enemy without is seen as a greater danger than the malaise within. But Helmut Schmidt was on the way to seeing the real threat, dimly in public and perhaps more clearly in private. He said:[35]

> The world economic crisis . . . is at least as great a strategic danger to the cohesion of the West as anything we have talked about so far [missiles]. . . . How to get down the rates of interest in the Western world is a question of at least the same importance to me right now early in 1982, as all this missile business.

Schmidt was referring to the proposed deployment of cruises and Pershing IIs. His apparent realization that, in spite of incessant propaganda to the contrary, resolution of the missiles controversy was no more important to Western Europe than interest rates could have been advantageously followed by an examination of the feared consequences of unilateral nuclear disarmament, in so far as they can be articulated. These are, in order of improbability:

A   The Russians could invade Western Europe and rule it directly through governors. This is beyond reasonable probability. Moscow lacks the personnel for imperialism on so great a scale and has not shown any desire to preside over the administrative shambles that would result from such an adventure. Russia has never had fanciful ambitions in Europe. Having convincingly defeated the Prussians in the Seven Years War (1756–63), it withdrew its forces without territorial gain; meanwhile Russian officers, in full control of Königsberg, had mixed with the Prussian aristocracy and attended lectures given by Kant.[36] After French forces had occupied the Kremlin in 1812, the Russians pursued them to Paris, then returned home. There is no reason to believe that they have any ambition today to set themselves up all over Europe. They have enough to do at home.

B *The Russians could invade Western Europe and set up puppet governments*. In the light of the Soviet Union's record since the war and of its present external and internal commitments, this is extremely unlikely. The Russians, as we have seen, have not intervened militarily in Europe beyond their *cordon sanitaire*; on the contrary, they have shown restraint in withdrawing from Austria and in restricting their interest in Finland to what they regard as the minimum requirement for their security. While they tried, eventually without success, to ensure the subservience of all European communist parties, their aim was mainly to counter what they believed were potentially aggressive Western policies; their Marxist interpretation of history precluded any attempt to topple capitalism before it was ripe to fall of its own accord. It is important to be clear about this point. In Russia Marxism has served as a religion. But what the Russians sought to spread in Europe was not the system that they thought the collapse of capitalism would lead to, but the belief that, for reasons advanced by Marx, capitalism was doomed; their aim was not immediate subversion but the education of a historically conscious vanguard that would be ready when the day of reckoning came. It is belief in what amounts to the teleological force of the material dialectic, which constitutes the core of the ideology. There is a millenarian element in the Marxist construction; but, as always in millenarianism, a period of excited expectancy is followed by recognition that the millennium has an increasing tendency to recede, and less is said of it. At the beginning of the 1970s, if not earlier, it was already being argued in a Soviet academic journal that economic techniques could sustain capitalism for longer than Marxists had expected.[37] Moscow, no less than the West, was deceived by the boom of the 1960s and early 1970s. The Eastern bloc became involved in substantial deals with the capitalists, and to some extent depended on the importation of Western technology to satisfy the rising expectations of its people. The Western recession reduced its export outlets and, consequently, its capacity to repay the loans that had financed the importation of capital goods. In this respect it was harder hit than even some Third World countries, probably because its economies, though stable in themselves if sensibly managed, lacked the flexibility needed to cope with those that were not. As Philip Windsor, of the London School of Economics, has pointed out, Moscow has developed an interest in the prosperity of capitalism, rather than in its downfall; this is evident in specialist journals, but not in newspapers.[38] The Soviet Union wants and needs economic co-operation with the West, not merely to improve its technology, but because of a change in world economic dynamics; its economists, like those in the West, 'attribute a major role to post-Second World War technological change as an influence favouring greater internationalization of production and exchange'.[39] Philip Hanson, Senior Lecturer in Soviet Economics at the University of Birmingham, finds that a reduction in East-West trade tends to reduce the growth rate of trade between nations in the Eastern bloc's COMECON.[40] Doubtless it is in the light of such trends that in January 1983, the Soviet Union, despite the cold war, began to negotiate observer status in the General Agreement on Tariffs and Trade (GATT), which for years it had branded as a mere instrument of capitalism.

Throughout the capitalist world Soviet commercial attachés are trying to sell technology, not merely buy it, with some notable successes, as we have seen. What the Russians regard as fruitful exchanges of this kind have become important to their economy. They are not too proud to see advantages in some Western methods; in December 1982 an economist writing in *Pravda* suggested that the Soviet Union should follow a Western tendency to break up large industrial conglomerates into smaller, more efficient, automated units. The evidence suggests that the Eastern bloc has more reason to be dismayed than pleased by the Western crisis, which, in addition to hampering economic plans, has probably raised fears that the United States is heading for a débâcle that could precipitate some desperate act. Doubtless the Kremlin will be watching the possibilities of a capitalist collapse with concern; but if the breakdown comes, it will not be because of Soviet intervention. The linking of Eastern and Western economies is already too advanced for the Kremlin to ignore the effect that sudden and pointless dislocation would have on the temper of people in its bloc. More vigorously and purposefully developed, East-West co-operation could provide opportunities that the West vainly seeks in the Third World.

If for some inconceivable reason the Soviets were tempted not to wait for history to work itself out in lands beyond their *cordon sanitaire*, they would be confronted by enough difficulties to restrain them. We have already seen in the previous chapter the dilemmas encountered by the Soviet Union in its relations with its satellites. As we noted, these relatively small countries represent between them a history of dictatorship, subjection to foreign domination and weak national identity. If Moscow finds difficulties there, the problems that would confront it in larger countries, more advanced technologically and with well-rooted Western traditions, would be insuperable – weak though Western society has become compared with its dynamic past and its potential; it would be Poland and Afghanistan multiplied many times. The well established tendency of groups in COMECON to combine when they have common interests would be accentuated. No force would be able to prevent nations from lining up with those in the West when seeking better bargains from Moscow. The USSR already has enough junior partners; expansion would weaken, not strengthen, its power. This point will not have escaped Soviet leaders, who are not blinded by missionary zeal, but, as two American specialists, Ginsburgs and Rubinstein, say, are 'committed to careful analysis of the empirical record (at least as they are able to perceive it)' and to formulation of 'routine policy moves on the basis of commendably accurate appreciation of the relevant data'.[41]

There is also a military constraint. Overcommitted to policing operations in Eastern and Western Europe, the Soviet Union would be more vulnerable to China, which already has nuclear weapons targeted on important Russian centres (see chapter 7). Having failed to control its birth rate, China could sacrifice to economic advantage a number equivalent to the entire populations of Eastern and Western Europe. The Soviets, with their fear of a Chinese invasion, would be extremely unlikely to put their Asian territory at risk for gains that would be a constant strain on their policing forces. In February 1982 the commander of the US Rapid Deployment Force, Lieutenant General Robert Kingston, said: 'I feel strongly the Soviets do not want a direct military confrontation with the United States at this time in Southwest Asia or anywhere else.' The reason given was that they were 'tied down' in Afghanistan and Poland. If this were so, they would be unlikely to undertake heavier commitments, even if their present problems were resolved. No country could rule a substantial part of Western Europe, directly or indirectly, without considerable minority consent and the co-operation of security forces in the subjugated nations; if this were forthcoming, the cause would lie not outside Western Europe, but inside it. The Russians might possibly be tempted to press for low-price food from the West; but since it is only political opposition that prevents the European Commission from virtually giving them the butter mountain, this would not create a threat that would justify the risk of nuclear destruction.

There is a special reason why Moscow would not seek to exercise control over Western Germany: the outcome would certainly be reunification. Although the Kremlin has toyed with the idea of a reunified Germany, provided it were effectively neutralized, like Austria, reunification today would be a nightmare to the Soviets, equalled only by their fear of China. The Russians have a profound respect for German efficiency and organization, and they would regard a united Germany as a danger, whether it were communist or not. For this reason they would almost certainly not welcome even a West German economic breakdown that led to communism, since they would then be sandwiched between communist China and a communist Germany armed with nuclear weapons taken over from NATO. If Moscow could not dictate to communist China, after having helped to put it on its feet, it could certainly not control a united Germany. One of the most significant events in the twentieth century is that whether the system is communist or capitalist, it is Germans who have made the best job of it. Eastern Germany, isolated from the mollifying influence of Western democracy, has developed a streak of communist nationalism, which would be hard to distinguish psychologically from national socialism; in January 1983 its rulers reprimanded Catholic bishops who had protested against militaristic education in schools. Eastern Germany spends 6.3 per cent of its gross national product on its armed forces, compared with from 1.4 per cent to 2.8 per cent in the other junior Soviet bloc countries.[42] The German problem, as it is usually called in specialists' works, has yet to be solved, and the Russians are sure to resist, rather than foster, any tendency towards a solution that they see as a danger. They would be unlikely to promote reunification, under any social system, unless peace was assured from the Atlantic to the Urals. Western leaders and their advisers almost certainly know that for these reasons the Soviet Union has no designs on Western Germany, the occupation of which would be essential to any significant westward encroachment. Their motives for insisting that nuclear weapons are needed to defend Western Europe are therefore open to question.

C   Finlandization. Faced with the improbability, if not impossibility, that the Soviets would either occupy or, we might say, Hungarianize the whole or parts of Western Europe, leader writers and politicians have fallen back on Finlandization as a horror more to be feared than nuclear destruction. Generally, the idea is that Moscow, even though it did not attack, would blackmail other countries, as it is said to have blackmailed Finland. This subject is examined from various aspects by ten specialists in a work, the editors of which acknowledge their debt to the Bureau of Intelligence and Research of the US Department of State.[43] From these analyses it emerges that the term, Finlandization, has little, if any, useful meaning. One of the contributors, C. G. Jacobsen, Adjunct Professor of Strategic Studies at the Institute of Soviet and East European Studies, Carleton University, Canada, says that 'ironically, its utility derives perhaps less from its validity than from the extent to which its emotive projection is at variance with reality.'[44] Another, Elizabeth Young, finds that while the concept is perhaps indispensable in examining Soviet policy, 'it seems rather to dissolve on close inspection.' For the purposes of discussion, the two editors of the work boil down a longer definition of the term to the following:[45]

Finlandization describes the behaviour of a country whose foreign policy and domestic politics are strongly conditioned by a conscious desire to mollify and maintain friendly relations with Moscow, at the expense if need be of close ties with formal allies and traditional friends or of its own sovereignty.

Whatever the definition, Finlandization does not seem to be a worry in Finland itself. Jacobsen says:[46] 'Finnish governments of the post-war era have consistently termed Western concepts of "Finlandization" as very far off the mark as concerns the reality of the Soviet-Finnish relationship.' He points out that Urho Kekkonen, who was President for twenty-five years until illness forced him to retire in October 1981, and Juho Kusto Paasikivi, who laid down Finland's neutrality in the 1940s, were both 'convinced that the historical experience disproved the thesis of inherently aggressive Soviet intent, military, political, or ideological'. Both had emphasized the Soviets' consistent restraint and 'the continuity between the prewar demands of a Moscow too feeble to expect compliance and the postwar moderation of a Moscow capable of enforcing far further-ranging designs'. Jacobsen continues:

Accepting the defensive nature and legitimacy of Moscow's posture, they [Finnish leaders] have determined to satisfy its implied requirements, expecting *quid pro quo* freedom to pursue

Finnish preferences in the domestic political, economic, and cultural domains. In their interpretation of history, Moscow will forego opportunities to affect these as long as it remains satisfied that its security needs are met.

If the Finns are right, it follows that a term coined to denote their experience of Moscow could have no application in a neutral Europe.

The present Kremlin view of its security needs in this region has nothing to do with either ideology or imperialism, but is similar to that of the tsars. We need not go into the situation arising from the vulnerability of the Leningrad hinterland and the geography of the northern rim. One example will suffice to illustrate the strategic nature of Moscow's interest in Finland and its restraint in pursuing it. In the autumn of 1961 the Soviets became alarmed at an increase in NATO activity in Norway, Denmark and the Baltic Sea; they were particularly concerned about the operations of a naval force, the Baltic Area Patrol (BALTAP), and of the growing West German presence in the Baltic and Northern Europe. Under the 1948 treaty, which is the 'foundation stone of Finnish foreign policy',[47] Moscow asked on 31 October for consultations with Helsinki, which could have led to the entry of Soviet forces into Finnish territory to defend Finland, and hence the USSR. The aim was to restore the strategic balance. The Finns resisted the proposal and when Moscow made a second demand, tension between the two countries rose. But Kekkonen went to see Kruschev and argued that if the treaty were invoked, the consequence would be a 'war psychosis', disadvantageous to the Soviet Union. Moscow then desisted. But the BALTAP remained in waters close to Soviet shores. This incident was doubtless among the factors that led to the Soviet Union's naval build-up, which, certainly at the outset, was 'clearly defensive'. At that time its naval forces were greatly inferior to those of NATO. Now, as a consequence of the arms race, Soviet submarines, which may be able to shelter under ice, can 'shower any part of the United States with nuclear missiles' launched from the Arctic Sea.[48]

The only political constraint imposed on Finland by the Soviet Union is that no force can arise that would threaten Finnish neutrality, as interpreted by Moscow, or lead to an abrogation of the 1948 treaty. This, in my view, is the only sense in which the term Finlandization has any meaning. Finlandization denotes a regional, strategic phenomenon arising from geography, It has no general application, and is therefore of little, if any, value as a term. As George Maude, Docent in International Relations at the University of Turku, Finland, says:[49] 'At any rate by virtue of the [1948] treaty, Finland will hardly serve.' While, as Maude emphasizes, Moscow's example illustrating the general character of Finlandization, then Finland will hardly serve, while, as Maude emphasizes, Moscow's influence on Finnish politics should not be exaggerated, the constraint is none the less firm within its limits, although it has never taken the form of a military threat. It was strongly apparent in the 1950s, for example, when politicians who were distrusted in Moscow – they included supporters of a man who had been gaoled as a war criminal – were included in the government, while communists, who had emerged as the largest party in the preceding election, were excluded. Moscow withdrew its ambassador and slowed down fulfilment of its trade agreements, which worsened unemployment. Kekkonen went to the Soviet Union in January 1959, came to an understanding and resolved to keep out of office elements whom Moscow disliked. Nevertheless, at a luncheon given in Helsinki on 4 September 1960, Kekkonen said to Kruschev, his guest of honour: 'Even if the whole of the rest of Europe becomes Communist, Finland will remain a traditional Scandinavian democracy, if the majority of the Finnish people so wish, which I believe they do.' Maude observes:

> In many respects Finnish society may be summed up as a more democratic society than many others in Western Europe, and more democratic than several of those societies whose press organs are prone to see Finland in the process of Sovietization.

With the exception of a small, extreme right, Finns are not troubled by their inability to elect leaders who would involve them in the East-West conflict. Doubtless their attitude has been influenced by the substantial economic gain derived from their relationship with the Soviet Union. Finland has enjoyed both economic worlds. It has found in the planned economy of the Soviet Union a constant, reliable outlet for its goods, immune from market aberration and uncertainty; at the same time, free to trade how and where it likes, it has been able to exploit opportunities in other parts of the world. As the Swiss Bank Corporation's journal, *Le Mois économique et financier*, points out, Finland's close collaboration with Moscow brought it an especial advantage when the oil price rose.[50] Under five-year agreements equipment and services were automatically paid for with Soviet oil. In 1950, the journal says, Finland resembled more a Third World than an industrialized country; 43 per cent of its workers were engaged in agriculture and forestry, 30 per cent in industry and 27 per cent in services. In 1978 the corresponding figures were 12 per cent, 34 per cent and 54 per cent. The percentage of workers in primary industry is still high compared with that in Britain, Sweden and Switzerland (4–5 per cent); but this is because Finland's large area of forests is still economically important. In 1979 and in 1980 Finland achieved the highest growth in the OECD – 7.6 per cent and 5 per cent. In 1980 the rate of investment in machinery and other capital goods rose 40 per cent; unemployment fell to 4.8 per cent from 6.1 per cent in 1979 and 7.5 per cent in 1978. Fears of an increase in the balance of payments deficit were dissipated, largely by a 'strong progression of exports to the Soviet Union'; in the first six months of 1981 the balance was in surplus. The Swiss journal forecast that in future the rate of increase in exports to the Soviet Union would probably slacken in favour of those to the West. Industry had been modernized and was competitive.

In a survey of Finland *The Economist* says that in the past decade, while shipbuilding, notably in neighbouring Sweden, has suffered badly, Finland has built three new yards and has increased the industry's work force by 4,000.[51] A quarter of wells being sunk in the North Sea are being drilled from Finnish rigs. In 1981 Finland delivered to Norway the biggest rig ever made. Finland has built half of the world's icebreakers. Finnish construction firms are working on seventy projects in eighteen countries. They are engaged in huge undertakings in the Soviet Union, where Finnish workers 'made history in February [1982] by staging a four-week strike on Soviet soil'. It is not only oil that Finland receives from the USSR, which supplied two of its four nuclear power plants.

Finland's striking economic transformation conveys two important lessons for Western Europe. One is that the economy has been cushioned – to borrow a word from *The Economist* – by association with a planned system, which, while not given to bursts of acceleration, is at any rate dependable, despite irregularities arising from the way it is run, rather than from its design. The other is that although the Soviet Union retains an export pattern dominated by primary products, as in the Third World, Finland's exports have become predominantly (61 per cent) and increasingly non-primary. This means that Finnish dynamism has not been inhibited by the greater political and military power of the Russians – a point worth taking into account when assessing the risks of possessing or not possessing nuclear weapons. Finland is not constrained in its formal trade relations with other countries. Since the middle of the 1950s it has joined the Nordic Council and the OECD, and has signed a free trade agreement with the European Economic Community (now part of the European Communities) and a special agreement with the European Free Trade Association (EFTA), despite initial EFTA resistance.

While the idea of Finlandization serves little purpose in the context in which it is usually placed, Jacobsen has been able to suggest a use for the underlying concept. He begins his argument:[52] 'Certainly formal or demonstrable Soviet control or influence over Finnish economy and culture appears nowhere near as extensive as that of the United States in relation to Canada.' Jacobsen recalls Prime Minister Pierre Trudeau's complaint that living next to the United States is in some ways like sleeping with an elephant. He says: 'Perceptual reality might be better served if Finland was called Austrianized, and if the phenomenon usually associated with the term Finlandization was renamed Canadianization or Romanianization.' Canada, he finds, bears the same relation to the USA as Romania does to the USSR, despite flamboyant declarations of independence by both smaller countries. But whatever name is given to what has been observed in Finland, Western Europe would need to be suicidally vainglorious, and devoid of historical realism, if it were to risk a nuclear war to avert it.

D *The Soviets could rob the West of its oil supplies.* It is strange that Western leaders should be willing to risk the destruction of European civilization for such a dwindling asset as Middle East oil. It was estimated at the end of 1979 that proved world reserves, 640,000 million barrels, would last less than thirty years at the consumption rate (which subsequently declined) then prevailing.[53] At the end of 1980, according to the Institute of Petroleum, London, only 55.5 per cent of world reserves were in the Middle East. Theoretically, techniques being devised to improve the recovery rate could increase the duration of the reserves by more than 60 per cent, but 'vast capital expenditure is needed even to maintain the existing level of production.' The technical difficulties of raising the recovery rate are formidable; valuable work has been done, but more research is needed. Shell has pointed out that 'obtaining adequately qualified staff could become a constraint; experienced people are in short supply and long training is necessary.' There is also the problem of capital. Sir Nevil Macready, President of the Institute of Petroleum and Managing Director of Mobil Oil Company Limited, said on 9 October 1981 that although oil company profits were devoted largely to reinvestment in energy, rising costs made the expenditure insufficient. He questioned whether the world's commercial banks could provide the increasing amounts of risk capital required. In the United Kingdom producer and consumer government levies took more than 75 per cent of the $45 selling price paid by customers for the typical barrel of 1979 OPEC crude. Sir Nevil concluded: 'It seems to me clear that in the future more of the money taken out of energy by governments will have to be put back into energy.' Also clear is that the solution of Western Europe's future energy problem does not lie in nuclear defence of the Middle East's diminishing reserves. Many of the world's sedimentary basins have only been partly explored, or not explored at all. A number of them are in 'remote locations in inhospitable climates or in difficult offshore waters where costs are extremely high'.[54] Some of these are in the USSR. Doubtless the Soviet Union would co-operate with the West in developing those in its territory, as it has in constructing the gas pipeline from Siberia; it has, in fact, already made agreements with BP and Japanese firms.

The myopic consumerism that prevented Western Europe from developing an adequate conventional defence system – as conceived by those who think militarily – has also soaked up funds required to ensure its energy supplies. Capital, which can only be accumulated by reducing consumption, is needed not merely to maintain existing oil production and develop new sources, but for the discovery of alternative supplies. Progress has already been made in the exploitation of tide and wind. But a development that could greatly reduce the need for oil was announced by the A & M University, Texas, in October 1982. Research workers there claim to have proved that hydrogen can be produced cheaply from the water molecule by electrolysis, using the sun to supply the necessary energy. The university has applied for patents of new types of anode and cathode. It says that factories to produce the hydrogen could be built by 1990. Practically all that remains to be developed is a container to replace the petrol tank in cars and a system of injection, which would require no carburettor. A promising method of liberating hydrogen from water by means of a photovoltaic cell has been developed at the University of California, Berkeley. Then there is atomic fusion, which has aroused increasing hopes of an almost inexhaustible energy source since the Russians designed their Tokamak experimental reactor, mentioned earlier in this chapter. Some physicists think it will take twenty years of costly research to produce a demonstration reactor and fifty years before fusion could be put to general commercial use. If the West believes that its falling oil supplies are under a future Soviet threat, it is obvious that it is of the greatest strategic importance not to waste money on nuclear weapons, but to switch large sums to research into energy sources that will, in any case, be essential within the foreseeable future. Except in the very short term – a moment in history – to fight for the oil would be to fight for a desert.

E   The Soviets could apply various pressures.   Having discounted A and B and seen the irrelevance of C and the transience of D, a prudent minority would look at other possible Soviet intervention – always with a view to measuring the risk of retaining nuclear weapons against that of scrapping them. It is often said that the Soviets could deprive Western Europe of vital raw materials, other than oil. This is undoubtedly correct, but it is necessary to ask why they should do so. The USSR is almost entirely self-sufficient in minerals, some of which it possesses in abundance. According to a report made by the Commission of the European Communities,[55] the USSR has half the world's known manganese reserves; communist countries including China, which has 60 per cent, share 80 per cent of the world's tungsten, which is vital to the war industry; and 96 per cent of known platinum reserves are in the USSR and South Africa. It is impossible to establish any motive that could lead the Soviet Union to deprive Western Europe of resources that it does not need itself. Its economic exchanges with the West are not haphazard, but are integrated within plans, the success of which is important to domestic harmony. Moscow would not wish to exacerbate the ill effects of the Western recession by the dislocation that would be caused if it sabotaged the entire West European economy. It has repeatedly emphasized its desire for economic co-operation with the West; its aim in this is clearly not to build up armaments, which it needs to reduce.

It is sometimes said that the Soviets would cut off Western Europe's supplies in order to precipitate an economic crisis that could lead to revolution. But the outcome would hardly be favourable to the power that had plunged the outraged masses into misery; more consistent with the Kremlin's Marxist views, and with common sense, would be to wait for capitalism to disgrace itself by collapsing of its own accord. If the Kremlin did, in fact, act against all reason and if, contrary to what is likely, Europe became dotted with puppet governments, Moscow's power would be weakened for the reasons given in B. The new satellites, along with those already established in Eastern Europe, and minorities in the USSR would soon become more than Moscow would handle. The proposition is, therefore, absurd.

Nevertheless, it is conceivable, although improbable, that Moscow would interrupt or slow down the supply of selected minerals or vegetable matter to increase its bargaining power for some particular purpose. But this would merely add to the no less serious hazards already foreseen by the European Commission, and could not be said to justify any nuclear risk. The Commission has pointed out that Western Europe is precariously dependent on the processing of imported raw materials; the time is long past when it had sufficient known mineral resources of its own. In the report already cited it points to the increasing tendency of countries in which the raw materials are situated to do the processing themselves. The Commission warns that if Europe is not continuously aware of this trend, it will find itself with an 'industrial structure starved of raw materials'. It says that the Community depends, or will soon depend, for many materials on a very small number of supplier countries. Supplies could be threatened either by political problems or by the unilateral imposition of unacceptable prices.

To avert the consequent predicament, the Commission recommends a concerted programme including establishment of reserve stocks, optimum recycling of waste, substitution by other materials and new manufacturing processes, and extension of product life by improving quality. This, it says, requires research, standardization and the dissemination of good practice. At the same time, a search should be made for new mineral resources in Europe; the Commission says that relatively recent discoveries of deposits of hydrocarbons, coal, uranium, lead, zinc, copper and fluorine show that these may be substantial. Solutions of recycling problems, the Commission suggests, may best be sought in the framework of environment policy. Quality improvement, accompanied by the introduction of a European quality mark, should be part of consumer protection. The report complains that the Community lacks not only information about resource prospects, but an instrument for assessing them and 'a prospecting service befitting Europe'. It says that while the problem is vast, it is long-term, and asks 'whether the Community will be able to take advantage of the absence of immediate pressure to set up, in an atmosphere of calm, those information, coordination and planning systems needed to map out a long term policy.'

That report was made in February 1975. Unfortunately, the Commission was obliged to send it to an ineffectual address; with its emphasis on careful assessment and long-term planning, the report reads as if it were written for the Kremlin. Very little has come of the proposals. The Council of Ministers rarely looks ahead and takes most of its important decisions, not calmly, but after periods of wrangling in which all concerned are exhausted by all-night sessions. To carry out the Commission's proposals would be costly, but a sum such as the £3,000 million estimated to be devoted to the Falklands War and its aftermath would have provided more than a beginning. A solution of the vital problems raised by the Commission would automatically dispose of any conceivable Soviet threat to resources. But it is to be expected in a non-creative, disintegrating civilization that the external bogey will be seen as a greater threat than the decay and lack of vision within, even though the consequence could be physical annihilation.

We are now perhaps in a better position than we were at the beginning of this chapter to compare the risk of retaining nuclear weapons with that of rejecting them. It is surely not going too far to say that no responsible person would shelve this problem; a calculation must be made, whatever the difficulty. Western Europe may be likened to a society living in ancient times on the slope of a volcanic mountain. For centuries intermittent eruptions kill the inhabitants in increasing numbers; eventually there is reason to fear that a gigantic explosion could annihilate them all. But Fate appears and says:

> Unaccustomed though I am to making offers of this kind, I shall give you a choice. I shall order the god of fire to stop all eruptions. But in return you must agree to accept the risk – and it is only a risk – that you will be subjected to a certain amount of pressure from your neighbours. How serious that would be for you, if it happened, would depend on your own character – on your spiritual and intellectual resources. Further advice I cannot give you. You must decide.

While the probabilities involved in the nuclear problem cannot be calculated with anything approaching mathematical precision, it should be possible to arrive at satisfactory orders of magnitude. In the simple, intuitive method proposed here the reader is invited to choose the figures. We shall assume that if Western Europe had no nuclear arms, the danger to be feared would be Hungarianization, as described in chapter 8; in fact, this author considers the danger to be much less, something negligible. The first step is to compare the probability of Hungarianization, in the event of unilateral nuclear disarmament, with that of a holocaust, if Western Europe retained its weapons. Some may consider, for instance, that Hungarian-ization, in the one case, would be about as likely as a holocaust, in the other; others might find it to be x times, or 1/x times, as likely. This is for the reader to decide. It then becomes necessary to weight each probability with the damage factor. For example, if we were to compare the likelihood of being killed while stepping under a painter's ladder with that of being killed when walking along a mountain path where boulders could fall, we should have to take into account the lethal power of a boulder compared with that of a paint tin. In each case the probability of being struck (expressed relatively) should be multiplied by the potential damage factor. I should say that the damage factor of a nuclear holocaust was near enough to an infinite number of times that of Hungarianization. Hence even if the risk of Hungarianization were a thousand times that of a holocaust, the weighted risk of the holocaust would still be very much greater – by a factor of one thousandth of something approaching infinity. If we exclude primitive emotions, there is no more to it than that.

Even if it were found that the weighted risk of a holocaust was less than that of Hungarianization, unilateral disarmament would remain Western Europe's surest defence. Seen as a weapon, it is double-edged. On the one hand, if the Soviets met it in good faith, peace throughout Europe would at last be established and the prospects of the entire world greatly improved; on the other hand, if they tried to take advantage of it by aggressive action, their policing requirements would exceed their capacity and in the ensuing revolts the USSR would almost certainly disintegrate. If Western Europe wishes to see more liberal policies and practices in the Eastern bloc – although these may be psycho-culturally less viable than is usually thought – it is unilateral nuclear disarmament, and not the incessant harassment of Moscow, which is the most effective means of achiev-ing it; for the Kremlin's most powerful lever in restraining dis-content at home and rebellion in the satellites is the potential danger, real or imagined, of Western aggression. It is not improb-able that if Western Europe dismantled its nuclear weapons, the

Kremlin's first reaction would be one of apprehension. The removal of all possibility of a West European attack could unleash forces that would destabilize the whole region. In that event it would be to Western Europe's advantage to co-operate with the Soviet Union in economic measures that would help to restore stability. Instability would help nobody and would certainly not lead to the emergence of capitalism – the dream of some Americans.

While it has been argued in this book that unilateral nuclear disarmament would serve Western Europe's interests, we have yet to consider why Russia cannot be expected to reciprocate. The answer is straightforward. Even if those elements in the United States who want to destroy the Soviet Union underwent a convincing change of heart, Moscow could not overlook its dispute with China.[56] Here it shares an interest with Western Europe. Because of its geographical position, Russia is Europe's guardian against the possibility, however remote it may be, that the Chinese will one day follow the path of Jenghiz Khan. It imputes no sinister motive to present Chinese leaders to say that China's bursting population could eventually provoke an overflow that would not stop at the Urals, unless it were checked. For this reason alone the Soviets will cling to nuclear weapons for some time, since China has them. If world peace is not established, the next historic clash could well be between a starving South, led by China, and the North. Compared with such a prospect the bickering between the two halves of Europe seems parochial and unreal. In this, no less than in other respects, the Western dominant minority, as befits the leaders of a declining civilization, are looking in the wrong direction and failing to come to terms with history. A situation could arise in which Europe could not survive unless it was united from the Atlantic to the Urals, east of which are resources and energy on which Russia is increasingly dependent. The China card may be a joker for America, but it has no place in the European pack.

Western Europe could play an important role in making the Soviet Union feel secure on its western flank and in mediating in negotiations for a settlement with China, which will have to be made. Here lies the greatest hope for world nuclear disarmament. For if, in the peace that followed, China agreed to abolish its nuclear weapons, which it has promised to do if others abolish theirs, a united Europe and China together could be strong enough to persuade other nations to follow suit. If it is hard to see this chain reaction of disarmament taking place, it is not hard to see what the alternative will be. To save the human race someone will have to make a start. This gives Western Europe a historic opportunity, which it can seize at negligible risk. For the purpose of preserving itself, of powerfully influencing events in Eastern Europe and of moving towards a more civilized future for the world, unilateral nuclear disarmament should be Western Europe's highest strategic priority – given the requisite moral strength.

Chapter 10

The end, or a beginning?

It is extremely unlikely that Western Europe will dismantle its nuclear weapons while the present minority (Toynbee's conception) remains dominant; for the rulers, with insignificant exceptions, still pipe the old tunes and most of the majority, as the Falklands affair showed, are only too happy to respond. In the days of bows and arrows, and even later, the suffering to which such dances led was relatively limited in its incidence, grievous though it was for the afflicted. But today the world is menaced by something like 50,000 nuclear warheads with a total destructive power more than one million times that of the Hiroshima bomb. It is no longer a question of how many would be killed, or even of how many would survive, but of whether the condition of the survivors and their equipment would permit resumption of the human function on the previous level. A qualitative, not merely quantitive, change has taken place in the consequences of war, but there has been no qualitative change in response to the unprecedented danger. Although the world is threatened with a holocaust, some Western leaders are as intemperate as in a petty brawl. Insult is heaped upon insult, negotiations for arms reduction are cynically treated as a public relations campaign to appease a frightened multitude, and madmen prepare for a limited castastrophe. Does all this mean that the end is approaching? The answer to that question lies in the answers to others. Does the growing disenchantment with the minority presage the emergence of entirely new leaders, with an entirely new vision, or is it merely a sign of impending disintegration? Will Western civilization see that it, and it alone, can put an end to the evil that its unparalleled inventiveness has created? Will it have the moral strength, the faith in the irrepressibility of its creativeness, to take such an initiative? Will it be able to free itself from tribal emotions sufficiently to realize that the danger entailed in abandoning nuclear weapons is negligible, all the more so when compared with the danger of retaining them? Will new, vital tunes be heard? Or will Western civilization dance its way to the nemesis that has overtaken sixteen others, by failing to respond to a new challenge in a new way?

The general view is not encouraging. We have seen in earlier chapters the unmistakable signs of decay. In a society that is spiritually out of joint the anti-nuclear movement itself is marred by eccentricity and disorder, and has even become an instrument for fomenting what is called the war of the sexes. A mob afraid of extinction does not constitute a regenerative force, although the second can emerge amid the first. The women of Greenham Common, or a significant number of them, sullied the reputation of their cause by disfiguring property and leaving behind a large quantity of litter, which could have been taken away just as easily as it was brought. Their leaders could not resist the opportunity to issue a facetious statement aimed at belittling men. The malaise is general. 'Better red than dead' is yet another expression of the civilization's impotence. More auspicious would be a confident assertion that a vital spirit is sure to persist, even in the face of conquest; but so far no new or regenerated spirit has been clearly articulated. The slogan also raises a false issue, since the alternative to nuclear weapons is not a change of ideological colour. Polish Catholics, although under communist rule, are not red, whatever else they are; nor is the Hungarian archbishop, mentioned in chapter 8, who got his way on a moral issue. 'Better red than dead' reflects society's failure to form a rational assessment of the risks of retaining or abandoning nuclear weapons.

It may be discouragingly significant that in Holland, where awareness of the nuclear danger is the greatest, the movement against it is perhaps the most bizarre. The Interchurch Peace Council (IKV), the most influential Dutch group working for unilateral nuclear disarmament, seeks an anti-nuclear alliance between Holland, Mexico, Rumania, Nicaragua, Yugoslavia and Sri Lanka. This political fantasy suggests that the IKV's plans for 'the construction of a completely different culture' belong to the category of futurism, identified by Toynbee as one of the signs of disintegration. Yet a different culture will have to be born if there is to be any culture at all. Despite the enormous publicity given to the nuclear issue, the present Western culture has produced too few people sufficiently aware of the danger to offer much hope of averting it. According to a poll published in *The Economist* on 18 December 1982 the percentage who regarded nuclear weapons as a 'great concern' was 49 in Holland, 40 in Norway, 32 in Western Germany, 28 in Britain, 27 in Spain, 21 in Italy, 18 in France and 18 in the United States. This inability to face reality is accompanied by a soothing withdrawal into drugs, alcohol and narcotic music. It is estimated in Britain that one in five women and one in ten men take tranquillizers every day; the number with a serious drink problem has been put at a minimum of 700,000; one-third of patients in British hospitals have psychiatric problems.

A society described by John Stuart Mill as having had no system of values since feudalism, disdained by Lord Acton as devoid of any directing ideals other than those included in the gospel of commercialism, and denounced by Max Weber as a nullity, might well think it time to take stock. It could ask whether its social and physical predicaments were the result of having failed to develop unifying moral principles, and whether such a concept as that of the permissive society was no more than a reflection of its total bankruptcy; on this point it could bear in mind Freud's statement that 'when the community has no rebuke to make, there is an end of all suppression of the baser passions.'[1] It might consider whether a generally accepted system of values, even though few could fully live up to them, and even though some of the creative minority that evolved them might exploit them cynically, was indispensable tó the inner security of the individual and the consequent unity and order upon which a society's survival depends. It would look at the effects of pollution, some of which are evident to the most inexperienced observer – ditches in which frogs can no longer live, seas in which fish cannot thrive, and food that is systematically robbed of important nutrients and contaminated by additives that man's evolution has not fitted him to assimilate without risk of disease. It would take more seriously the damage being done by lead to the nervous systems of children and the general health of adults, and would note, in passing, that lead is excluded from petrol in the USSR. It would examine, not without anxiety, studies that have been made of the threat of man-made carbon dioxide to the climate, the increase in acid rain and the steady expansion of deserts. In short it would pause to consider how much truth there is in the warning of the head of the United Nations Environment Programme that by the end of the century the world will face 'an environmental catastrophe', which will produce 'devastation as complete, as irreversible as any nuclear holocaust'.[2] Finally, a society concerned with survival would ask whether the voracious consumerism that caused all this destruction arose from a deeper malady; whether a spiritually empty society corresponds to the patient, familiar to psychiatrists, who eats and drinks to excess because he has been parentally deprived; and whether this avid hunger, unbridled by reason, could lead to the annihilation, in one way or another, of the society itself.

Yet there are hopeful signs. Of these the most striking and perhaps the most significant is the protest within the Church of England against nuclear weapons. The church's doctrine, discipline and government are established by act of parliament. An Anglican clergyman, 'like a soldier of the National Army, is subject to duties and courts to which other Englishmen are not subject. He is bound by restrictions.'[3] Yet despite its integration within the institutional framework established by the rulers, the established church has given birth to a coherent, purposeful movement that rejects the government's policy on an issue vital to national security, whichever way it is looked at. The dissenters have found the spiritual strength to triumph over formidable tribal fears, which afflict all of us, and proclaim that nuclear arms must be abolished because they violate the gospel. This radically new vision, arising on such a scale, could mark a turning point in the history of the church, of the United Kingdom and of Europe. In the past the church, like churches throughout the world, has been virtually united in supporting the government's wars, however unjust, in the belief that God was on the nation's side. By contrast, William Howard Russell, correspondent of *The Times* at Balaclava, Lucknow, Bull Run, Sadowa and Sedan, saw Queen Victoria's reign as 'an incessant record of bloodshed'.[4] He expressed his disgust in his diary upon learning of an expedition to Afghanistan, following those planned against the Maoris and Burmese; he had already observed repression by drunken British soldiers of both blacks and Boers. But throughout Queen Victoria's reign, as before and afterwards, the church did not falter in its blasphemous assumption that the blessing of God was upon the government's aggression. This relic of primitive superstition was substantially eroded when the Archbishop of Canterbury enraged the Prime Minister (on 12 October 1982) by thanking God only for the end of the Falklands War, and not for victory. The Archbishop's interpretation of God's beneficence, at once more rational and more devout, was a promising sign. But the revolt of a substantial number of the clergy on the nuclear issue goes much farther. It is a qualitative leap, in which both disintegration and regeneration are simultaneously manifest; it is a positive response within the establishment itself to at least one element in today's historic challenge.

In a sense the Falklands campaign, though lamentable and culpable, produced another good sign. The victory was over a Third World junta, which was less well-equipped than its enemy in the air and at sea, and dependent on badly-trained conscripts, who were terrified by portable anti-tank weapons and modern air and artillery bombardment. Yet, conducted at such a distance in freezing Atlantic winds, on territory where all supplies had to be brought in, the operation required the organization, skill, stamina and valour that had made imperial expansion possible. Those qualities, which were squandered on such a futile enterprise, could be used for a more constructive purpose. They recall the highly important words of Toynbee:[5]

> The biological heritage of the epigoni is the same as that of the pioneers, and all the pioneers' endeavours and achievements are potentially within their descendants' reach. The malady which holds the children of the decadence fast bound in misery and iron for generation after generation is no paralysis of their natural faculties as human beings but a breakdown and disintegration of their social heritage, which debars them from finding scope for their umimpaired faculties in effective and creative social action.

It does not follow, of course, that the qualities required for military conquest are suited to higher purposes. But the way in which the Falklands operation was carried out does suggest that the vitality that made all past British – and European – achievements possible is not dead, as might have been thought from observation of other activities. Properly directed, this latent creativeness could cope with economic reconstruction, pollution, development of new energy sources, and new diplomatic relationships consequent upon nuclear disarmament. But where is the direction to come from? It is unlikely to be found among the three factions of the dominant minority; faced with problems going to the roots of the civilization, these have produced nothing more original than the anachronism of an Iron Lady, apparently modelled on Queen Victoria, who, herself, was hardly in the forefront of enlightened thinking. The Falklands campaign is sufficient to illustrate the rulers' inadequacy; leaders of all three factions supported it, although some expressed ineffectual and self-contradictory reserve. Britain had far more pressing needs than this costly expedition. The bill for the campaign and its aftermath is estimated at £3,000 million, or more than £1,500,000 for each of the 1,800 islanders, most of whom would almost certainly have settled for much less if they had been moved out. The moral arguments in favour of the operation are inadmissible. It was said that Britain had a duty to the world to show that territory could not be gained by aggression. What it showed was no more than the obvious – that territory can be gained, or held, by a superior force. This lesson, if any, was the one learned by Israel, which soon after the campaign struck at Lebanon with an impunity that is said to have influenced the South African Government in its attack on Lesotho. Violence does not prevent violence, but creates the climate in which it breeds – to such an extent that some sociologists liken the spreading of war to an epidemic disease. It was also claimed that Britain was fighting for the right of people to determine their own future. This was clearly not a matter of general principle; for as recently as 1973 the protesting inhabitants were evicted from the British possession, Diego Garcia, in the Indian Ocean, to make way for an American military base. In fact, as everyone in the minority knows, the islanders will eventually have little say in what happens to them. Their insular lives have already been dislocated by the presence of troops far more numerous than themselves; and Britain, certainly when it has run out of oil, will be unable to afford to defend indefinitely this vestigial remnant of imperialism. For no cogent reason 250 men were sent to their deaths, while nearly 800 were disabled or seriously wounded. One of those who died, Lieutenant David Tinker, aged twenty-five, had this to say in a letter to his father, Professor Hugh Tinker, who has published it in a book:[6]

> The pity for us is that there is no cause for this war, and, to be honest, the Argentinians are more patriotic about the Malvinas than we are about the Falklands. And the iniquitous thing is that we trained and equipped them.

David Tinker condemned the Prime Minister, Defence Minister, the high command, the disinformation of the defence ministry, and the press. His father wrote: 'David had to die because of crass error, and weakness disguised as boldness in high places.' It cannot be expected that rulers who have exhibited such ineptitude and lack of humanity in the comparatively simple problem of the Falklands will be wiser in handling the threat of nuclear war. It was such people who perpetrated the First World War, which, quoting Kissinger again, was senseless in its origin and pointless in its outcome. There has been no improvement at the top since Bertrand Russell wrote, just after the war broke out, that those who had led the British people into it were 'mostly stupid, and all without imagination or heart'.[7]

As Bertrand Russell was one of those philosophers who might at any stage of history be expected to criticize politicians, no special social significance can be attached to his comment; but since he wrote, a marked collapse of deference, one of the hallmarks of decline, has spread in and close to the Palace of Westminster, not only among extremists. When Lord Carrington resigned on the ground that he had failed in his responsibility, Robert Carvel, political editor of the *Standard*, said:[8]

> Let others now follow the Carrington code – both in Government and Opposition. If only they would, in next to no time we would have an entirely new set of politicians in command – on both sides of the House. That could not be a change for the worse.

It is doubtful whether even as recently as a dozen years ago such a comment could have appeared in such a newspaper. But there was an important precedent among the parliamentarians themselves. John Pardoe said in January 1976 that it was 'time to sweep away the mandarins of British politics', who had 'fed themselves fat on the spoils of an outdated political system'. He subsequently wrote that what the nation needed was 'its first chance since the first Puritan revolution to "make things new" '.[9] Pardoe's insight did not enable him to succeed in his bid for the Liberal Party leadership; nor did it avert the loss of his seat in the Commons.

If Toynbee was right, the new rulers would have to overhaul the institution of Parliament itself. In a section on the 'nemesis of creativity' he likened worship of the 'mother of parliaments' to the 'crushing incubus' of idolization of the Egyptian divine king.[10] The industrial revolution, he said, had undermined the village foundations of the electorate, which now required an occupational basis of representation. He thought, however, that it was improbable that England would 'cap its seventeenth-century feat by becoming for the second time the creator of those new political institutions which a new age requires'. These innovations were more likely to arise in other countries. But we may add that in the troubled times in which such changes would occur, the United Kingdom's monarchy and its flexible constitution could help to effect a relatively smooth transition. The new, creative minority would require much time to reorganize society, and it would be out of the question to hold a second, destabilizing election within five years of its having assumed office. Since the constitution sets no limit on the life of the Commons, the new leaders would merely need to ask the electors for a mandate of ten years or more, which could be enacted by parliament. Thus, unlike in countries with rigid constitutions, authority could be strengthened without dictatorship. This has already been done. The Parliament elected in December 1910 lasted eight years, solely by its own decision, to avoid wartime elections; that of 1935 remained in office until 1945.

The Monarch could play a valuable, unifying role in a period of transition. According to Dicey, the Victorian authority on the constitution, there is a relatively new convention by which the monarch is seen 'to share and give expression to the moral feelings of British subjects'.[11] It is not inconceivable that in a critical time there would be a strengthening of the royal influence in government, which even today is not entirely absent. The royal prerogatives are now exercised, in practice, by the cabinet, which, by virtue of them, may make war or peace, disband the armed forces or dismiss certain civil servants without consulting parliament. But the sovereign retains the right to choose the prime minister; and the convention that limits the choice to that of a party leader who can command a majority in the Commons 'to some extent lacks the binding force of other conventions'.[12] In unforeseen circumstances the rule could be deprived of its force, Dicey says. It may perhaps be conjectured that such a situation could arise when parties patched up a coalition that seemed to frustrate the people's will. The present Prince of Wales would not be unprepared if called upon. Asked if he saw the monarch as becoming more involved in the nation's affairs, he replied:[13] 'I've always believed in trying to lead from the front.' His answer to criticism of his competence in industrial matters was: 'I haven't myself worked in industry, which is always the criticism that is thrown at me; I accept it. But how many politicians have actually worked in industry, or in any of the areas they pronounce upon?' Politicians, in the name of democracy, are sure to try and drive a wedge between the people and any attempt of the monarch to express their will. King Edward VIII sought to develop the moral convention 'by his closer contacts with the lives of the more humble and more distant of his father's subjects'. There is evidence that 'Ministers feared the pace at which the convention had been allowed to develop.'[14]

But who is to inspire the moral and social consensus without which no radical change can take place? While extreme leftists favour unilateral nuclear disarmament, they are not qualified for the larger role. Some of them fit into Toynbee's conception of futurists, in that they claim to possess a formula that opens the gate for a painless step into paradise. The futurist's fundamental error is to assume that class revolutions, or so-called class revolutions, are enough to reform people, and that economic relationships and other factors in the physical environment are more important in the development of morality than questioning the actions and motives of the self. This theory persists, despite strong evidence to the contrary, in the Soviet Union, where only living conditions, not mankind, have been improved. Poverty can lead to delinquency, but is not the primary cause of it. Drunkenness and crime rose in England when jobs were plentiful and when incomes were beyond the hopes of the previous generation; the continuation of this tendency is not mainly the result of either unemployment or low pay, but is part of the spiritual illness that afflicts the entire civilization. Anyone who has lived in a poor area will know that something more than poverty is required to provoke delinquency. Whether we look at Western Europe, the USA or the USSR, there seems to be a co-relation between delinquency and consumerism.

In general the extreme leftist's picture of the world is a social and moral distortion. Romanticizing the creativity of the working class, he overlooks the fact that it was the middle class, not the proletariat, to whom Marx and Engels credited the great surge in West European production and that an increasing amount of proletarian work can now be performed by robots. He confuses his dream of utopia with what is practicable under the present system. While he asserts that various services are the people's right, he rarely adds the qualification that nobody is entitled to a better lot than that of the most miserable Indian landless labourer, except in so far as society produces it. Unable to supply any remedies for the problems of capitalism, and with no revolution in sight, he is reduced to pressing for measures that can only increase economic dislocation and make life worse for everybody. There is an element of sabotage in this agitation. But generally extreme leftists are prone to exceptionally muddled thinking in economics. To some extent hedonists, they believe they can increase consumption by raising company taxation, although this reduces the investment required for higher production. Most, if not all, shut their eyes to the fact that a contributing cause of the rise in unemployment is that real wages and sharp increases in labour-related taxes on employers outpaced productivity gains by a wide margin in the first half of the 1970s. Some extreme leftists seize upon Marx's 'absolute law of capital accumulation' as foretelling the doom of capitalism, without being aware that the theory has been demolished in their own camp; one goes as far as to propose it as 'an important source of theoretical consensus in the labour movmement'.[15] The impotence of the right is thus matched in the left. Automation is condemned as being deployed against the workers; instead, it is mostly a means of saving industries – and jobs – from being wiped out by competition. Leftists invoke the class struggle as if it were a conflict between good and evil, and confuse the long-term, historical concept of it, which is itself dubious, with present problems. Today, in the important issue of unemployment, the relevant class division is less between employer and worker, although the worker is more vulnerable when jobs are scarce, than between workers whose incomes have been increased by new technology and those who have lost their jobs because of it. The solution of unemployment is the sharing of work. But if at a given level of production hours are reduced to provide more jobs, wages must come down proportionately. Most of those working in a society gripped by consumerism would sooner see millions on the dole than accept the wages cuts needed to get them back to work. The problem, like the others confronting the civilization, is moral; so far the extreme left has not informed the workers of this. Nor, while condemning arms sales to Third World juntas, has it mentioned the loss of work that cessation of this substantial and growing traffic would entail. Despite the fact that the Eastern bloc has become increasingly dependent on arms sales to the Third World, the left still imagines that such evils would vanish in a socialist society; but most people would take a great deal of convincing before they sacrified even a set of video tapes for a moral purpose of that kind.

What is needed to guide Europe to moral and physical salvation is not merely new leaders, but a new type of leader, capable of making the necessary qualitative leap. It is an almost constant social paradox that whereas only wise men should govern, wise men have profounder interests and eschew the banality and degradation of politics. The political leader is not only corrupted intellectually and morally by the power for which he thirsts; the very limitation of his ethos makes him unfit for his role. He lacks depth. He has become less a thinker and creator and more a purveyor of shibboleths, imprisoned within the routine of administration, except when devising strategy for his re-election. In such a time as the present his circumscription is not only a handicap but a danger; as Emile

Durkheim, the French sociologist, said, the politician is the least well placed to see the causes that lead to his actions.

The task of moral and social regeneration requires a different kind of leader, whose sole desire is the acquisition of knowledge and wisdom and the improvement of mankind; one who is drawn to power, not by lust for it, but by a feeling of *noblesse oblige*, which overcomes his natural disinclination; in short, someone with the qualities of a philosopher-king. Post-classical Europe has provided an example of such a man in Pope Gregory the Great (590–604), who at first resisted his election by clergy and people, but emerged from his monastery to initiate the expansion of Western Christendom and to become the first pope in history to exercise political power. It seems that there are two possible future sources of such a leader – the churches and the Green movement. Clergymen of all denominations are becoming more aware of socio-economic problems. Organizationally, the Roman Catholic church would be adequately equipped to initiate a widespread European reform, if the hierarchy became sufficiently enlightened; but this would require a pope with a minimum of emotional involvement with the soil on which he happened to be born. In the United Kingdom the Anglican anti-nuclear movement, spreading throughout the parishes, could well embrace the entire complex of problems, none of which is likely to be solved without a will that could overcome them all. One is not thinking of the next election, or of the one after that . . . but of the time when mere disillusionment has been followed by despair, when imitation of the minority, now faltering, has ceased altogether, and when a helpless majority looks for a new, creative leadership.

But if we are to identify an entirely original movement, which could provide the basis of a new or regenerated civilization, it is to the environmentalists that we must turn. While they are not without the neurotic streak that is to be expected of such a movement in a disintegrating society, they are no more bizarre than some of the early Christians and may eventually produce creative leaders. Long before the Green movement reached its present strength, Toynbee saw a possible future for it and went so far as to say that it might form a new religion – a phenomenon that has been associated with the birth of civilizations. If for 'religion' we substitute 'system of values', for which adherents are willing to make material sacrifices, the Green movement has already begun to qualify in that respect. It may be significant that the Greens are strongest in Germany, where in the sixteenth century Lutheranism generated a wave that is still felt throughout northwestern Europe and across the Atlantic.

One of the first tasks of the new rulers would be to set Western Europe on the path of making a completely honest living. This would mean stopping arms sales to the Third World and a consequent economic reconstruction, whatever sacrifices it might entail. It is of little use calling for unilateral nuclear disarmament by a society that is content to enjoy luxuries made possible through selling the means of destruction to backward peoples. The moral strength needed to abandon nuclear weapons could only arise from a consensus sufficiently wide and profound to encompass responsibility towards the entire world. Fear of the weapon is not enough; dread of the tribal enemy will remain stronger than that until a new society emerges. Those who say that the Third World is only being sold what it wants are using the argument of the drug pedlar. If Western Europe wishes to show itself to be morally superior to the Soviet Union, here is its chance. Mitterrand's statement that France could not maintain its defence industry without a flourishing export trade in arms reflects a widespread, irresponsible cynicism. At the Aldershot exhibition weapons are advertised and demonstrated on closed television circuits. A tape of this operation, broadcast on the BBC World Service, exuded an atmosphere of engulfing evil, which seemed to bode ill for the civilization that produced it. An eerie voice broke through sinister sound effects to boast of one weapon: 'It's accurate – and it kills!' Salesmen, and a saleswoman, interviewed for the broadcast, gloated and cackled over their triumphs, as if they were demons in hell. One salesman was beside himself with joy when he described the queuing up of buyers for his portable anti-tank weapon, which had proved such a winner in the Falklands.

The only real conflict of interests in the world today is between the North and the Southern élite. It is unimaginable that, with weapons increasing in deadliness and range, some of those sold to the South will not be used against the suppliers; the Falklands expedition has already provided a foretaste. It should be obvious that there is no future without a moral future. This is realism; it is those who imagine themselves to be hard-headed realists, who hope to survive as the fittest in a military and economic jungle, who are, in fact, the perpetrators of fantasy. In the past morality has never been essential to survival; now technology has made it so. Failure to see so obvious a point reflects a possibly fatal incompetence.

If and when the truth dawned, the sacrifice required to abolish the export of arms and useless projects to the Third World would be smaller than it would be now. Unable to pay its debts and with little or no oil to sell, the Third World could not afford imports on the present scale, which are, in any case, not as important as is sometimes claimed. Figures showing Europe's exports to the Third World as a percentage of its total exports to non-EEC countries are misleading, since the ten members do about 54 per cent of their trade among themselves. Exports to the Third World are about 25 per cent of the total of intra-EEC and extra-EEC exports, which are equivalent to 25 per cent of the Gross National Product. Exports to the Third World therefore represent less than 7 per cent of the GNP. Thus even at present the price of a clear conscience would only be the loss of certain luxuries – given a rational planning of employment to avert loss of jobs. As Alan H. Smith says, when he compares the possible effects of a reduction in the rate of growth of consumer goods in the Eastern bloc with that in the West:[16] 'Even a cut-back in absolute income levels [in Western Europe] could be largely reflected in a slow-down in the rate of accumulation of consumer durables rather than in an absolute cut in living standards for many consumers.' What was left would be much more than was available at the beginning of the century, when Weber thought that consumerism was already going too far.

Consumption and amenities should not be regarded as synonymous with living standards. Already the high cost of fuel and train fares has forced not a few people to live better. Cycling and walking to work, Douglas Brown finds, has made many people fitter.[17] Unemployment has stimulated creativity; many have learned handicrafts and set themselves up in business. This is a promising development. Technology, which reduced people to slavery on the production line, has now thrown millions out of work. But the creative response, small though it is at present, suggests a richer future. A more civilized and capable society that rationally planned the use of automation and shared the remaining work would have the leisure to find self-expression in arts and handicrafts and to engage in science and mechanics, all of which provide opportunities for different levels of experience and talent. Most important of all, there would be time for reflection – the lack of which is one of the underlying causes of present confusion. Thinking has declined seriously as a pursuit. The historian, Jasper Ridley, emphasizes the significant fact that William Russell's well-written, revealing dispatches from the Crimea to *The Times* were of 15,000 words each (longer than all except one of the chapters in this book), printed in unbroken columns in very small print with no sub-headings.[18]

As it is, those who see man as Frankenstein and technology as his monster are not being fanciful. The construction of increasingly deadly weapons has acquired a momentum of its own. Each new device is a challenge that demands improvement; engineers, obsessed with what they have created, are irresistibly drawn to fresh invention. A morbidly fascinated public watches while missiles streak across television screens, but gives little or no thought to the fact that any one of them, if loaded, could destroy a town. Technology is even taking over pop music; asked what he thought about this a record producer said: 'I don't mind, because technology is taking over everything; there is even a disc about it.' Everything, including man himself. It will take more than a revolution, as normally conceived, to arrest this dangerous process. Europe, from the Atlantic to the Urals, needs a new message. The Soviet Union is suffering from a moral crisis related to, and no less grave than, that in the West. Soviet urban youth, infected by Western decay, are resorting to the abandon that disguises sterility and stagnation as vitality and progressiveness. It is this, not communism, that is Europe's dangerous virus. In one of his last important speeches Brezhnev devoted a chapter heading to 'the formation of a new type of man'.[19] But he was obliged to condemn irresponsibility in high places, drunkenness, the payment to workers of unearned premiums and the collection of wages for merely turning up and doing nothing. Crime is rising. In January 1983 the Soviet head of law and order said that criminals, hooligans, embezzlers and drunkards were on the rampage in various parts of the country; residents of Gorki were complaining that it was dangerous to go out at night.

Soviet society has clearly been dislocated by rapid and culturally incompatible industrialization. But the underlying cause is the absence of a system of values – or, rather, one that intelligent people can accept. While the West clings to old shibboleths, the Russians have produced one of their own. The entire Soviet ideology rests on a stupendous fallacy. The Soviet Union has no Marxist basis, either historical or moral. Marx's prophecy that capitalism would develop until its contradictions caused it to break down and give place to communism has not been fulfilled in Russia, which, as was recalled in chapter 3, could not be classed as a capitalist country; his adaptation of the Hegelian dialectic cannot be said to have worked out there. Similarly, on the moral side, Marx has been negated. He expected socialism to end the alienation of the worker from his function, which he saw as one of the great evils of modern capitalism. But, as Brezhnev's remarks suggest, there is no country in the world where alienation is more apparent than in the Soviet Union; the reason, as we saw, is cultural. Marxist myths were useful as an instrument of revolution; indeed, Lenin saw philosophy as no more than a weapon in the class struggle. But their perpetuation ossifies thought and distorts vision. Brezhnev, though he may not have understood the cause, was aware of the effect when he said that Soviet thinkers often preferred to prove what had already been proved (as he saw it), rather than explain new phenomena. What has happened is that dialectical materialism, one of the various philosophic theories that captivated the Russian intelligentsia in the nineteenth century, has been officially codified.

Europe is therefore divided into two rotting halves, one with a bogus ideology and the other with no effective values except consumerism. The Western civilization, lacking harmony in its parts, both within and between the nations that comprise it, has lost its capacity for self-determination, thus producing Toynbee's important symptom of impending disintegration. On the other hand, the socio-economic organization of the entire Eastern bloc is a sham. While lip-service is paid to dogma, black markets in goods and services, including medical practice, are not only tolerated, but in some countries are tacitly approved as essential to the economy. This contradiction between principle and practice promotes cynicism and undermines morality in all its aspects. Corruption, which has a strong tradition among Slavs, is exacerbated; according to Hedrick Smith, under-the-counter trade makes every Soviet retailer a thief. In Eastern Germany the pressures of supply and demand defeat the law. Garage mechanics finance house-building from illicit earnings; citizens, mocking the principle of collectivism, steal whole fences for their gardens. Foreign businessmen pay bribes to expedite formalities. At the same time the race to catch up with Western Germany is too fast for some people, and the suicide rate, significantly kept secret, is said to be high. While the government vaunts the rise of socialist man, some East Germans, including the novelist, Christa Wolf, find it necessary to urge the need for a new morality.

Yet Brezhnev's speech, already mentioned, has an impressively responsible tone. With its allusions to spiritual life and efforts to make work more creative, its confessions of failure, its urging of the scientific study of public opinion and its aspiration towards a better type of man, it contrasts favourably with the unmitigated materialism, Darwinian morality, false promises and demagogy found in the speeches of Western politicians. On the whole, most of what is bad in Russia is traditional and much of what is good is new. As the experience of the nineteenth century shows, it is to Russian idealism that the West must address itself if it wishes to be an influence. There can be no message without principle; and at present Western Europe has no principle to offer. Unrestrained democracy, which has been condemned by every thinker who has given it attention, is unattractive to most Russians and is almost certainly doomed in Western Europe, which will have to reconsider such opinions as Lord Acton's, 'It is bad to be oppressed by a minority, but it is worse to be oppressed by a majority.'[20] Nor does the Western economy, which stands convicted of having produced both consumerism and unemployment, make an appealing model. Made possible in the first place by the unprecedentedly rational calculation of individuals, it has become irrational in its macro-operation. While the economic crisis deepens, its victims can only pray, as to some angry fetish, that the mystic and unpredictable market forces will cease their malevolence. A rational society, instead of waiting for a solution to turn up, would give the system a deadline by which it must function properly. It would then eschew the religious war between those for and against nationalization, reject the vague concept of mixed economy and get down pragmatically to a drastic reorganization, in which planning would have to play a very important part. The new economy would have to be applied at least throughout Western Europe; it would be even more self-sufficient if it were integrated from the Atlantic to the Urals.

Both parts of Europe are held back by ideological constraints. This gives Western Europe a chance to show the way forward. For centuries science has widened the gap between rationality and spirituality. Now, to devise a new socio-economic structure with a moral foundation, Europe and the world need more of both. If Europe can establish values that will deal an effective blow to consumerism, values that will include the idea of sacrifice should that be necessary, it will have taken the first step towards establishing a new civilization. Here the nuclear weapon provides a focus; for the moral force that would be required to abolish it would be strong enough to inspire the serious tackling of the other problems – and they are many – with which the whole of Europe is confronted.

The crucial issue is whether or not leaders who are at once competent and moral, will emerge in time. It may well be that the majority, or what is left of it, will not heed new voices until a holocaust has dissipated the last of its illusions. Relative international calm, resulting from some agreement on arms control, could be deceptive. In the West the danger of serious economic dislocation is great; in the East unfulfilled expectations, fostered when communist leaders geared their economies to the Western boom, could cause serious unrest. These situations could lead to nuclear war, as long as the weapons remained. But pressure on rulers to stop the nuclear build-up would tend to restrain them; and while the danger would be ever present, the time available for a new beginning could be extended.

Meanwhile what we have seen so far is the triumph of irrationality and irreligiousness. An observer on a more civilized planet would note that three-quarters of the inhabitants of this one still consisted of 'Neolithic-Age peasantries' with a mostly parasitic, alien top-dressing;[21] that the remainder had yet to develop the rationality and morality needed to protect them from the consequences of their inventiveness; and that a qualitative change from veneered savagery to a higher civilization would be essential to survival.

Notes

Preface

1   A. Toynbee, *A Study of History*, London, Thames & Hudson, 1972, p. 443.

Chapter 1   Signs of war

1   F. A. Beer, *Peace Against War*, San Francisco, W. H. Freeman & Co., 1981 provides a useful review of war studies.
2   Ibid., pp. 41–3, 46.
3   R. Neild, *How to Make up Your Mind About the Bomb*, London, André Deutsch, 1981, p. 42.
4   Ibid., p. 46.
5   Ibid., p. 44.
6   *The Guardian*, London, 10 August 1982.
7   Beer, op cit., p. 3; the author was also informed of Idi Amin's disease by a former British civil servant, who worked with him in Uganda.
8   Ibid., p. 210.
9   Hugh L'Etang, *Fit to Lead?*, London, William Heinemann Medical Books, 1980, pp. 1, 4.
10 Ibid., p. 32.
11 Ibid., pp. 108–9.
12 Ibid., p. 7.
13 Ibid., p. 144.
14 The *Standard*, London, 14 April 1982.
15 Beer, op. cit., p. 14.
16 Ibid., p. 15.
17 *The Autobiography of Bertrand Russell*, vol. 2, London, George Allen & Unwin, 1968, pp. 42–3.
18 *Encyclopaedia Britannica*, vol. 23, London, 1951, p. 766.
19 H. Kissinger, *The White House Years*, London, Weidenfeld & Nicolson and Michael Joseph, 1979, p. 85.
20 *The Guardian*, London, 17 February 1982.
21 S. Britten, *Science and Public Policy*, London, 1982, vol. 9, no. 2, April, p. 74.

22 Ronald Segal, *America's Receding Future*, London, Weidenfeld & Nicolson, 1968, p. 272.

23 G. Lewy, *America in Vietnam*, New York, Oxford University Press, 1978, p. 453.

24 *International Herald Tribune*, Paris, 23 January 1978.

25 Beer, op. cit., p. 332, n. 31.

26 Ibid., p. 301.

27 S. Britten, op. cit., p. 73.

28 Ibid., p. 73.

29 Ibid., p. 73.

30 Ibid., p. 73.

31 R. Halloran, *International Herald Tribune*, Paris, 10 September 1980.

32 *Daily Telegraph*, London, 10 April 1940.

33 *The Economist*, London, 25 April 1981, p. 25; *The Guardian*, London, 23 June 1980.

34 Beer, op. cit., p. 91.

35 Ibid., pp. 302 ff.

Chapter 2 The Americans

1 H. Kissinger, *The White House Years*, London, Weidenfeld & Nicolson and Michael Joseph, 1979, p. 59.

2 G. Ginsburgs and A. Z. Rubinstein, *Soviet Foreign Policy toward Western Europe*, New York, Praeger Publishers, 1978, p. 279.

3 F. A. Beer, *Peace against War*, San Francisco, W. H. Freeman & Co., 1981, p. 37.

4 D. J. Boorstin (ed.), *American Civilization*, London, Thames & Hudson, 1972, p. 9.

5 A. Toynbee, *A Study of History*, London, Thames & Hudson, 1972, p. 371.

6 D. Purgrave, *Daily Mail*, London, 15 March 1982.

7 R. C. Toth, *International Herald Tribune*, Paris, 19 April 1978.

8 D. S. Greenburg, ibid., 5 December 1978.

9 C. Dickens, *American Notes and Master Humphrey's Clock*, London, T. Nelson & Sons, undated, p. 130.

10 M. Balfour, *The Adversaries*, London, Routledge & Kegan Paul, 1981, p. 112.

11 J. Barry, *The Times*, London, 14 January 1982.

12 M. Balfour, op. cit., p. 10.

13 Kissinger, op. cit., p. 14.

14 Interview on BBC World Service, 10 November 1981.

15 J. Doyle, *Newsweek* chief political correspondent, BBC World Service, 10 November 1981.

16 , Kissinger, op. cit., p. 59.

17 *Encyclopaedia Britannica*, vol. 22, London, 1951, p. 836.

18 Kissinger, op. cit., p. 60.

19 Boorstin (ed.), op. cit., p. 321.
20 Ibid., p. 321.
21 Kissinger, op. cit., p. 60.
22 Balfour, op. cit., pp. 17–18.
23 Ibid., p. 35.
24 Ibid., p. 95.
25 Ibid., p. 90.

Chapter 3 The Russians

1 Cited in C. Duffy, *Russia's Military Way to the West*, London, Routledge & Kegan Paul, 1981, p. 1.
2 R. Pipes, *Russia under the Old Regime*, London, Penguin Books, 1979, pp. 27 ff.
3 Duffy, op. cit., p. 2. While the Mongols led the force that subjugated Russia, most of their troops were Tatars, who eventually assimilated them.
4 Cited in Duffy, op. cit., p. 1.
5 A. Toynbee, *A Study of History*, London, Thames & Hudson, 1972, p. 184.
6 Ibid., p. 185.
7 C. M. Cipolla (ed.), *The Fontana Economic History of Europe*, London, Collins/Fontana Books, vol. 1, 1975, p. 156.
8 Cited in Umberto Melotti, *Marx and the Third World*, London, Macmillan, 1977, p. 29.
9 W. Miller, *Who are the Russians?*, London, Faber & Faber, 1973, p. 15.
10 Ibid., p. 50.
11 W. H. Bruford, *Chekhov and his Russia*, London, Routledge & Kegan Paul, 1971, pp. 61–2.
12 Hedrik Smith, *The Russians*, London, Sphere Books, 1976, p. 145.
13 Ibid., p. 155.
14 Milovan Djilas, *Conversations with Stalin*, London, Rupert Hart-Davis, 1962, p. 106.
15 Pipes, op. cit., pp. 232–3.
16 R. Auty and D. Obolensky (eds), *An Introduction to Russian History*, Cambridge, Cambridge University Press, 1976, p. 321.
17 Djilas, op. cit., pp. 97–8.
18 Smith, op. cit., pp. 243–5, 301–2.
19 *A Handbook of Marxism*, London, Victor Gollancz, 1935, p. 961.
20 Duffy, op. cit., p. 239.
21 A. D. Sakharov, *My Country and the World*, London, Collins & Harvill Press, 1975, pp. 29–30.
22 Smith, op. cit., p. 338.
23 Ibid., p. 341.

24 M. Weber, *The Protestant Ethic and the Spirit of Capitalism*, London, Unwin University Books, 1974, pp. 18–19.
25 Ibid., pp. 21–2.
26 Ibid., p. 181.
27 Pipes, op. cit., p. 205.
28 Ibid., p. 206.
29 *An Introduction to Russian History*, op. cit., p. 53.
30 Duffy, op. cit., p. 40.
31 Ibid., p. 40.
32 Bruford, op cit., p. 142.
33 Duffy, op. cit., p. 72.
34 *An Introduction to Russian History*, op. cit., p. 172.
35 Cited in G. Alexinsky, *Russia and Europe*, London, T. Fisher Unwin, 1917, p. 204.
36 Alexinsky, op. cit., p. 76.
37 Ibid., p. 150.
38 Ibid., p. 152.
39 Ibid., p. 134.
40 For a still much needed account of what feudalism amounted to see M. Bloch, *Feudal Society*, London, Routledge & Kegan Paul, 1962.
41 Alexinsky, op. cit., p. 229.
42 Ibid., p. 144n.
43 Herzen cited in A. G. Mazour, *Russia Tsarist and Communist*, London, Princeton, D. van Nostrand, 1962, p. 236.
44 Alexinsky, op. cit., p. 153.
45 Mazour, op. cit., p. 238.
46 *An Introduction to Russian History*, op. cit., p. 235.
47 J. Stalin, *Leninism*, London, George Allen & Unwin, 1940, p. 365.
48 Bruford, op. cit., pp. 42–3, 48, 54.
49 Alexinsky, op. cit., p. 159.
50 Smith, op cit.; see particularly Authority in the index.
51 Mazour, op. cit., p. 386.
52 *An Introduction to Russian History*, op. cit., p. 324.
53 Cited in Miller, op. cit., p. 105.
54 Ibid., p. 105.
55 *An Introduction to Russian History*, op. cit., p. 219.
56 Ibid., p. 220.
57 Alexinsky, op. cit., pp. 47–56.
58 W. S. Maugham, *The Summing Up*, London, Penguin Books, 1969, p. 133.
59 G. Pavlovsky, *Agricultural Russia on the Eve of the Revolution*, London, George Routledge & Sons, 1930, pp. 249–51.
60 *The Essentials of Lenin*, vol. I, London, Lawrence & Wishart, 1947, p. 477.
61 *A Handbook of Marxism*, op. cit., p. 957.
62 Miller, op. cit., p. 158.

63 Stalin, op. cit., p. 334.
64 *An Introduction to Russian History*, op. cit., p. 25.
65 Karl-Eugen Wädekin, *Foreign Affairs*, New York, 1982, vol. 60, no 4, spring, p. 903.
66 Harry G. Schaffer (ed.), *Soviet Agriculture; An Assessment of its Contributions to Economic Development*, New York, London, Praeger, 1977, p. viii.
67 Ibid., pp. 56–105.
68 *An Introduction to Russian History*, op. cit., p. 25.
69 Smith, op. cit., p. 80.
70 Ibid., pp. 106–7.
71 *The Economist*, London, 8 January 1983, p. 61; *The Guardian*, 10 January 1983; *The Times*, 10 January 1983; *International Herald Tribune*, 27 December 1982.
72 Miller, op. cit., p. 218.
73 Mazour, op. cit., p. 875.
74 Smith, op. cit., p. 614.
75 Sakharov, op. cit., pp. 26–7.
76 Bruford, op. cit., p. 94.
77 Sakharov, op. cit., p. 46.
78 A. Arnold, cited in R. Graham, *Iran: the Illusion of Power*, London, Croom Helm, 1978, p. 129.
79 Miller, op. cit., pp. 162–4.
80 Smith, op. cit., p. 143.
81 M. Weber, *The Religion of China*, New York, The Free Press, 1968, pp. 236–7.
82 Smith, op. cit., p. 265.
83 K. Dawisha and P. Hanson (eds), *Soviet-East European Dilemmas*, London, Heinemann/The Royal Institute of International Affairs, 1981, pp. 163–4.
84 B. May, *The Third World Calamity*, London, Routledge & Kegan Paul, 1981.
85 V. Kirichenko, cited in Smith, op. cit., p. 258.
86 R. Hutchings, *Soviet Science, Technology, Design*, London, Oxford University Press, 1976, p. 204.
87 Smith, op. cit., p. 309.
88 Hutchings, op. cit., p. 145.
89 K. Marx, *Capital*, London, J. M. Dent & Sons, 1932, vol. II, p. 614.
90 K. Marx, *Grundrisse*, London, Penguin Books, 1977, pp. 104–5.

Chapter 4   The West Europeans

1 A. Toynbee, *A Study of History*, London, Thames & Hudson, 1972, p. 245.
2 A. Toynbee, *A Study of History*, London, Oxford University Press/ Humphrey Milford, 1939.

3   Ibid., vol. 4, p. 321n., vol. 6, pp. 312–21.
4   Toynbee (1972), op. cit., p. 247.
5   Toynbee (1939), op. cit., vol 4, p. 125.
6   Ibid., p. 5.
7   *The Guardian*, London, 21 October 1981.
8   Toynbee (1972), op. cit., p. 241.
9   Toynbee (1939), op. cit., vol. 5, p. 376.
10 Toynbee (1972), op. cit., p. 242.
11 Toynbee (1939), op. cit., vol. 5, p. 377.
12 Toynbee (1972), op. cit., p. 245.
13 Ibid., p. 34.
14 Ibid., p. 171.
15 *A Handbook of Marxism*, London, Victor Gollancz, 1935, p. 28.
16 Toynbee (1939), op. cit., vol. 5, p. 153.
17 Carlo M. Cipolla (ed.), *The Fontana Economic History of Europe*, London, Collins/Fontana Books, vol. 4, 1973, pp. 658–9.
18 M. Weber, *The Protestant Ethic and the Spirit of Capitalism*, London, Unwin University Books, 1974, pp. 181–2.
19 Kathy Sawyer, *International Herald Tribune*, Paris, 5 December 1977.
20 Toynbee (1972), op. cit., p. 247.
21 Toynbee (1939), op. cit., vol. 5, p. 482.
22 I think the point was made by W. B. Fagg, but I regret that I cannot find the reference.
23 Toynbee (1972), op. cit., p. 244.
24 Ernst Roth, *The Business of Music*, London, Cassell, 1969, pp. 248–9.
25 C. P. E. Bach, *Essay On the True Art of Playing Keyboard Instruments*, London, Eulenburg Books, 1974, p. 34.
26 Toynbee (1939), op. cit., vol. 5, pp. 439–80.
27 G. M. Trevelyan, *A Shortened History of England*, London, Penguin Books, 1967, p. 553.
28 F. M. Cornford (translator), *The Republic of Plato*, London, Oxford University Press, 1955, pp. 282–3.
29 Sari Gilbert, *International Herald Tribune*, Paris, 14 February 1978.
30 Toynbee (1939), op. cit., vol. 5, p. 16.
31 Ibid., vol. 3, p. 167.

Chapter 5   Economic débâcle and nuclear danger

1   M. W. Thring, 'Values in engineering', *Science and Public Policy*, London, 1981, vol. 8, no. 6, December, p. 444.
2   G. Merritt, *World out of Work*, London, Collins, 1982, p. 44.
3   Ibid., p. 82.
4   Ibid., p. 27.
5   *Financial Times*, London, 26 April 1982.
6   Merritt, op. cit., p. 116.
7   Ibid., p. 42.

8   *The Economist*, London, 29 May 1982, p. 91.

9   Merritt, op. cit., p. 61.

10 Ibid., p. 54.

11 *The Economist*, 29 May 1982, p. 50.

12 Ibid.

13 Ibid., 31 July 1982, p. 51.

14 Ibid., 24 July 1982, pp. 9–10.

15 B. May, *The Third World Calamity*, London, Routledge & Kegan Paul, 1981; see 'Cultural and social dislocation' in the index.

16 *The Impact of the Newly Industrializing Countries*, Paris, OECD, 1979, p. 45.

17 UNCTAD/TDR/2, vol. 1, 31 July 1982, p. 1.

18 M. A. Adesiyan, report on the Seminar on Planning Strategy, Oyo State, Ibadan, Ministry of Finance and Economic Development, May 1978, p. 18.

19 *Annual Survey of Industries 1975–76*, Summary results for factory sector, New Delhi, Central Statistical Organization, Ministry of Planning, p. 6.

20 OECD, op. cit., pp. 18–22.

21 M. Morishima, *Why has Japan 'Succeeded'?*, Cambridge, Cambridge University Press, 1982.

22 May, op. cit.; see particularly chapters 1, 4 and 9. One critic has argued that the success of Indian businessmen in England shows that they have no cultural disability that would prevent development in India. But communal ties and family acceptance of responsibility for a member's debts are important factors in the rise of the immigrant Asian capitalist. These enable him to take advantage of a going system, but, as Max Weber has shown, were a barrier to the formation of impersonal institutions, which were essential to the growth of modern capitalism. Cultural traits that prevented the birth of capitalism in India persist, and impede Western-style development.

23 *The Economist*, 11 December 1982, p. 22.

24 *International Reports*, New York, 10 September 1982, pp. 914–15.

25 *The Economist*, 24 July 1982, p. 69.

26 Peter Singer, *Marx*, Oxford, Oxford University Press, 1980, p. 38.

27 Merritt, op. cit., p. 210.

28 BBC World Service, 14 January 1982.

29 M. C. Howard and J. E. King, *The Political Economy of Marx*, London, Longman, 1975, p. 194.

30 Ibid., p. 203.

31 Ian Steedman, *Marx after Sraffa*, London, Verso, 1981, p. 206.

32 Howard and King, op. cit., p. 202.

33 Merritt, op. cit., p. 119.

Chapter 6   Helsinki, Afghanistan, Poland and morality

1   Yuri Kashlev, *Europe Five Years After Helsinki*, Moscow, Novosti, 1980, pp. 47–56.

2   Percy A. Scholes, *The Oxford Companion to Music*, London, Oxford University Press, 1980, pp. 901–4.

3   Ibid., p. 904.

4   R. Auty and D. Obolensky (eds), *An Introduction to Russian History*, Cambridge, Cambridge University Press, 1976, p. 208; the Russian threat is described as 'a myth without substance'.

5   Fred Halliday, *Threat from the East?*, London, Penguin Books, 1982 provides material gathered in Afghanistan after Soviet intervention.

6   See also Arnold Kohen and John Taylor, *An Act of Genocide: Indonesia's Invasion of East Timor*, London, Tapol, 1979.

7   B. May, *The Indonesian Tragedy*, London, Routledge & Kegan Paul, 1978, chapter 3.

8   Ibid., chapter 5.

9   Pramoedya Ananta Toer, *This Earth of Mankind*, Ringwood (Australia), Penguin Books, 1982.

10   *Le Monde*, Paris, 24 October 1981.

11   May, op. cit., pp. 376–7.

12   *International Herald Tribune*, Paris, 5 June 1978.

13   R. Portes, *The Polish Crisis: Western Economic Policy Options*, London, The Royal Institute of International Affairs, February 1981, p. 23.

14   *The Guardian*, London, 17 February 1982.

15   *The Times*, London, 22, 23 February 1982.

16   Cited by Jonathan Power, *The Guardian*, 17 February 1982.

17   A British correspondent with considerable experience in Central Europe told the author that the emotional involvement of Western correspondents with Solidarity had led to bad reporting.

18   K. Dawisha and P. Hanson (eds), *Soviet-East European Dilemmas*, London, Heinemann/The Royal Institute of International Affairs, 1981, p. 141.

Chapter 7   Soviet contraction

1   K. Kaiser, W. Lord, T. de Montbrial, D. Watt, *Western Security*, New York, Council on Foreign Relations, Inc., 1981.

2   J. K. Galbraith, 'Russia: Thinking About Imperialism', *International Herald Tribune*, Paris, 20 March 1981.

3   *The Military Balance 1981–1982*, London IISS, 1981, p. 47.

4   B. May, *The Third World Calamity*, London, Routledge & Kegan Paul, 1981, p. 94; see also R. G. Gidadhubli, 'Soviet Central Asia: Challenges and New Approaches', *Economic and Political Weekly*, Bombay, vol. xvii, no. 37, 11 September 1982, p. 1488, which discusses cultural persistence in Tadjekistan.

5 J. F. Hough, *Soviet Leadership in Transition*, Washington, The Brookings Institution, 1980, p. 165.

6 In *The Indonesian Tragedy*, Routlege & Kegan Paul, London, 1978, p. 387, the author said it was possible that if Indonesia disintegrated politically, the USSR could support a Sumatran faction and gain control of oilfields. This speculation was made in the light of a CIA forecast that the USSR would need to import oil in the 1980s, which now appears to be erroneous.

7 See *The Military Balance 1981–1982*, op. cit. and M. Leifer, 'The Security of Sea-lanes in South-east Asia,' *Survival*, London, IISS, 1983, vol. xxv, no. 1, pp. 16–24.

8 *The Military Balance*, op. cit., p. 92.

9 *Western Security*, op. cit., pp. 24, 33.

10 R. Graham, *Iran: The Illusion of Power*, London, Croom Helm, 1978, p. 68.

11 K. Dawisha, *Soviet Foreign Policy Towards Egypt*, London, Macmillan, 1979, pp. 40–1.

12 F. Halliday, *Threat from the East?*, London, Penguin Books, 1982, p. 120.

13 May, op. cit., chapter 2, 'The Lesson of Iran'.

14 Halliday, op. cit., pp. 71–2.

15 M. Balfour, *The Adversaries*, London, Routledge & Kegan Paul, 1981, p. 38.

16 Ibid., p. 12.

17 Ibid., p. 12.

18 Ibid., pp. 8–9.

19 *Western Security*, op. cit., p. 22.

20 Ibid., pp. 27–8.

21 K. Dawisha and P. Hanson, *Soviet-East European Dilemmas*, London, Heinemann/The Royal Institute of International Affairs, 1981, p. 21.

22 G. Ginsburgs and A. Z. Rubinstein (eds), *Soviet Foreign Policy toward Western Europe*, New York, Praeger, 1978, p. 165.

23 Dawisha and Hanson, op. cit., p. 10.

24 Ibid., p. 20.

25 *International Herald Tribune*, 15–16 January 1983.

26 A. Toynbee, *Civilization on Trial*, New York, Oxford University Press, 1948, pp. 168–9.

27 Dawisha and Hanson, op. cit., p. 135.

28 F. A. Beer, *Peace against War*, San Francisco, W. H. Freeman & Company, 1981, p. 119.

29 *International Herald Tribune*, 22 November 1982.

30 Z. A. Medvedev, *Soviet Science*, Oxford, Oxford University Press, 1979, p. 150.

Chapter 8   The worst case

1   *The New York Review of Books*, New York, 17 December 1981, p. 4.
2   The *World Bank Atlas* for 1976 showed the GDR's GNP per head as higher than Britain's in 1974, but added that because of methodological difficulties the comparison was unsatisfactory. Problems include evaluation of the mark, which is not floating, differences in the relationship between cost and price and the fact that COMECON countries use the concept of Net Material Product, which is not the same as GNP. Since 1976 the World Bank has shown Britain's GNP per head as higher than the GDR's. Yet during the five-year plan, 1976–80, the GDR's NMP rose at an average annual rate of 4.1 per cent compared with 1.1 per cent in Britain's GNP. For some years the bank has said that it is working on a new methodology, but so far has not applied it. At the beginning of 1983 the OECD initiated a comparative study of the GNPs of COMECON and Western countries.
3   *Economic Survey of Europe in 1981*, United Nations, chapter 3, p. 28.
4   J. Steele, *Socialism with a German Face*, London, Jonathan Cape, 1977, p. 53.
5   Ibid., pp. 131–2.
6   Author's calculation from *National Accounts vol. 1: Main Aggregates 1951–1980*, Paris, OECD, 1982.
7   Information given by a clock factory manager to the author. His first explanation of the differential was a dry 'because we are a workers' state'.
8   *Questions et Réponses*, East Berlin, Panorama, 1981, p. 97. (Also available in English.)
9   Steele, op. cit., p. 148.
10   Ibid., p. 171.
11   Ibid., p. 11.
12   *Questions et Réponses*, op. cit., p. 149.
13   B. Szajkowski (ed.), *Marxist Governments: A World Survey*, London, Macmillan, 1981, vol. 2, p. 340.
14   Ibid., p. 339.
15   Steele, op. cit., p. 149.
16   *Economic Survey of Europe*, op cit., p. 1.
17   *Le Mois économique et financier*, Basle, Swiss Bank Corporation, February 1983, p. 28.
18   *Economic Survey*, op. cit., p. 15.
19   Ibid., p. 17.
20   Ibid., p. 31.
21   Ibid., p. 31, n.1.
22   Steele, op. cit., p. 125.
23   Ibid., p. 144.
24   H. Wassmund in Szajkowski (ed.), op. cit., p. 333.
25   Steele, op. cit., p. 133.

26 *Questions et Réponses*, op. cit., p. 107.
27 M. Bloch, *Feudal Society*, London, Routledge & Kegan Paul, 1962, pp. 329–31.
28 R. Bahro, *The Alternative in Eastern Europe*, London, Verso, 1981, p. 385.
29 Z. A. Medvedev, *Soviet Science*, Oxford, Oxford University Press, 1979, p. 205.
30 Ibid., p. 90.
31 B. Kovrig in T. Rakowska–Harmstone and A. Gyorgy (eds), *Communism in Eastern Europe*, London, Indiana University Press, 1979, p. 83.
32 *The Guardian*, London, 1 December 1981.
33 Kovrig, op. cit, p. 92.
34 A. Pravda in *Marxist Governments*, op. cit., p. 269.
35 Ibid., p. 270.
36 Malcolm Mackintosh in K. Dawisha and P. Hanson (eds), *Soviet-East European Dilemmas*, London, Heinemann/Royal Institute of International Affairs, 1981, p. 144.
37 E. Moreton, ibid., p. 179.
38 P. Hanson, ibid., pp. 94–5.
39 Ibid., p. 99.
40 A. H. Smith, ibid., p. 113.
41 Ibid., p. 130.
42 W. Brus, ibid., p. 87.
43 E. Moreton, ibid., pp. 180–1.
44 R. Johnson, 'Has Eastern Europe Become a Liability to the Soviet Union?' in C. Gati (ed.), *The International Politics of Eastern Europe*, New York, Praeger, 1976.
45 P. Windsor in *Soviet-East European Dilemmas*, op. cit., p. 198.

Chapter 9   The risks: an assessment

1 M. Balfour, *the Adversaries*, London, Routledge & Kegan Paul, 1981, p. 9.
2 Ibid., p. 5.
3 Ibid., p. 9.
4 G. Ginsburgs and A. Z. Rubinstein (eds), *Soviet Foreign Policy toward Western Europe*, New York, Praeger, 1978, p. 3.
5 *Report of the European Fusion Review Panel*, Brussels, Commission of the European Communities, 3 December 1981.
6 R. Hutchings, *Soviet Science, Technology, Design*, London, Oxford University Press, 1976, p. 245.
7 *Actualités 1*, Moscow, Licensintorg, 1981, p. 3.
8 *Foreign Affairs*, New York, 1982, vol. 60, no. 4, p. 754.
9 *The New York Review of Books*, 28 May 1981, pp. 15–19.
10 *Newsweek*, New York, 26 April 1982, p. 25.

11 *The Guardian*, London, 10 August 1982.

12 *The Military Balance 1981–1982*, London, IISS, 1981, p. 123.

13 *Foreign Affairs*, op. cit., p. 764.

14 Gregory Treverton, *Nuclear Weapons in Europe*, Adelphi Papers no. 168, London, IISS, 1981, pp. 2, 6, 7.

15 *Foreign Affairs*, op. cit., p. 755.

16 Treverton, op. cit., p. 9.

17 Ibid., p. 6.

18 Ibid., p. 10.

19 *Newsweek*, op. cit., p. 24.

20 Ibid., p. 25.

21 Ibid., p. 25.

22 *Foreign Affairs*, op. cit., p. 757.

23 *The Guardian*, 15 May 1981.

24 *Newsweek*, op. cit., p. 25.

25 *Foreign Affairs*, op. cit., p. 753.

26 Letter to *The Times*, London, 4 November 1981.

27 *Foreign Affairs*, op. cit., p. 766.

28 H. Kissinger, *The White House Years*, London, Weidenfeld & Nicolson and Michael Joseph, 1979, p. 84.

29 *The Economist*, London, 24 July 1982, p. 45.

30 Ibid., 4 December 1982, p. 47.

31 F. A. Beer, *Peace against War*, San Francisco, W. H. Freeman & Company, 1981, p. 225.

32 Ibid., pp. 206–9.

33 Cited ibid., p. 206.

34 *Foreign Affairs*, op. cit., p. 765.

35 *The Guardian*, 19 February 1982.

36 C. Duffy, *Russia's Military Way to the West*, London, Routledge & Kegan Paul, 1981, p. 82.

37 W. Miller, *Who are the Russians?*, London, Faber & Faber, 1973, p. 185.

38 BBC World Service; I regret that I did not note the date.

39 K. Dawisha and P. Hanson (eds), *Soviet-East European Dilemmas*, London, Heinemann/The Royal Institute of International Affairs, 1981, p. 101.

40 Ibid., p. 102.

41 Ginsburgs and Rubinstein, op. cit., p. 282.

42 Dawisha and Hanson, op. cit., p. 187.

43 Ginsburgs and Rubinstein, op. cit.

44 Ibid., p. 152.

45 Ibid., p. 5.

46 Ibid., p. 152.

47 Ibid., pp. 49–52.

48 Ibid., p. 174.

49 Ibid., p. 62.

50 *Le Mois économique et financier*, Basle, 1982/1, pp. 17–19.

51 *The Economist* (supplement), 'Kovisto's new Finland', 28 August 1982.

52 Ginsburgs and Rubinstein, op. cit., pp. 152–3.

53 E. S. Tucker, 'Stretching the world's resources', *Petroleum Economist*, May 1980, pp. 212–13.

54 Ibid.

55 *The Community's Supplies of Raw Materials*, Bulletin of the European Communities, Supplement 1/75.

56 De Gaulle told Nixon that the Russians viewed their relations with the West in the light of problems they expected to have with China, which was their principal concern. See Kissinger, op. cit., p. 108.

Chapter 10   The end, or a beginning?

1 S. Freud, *Civilization, War and Death*, London, Hogarth Press, 1939, pp. 5–6.

2 *The Guardian*, London, 11 May 1982.

3 A. V. Dicey, *Introduction to the Study of the Law of the Constitution* (revised), London, Macmillan, 1959, p. 310, n. 3.

4 Alan Hankinson, *Man of Wars: William Howard Russell*, Heinemann Educational, reviewed in *The Economist*, 20 November 1982, p. 99.

5 A. Toynbee, *A Study of History*, London, Oxford University Press/ Humphrey Milford, vol. 4, 1939, pp. 15–16.

6 H. Tinker, *A Message from the Falklands*, Junction Books, reviewed in *The Economist*, 18 December 1982, p. 111.

7 *The Autobiography of Bertrand Russell*, vol. 11, London, George Allen & Unwin, 1968, p. 42.

8 *Standard*, London, 6 April 1982.

9 *The Guardian*, 13 September 1975, 7 January 1976.

10 Toynbee, op. cit., pp. 414f.

11 Dicey, op. cit., p. clxvi.

12 Ibid., p. cliv.

13 *Sunday Times*, London, 22 November 1981.

14 Dicey, op. cit., pp. clxvi-vii.

15 B. Jordan, *Automatic Poverty*, London, Routledge & Kegan Paul, 1981, p. 175.

16 K. Dawisha and Philip Hanson, *Soviet-East European Dilemmas*, London, Heinemann/The Royal Institute of International Affairs, 1981, p. 132.

17 'Reflections', BBC World Service, 29 January 1982.

18 J. Ridley, *The History of England*, Routledge & Kegan Paul, 1981, p. 275.

19 L. I. Brezhnev, Report of the Central Committee of the CPSU to the twenty-sixth Party congress, 23 February 1981.

20 J. E. E. Dalberg-Acton, *The History of Freedom and other Essays*, London, Macmillan, 1901, p. 11.
21 A. Toynbee, *A Study of History*, London, Thames & Hudson, 1976, p. 442.

Index

Unemployment, 86, 99, 100–2, 103–4
United Kingdom: connivance in repression, 123–5; dependence on USA, 35; dictatorship of circumstance, 96; economy, 154; liberty, 43, 163–4; monarchy, 217–18; neurosis, 213; nuclear force, 182; Parliament, 94, 96, 217–18; in South Arabia, 122–3; and Third World, 106–7, 109; unemployment, 100–1, 103, 152; war casualties, 22
United Nations, 20, 123–4, 125; Environment Programme, 213
USA: anti-communism, 13, 152–3, 209; armed forces, state of, 17–18; conflict with Europe, 22, 188–9, 190; corruption, 25–6; crime, 24; cultural attitude, 22–3; economy, 102–3, 104–5, 111, 112, 152, 191; ethnic heterogeneity, 27–8, 30; intervention in Third World, 139; involvement in Europe, 22, 29–37, 174; isolationism, 32; Jewish lobby, 26–7; and League of Nations, 32; lend-lease, 33, 35; military lobby, 191; missionary zeal, 34; moral failure, 24; neutrality, 29–31; Open Door, 34–7; Polish lobby, 27; political alienation, 25; protectionism, 35; scholarship, 21, 25; technology, 24–5; Tehran operation, 17; unemployment, 104, 152; war casualties, 22; war profits, 31; as Western leader, 21–4, 28–9, 32, 186–7, 190–1; westward expansion, 34
USSR (see also Russia, tsarist): agriculture, 68–70; cheka, 65; *cordon sanitaire*, 132, 133, 144–7, 149, 173; corruption, 225; dilemmas in Eastern Europe, 170–3; diminished influence, 135–8; dissidents, 47, 72; dominance in Europe, 38, 147, 174; economy, 70–2, 74, 159, 160; education, 73; encirclement, fear of, 121, 149–50; idealism, 74–5, 175; imperial burden, 80; kulaks, 67, 68; living standards, 70–1; Marxism, 143–4, 195, 224–5; moral failure, 1, 75, 224; naval build-up, 137, 200; *nomenklatura*, 73, 75; pluralism, 149; quality of goods, 77–8; restraint in foreign relations, 140–1, 146, 147, 199, 200; science, 78–9, 165–6, 177; technology, 70, 78–9, 176–7; terror, 76; Third World characteristics, 77–8; war casualties, 22; West, fear of, 36, 148, 150–2, 175; West, interdependence with, 196, 205

Victoria, Queen, 214, 215
Vietnam, 14–15, 122
Vladimir I, 40
Voltaire, 58

Walesa, Lech, 129, 130, 131
War (see also nuclear war): casualties, 15–22; domestic factor, 15–16; haphazardness, 13; law on, 18–19; miscalculation, 11–12, 14, 17; pathological factor, 9–11; propaganda, 14, 15; prospects, 19–20; psychological factor, 10, 16–17, 18, 20; unemployment factor, 16, 35, 114, 152; signs of, 7
Warnke, P., 179, 184
Warsaw Pact, 148, 180, 182
Washington, George, 29
Wassmund, H., 157–8, 162
Wajda, Andrzej, 128
Webb, S. and B., 175
Weber, Max, 49–50, 77, 89–90, 110
Weinberger, C., 28, 187
Western bloc: aggressive potential, 152–3; dominance in Third World, 143
Western Europe: challenge to, 1, 3, 83, 210; dynamism, 1, 88; economy, 88, 194, 226; imprudence, 120, 132–4; intervention in Third World, 122–6; moral posture, 122, 126, 133, 216; regeneration, 2, 3, 84, 91, 212, 214–15, 221; violence in, 85–6, 90, 96
West European decline, 2, 82–98; abandon and drug culture, 87, 92; archaism, 87; art, 91; collapse of deference, 217; cultural promiscuity, 91–2; dependence on USA, 22, 36, 38–9, 176, 186–7, 192; disenchantment, 84, 85, 86, 90–1, 95, 97, 217; economic ills, 99–114; fatalism, 90; futurism, 87, 90–1, 212; lethargy, 97; loss of harmony, 225; moral failure, 1, 89–90, 222; music, 92–4; nationalism, 82, 87, 176; passivity, 89, 90; proletarianization, 93, 94; relative to Russia, 38–9, 174–6, 193; self-indulgence, 175–6; spiritual impotence, 91, 213–14; terrorism, 90
Wilson, Woodrow, 13, 30, 31, 32
Windsor, P., 195–6
Witte, Serge, 62
Wolf, Christa, 225
World Council of Churches, 132